ENVISIONING WOMEN IN WORLD HISTORY

PREHISTORY–1500, VOLUME 1

CATHERINE CLAY

Shippensburg University

CHANDRIKA PAUL

Shippensburg University

CHRISTINE SENECAL

Shippensburg University

McGraw-Hill
Higher Education

Boston   Burr Ridge, IL   Dubuque, IA   New York   San Francisco   St. Louis
Bangkok   Bogotá   Caracas   Kuala Lumpur   Lisbon   London   Madrid   Mexico City
Milan   Montreal   New Delhi   Santiago   Seoul   Singapore   Sydney   Taipei   Toronto

McGraw-Hill
Higher Education

Published by McGraw-Hill, an imprint of The McGraw-Hill Companies, Inc., 1221 Avenue of the Americas, New York, NY 10020. Copyright © 2009. All rights reserved. No part of this publication may be reproduced or distributed in any form or by any means, or stored in a database or retrieval system, without the prior written consent of The McGraw-Hill Companies, Inc., including, but not limited to, in any network or other electronic storage or transmission, or broadcast for distance learning.

This book is printed on acid-free paper.

1 2 3 4 5 6 7 8 9 0 DOC/DOC 1 0 9 8

ISBN: 978-0-07-351322-5
MHID: 0-07-351322-9

Editor in Chief: *Michael Ryan*
Publisher: *Lisa Moore*
Senior Sponsoring Editor: *Jon-David Hague*
Editorial Coordinator: *Sora Kim*
Executive Marketing Manager: *Pamela Cooper*
Production Editor: *Karol Jurado*
Production Service: *Anne Draus, Scratchgravel Publishing Services*
Manuscript Editor: *Carol Lombardi*
Designer: *Margarite Reynolds*
Senior Production Supervisor: *Tandra Jorgensen*
Composition: *10/13 Palatino by Laserwords*
Printing: *45# New Era Matte Plus, R.R. Donnelley & Sons*

Library of Congress Cataloging-in-Publication

Clay, Catherine.
  Envisioning women in world history / Catherine Clay, Chandrika Paul, Christine Senecal.
    —1st ed. p. cm.
  Includes index.
  ISBN-13: 978-0-07-351322-5 (alk. paper)
  ISBN-10: 0-07-351322-9 (alk. paper)
    1. Women–History. I. Paul, Chandrika. II. Senecal, Christine. III. Title.
HQ1121.C623 2009
908.2—dc22   2007032970

The Internet addresses listed in the text were accurate at the time of publication. The inclusion of a Web site does not indicate an endorsement by the authors or McGraw-Hill, and McGraw-Hill does not guarantee the accuracy of the information presented at these sites.

Photo Credits:
Figure 1-1: © Erich Lessing/Art Resource, NY. Figure 1-2: © Gail Mooney/Corbis. Figure 2-1: © Scala/Art Resource, NY. Figure 3-1: © The Art Archive. Figure 3-2: © Borromeo/Art Resource, NY. Figure 4-1: Thanks to Alan Cresswell. Figure 4-2: Photo courtesy of Shippensburg University Fashion Archives and Museum. Used by permission. Figure 5-1: © Justin Kerr, K2887. Figure 5-2: © Werner Forman/Art Resource, NY. Figure 5-3: © Bildarchiv Preussischer Kulturbesitz/ Art Resource, NY. Figure 7-1: © Fototeca Storica Nazionale/Getty Images.

www.mhhe.com

◖ TABLE OF CONTENTS ◗

❰ NOTE FROM THE ❱ SERIES EDITORS

World History has come of age. No longer regarded as simply a task for amateurs or philosophers, it has become an integral part of the historical profession and one of its most exciting and innovative fields of study. At the level of scholarship, a growing tide of books, articles, and conferences continues to enlarge our understanding of the many and intersecting journeys of humankind framed in global terms. At the level of teaching, more and more secondary schools as well as colleges and universities now offer, and sometimes require, World History of their students. One of the prominent features of the World History movement has been the unusually close association of its scholarly and its teaching wings. Teachers at all levels have participated with university-based scholars in the development of this new field.

The McGraw-Hill series—Explorations in World History—operates at this intersection of scholarship and teaching. It seeks to convey the results of recent research in World History in a form wholly accessible to beginning students. It also provides a pedagogical alternative to or supplement for the large and inclusive core textbooks that are features of so many World History courses. Each volume in the series focuses briefly on a particular theme, set in a global and comparative context. And each of them is "open-ended," raising questions and drawing students into the larger issues that animate World History.

Women's history may be the only field of historical study more vigorous than World History over the last 40 years. Nevertheless, the sheer volume of research and writing, after millennia of neglect, has made it difficult for most scholars in women's history to reach beyond the established conceptual traditions of national histories. World History has taught us to ask and try to answer larger questions about women than those posed by national histories. What patterns can be discerned from the separate histories of women over the globe? Have women always been subordinate to men, or is patriarchy a particular historical development with a beginning, middle, and perhaps an end? What historical conditions or institutions repress or liberate women? What have women been able to accomplish to shape their own destinies?

The authors of this book are ideally suited to help us answer these questions. Catherine Clay, Chandrika Paul, and Christine Senecal are all specialists in women's history within particular cultures: Eurasia, India, and ancient and medieval Europe, respectively. They are also all passionate, practicing world historians. We are proud to offer the fruits of a collaboration that finally introduces, in engaging prose, the other half of world history.

Robert Strayer
Kevin Reilly

⬕ Acknowledgments ⬔

This project involved the assistance of many people, and the authors would like to extend our sincere gratitude to the following: Sandy and Sarah Hughes, whose involvement first made this project possible and who provided indispensable assistance in our research; Robert Strayer and Kevin Reilly, who read early drafts of this book and gave sage advise about shaping the major themes; Winston Black, Sabrina Joseph, Charles Loucks, Jennifer Ottman, Jonathan Skaff, Susan Spicka, Robert Babcock, Robin Fleming, and Vera Reber, whose scholarly expertise helped us on individual chapters; the editors at McGraw-Hill and Scratchgravel Publishing Services, including Anne Draus, Karol Jurado, and Sora Kim, whose work saved us from many errors; the students of World History I, Honors and general sections of Asia/Pacific History, and Comparative Women's History classes at Shippensburg University who test-drove early drafts and provided student feedback; and our department chair, David F. Godshalk, department secretary, Mrs. Reed, graduate assistant, Racheal Teates, and all our colleagues at Shippensburg University who were extremely supportive of our writing endeavors. The authors also acknowledge the legacy of the scholars of women's history, whose work provided the foundation for this book. Of course, any errors in our book are entirely our responsibility, and not that of these excellent scholars.

On a personal level, we each owe an irredeemable debt to our parents for their loving upbringing. In addition, Catherine Clay would like to thank Alan, Josefine, Evan, and Nathaniel for competing so stoically and lovingly with this project. Chandrika Paul would like to thank her close friend David Godshalk for his support and help during this project. Finally, Christine Senecal would also like to thank her husband, David De Bruin, and children, Peter and Gabrielle, for making her life so enjoyable.

◀ INTRODUCTION ▶

*Humanity is male and man defines woman not in herself but as relative to him; she is not
regarded as an autonomous being. . . . And she is simply what man decrees; thus she is
called "the sex." . . . She is defined and differentiated with reference to man and he with
reference to her; she is incidental, the inessential as opposed to the essential. He is the
Subject, he is the Absolute—she is the Other. . . . But it will be asked at once: how did all
this begin? . . . How is it that this world has always belonged to men? (de Beauvoir, 1980)[1]*

*Over and over again women heard in voices of tradition . . . that they could desire
no greater destiny than to glory in their femininity. Experts told them how to dress,
look, and act more feminine. . . . They were taught to pity the neurotic, unfeminine,
unhappy women who wanted to be poets or physicists or presidents. . . . (Friedan, 1963)[2]*

In 1953, the English translation of Simone de Beauvoir's *Le Deuxieme Sexe
(The Second Sex)* was published in the United States. De Beauvoir offered
an explanation of the lower status of women in society. Her book, along
with Betty Friedan's *The Feminine Mystique* (1963), became the seminal
works defining the early 1960s women's movement in the United States.
As the above quotes demonstrate, de Beauvoir and Friedan are in agree-
ment that from beginning of historical time, women have led a peripheral
existence in comparison with men. Their works intensified the intellectual
debate on the origins of patriarchy—that is, the institutional domination
of men over women. Some scholars disagreed with their analyses, argu-
ing that some societies have existed where women shared a rough parity
with men. Largely because of the vast differences in women's experiences in different societies, historians have yet to develop either a simple
explanation for the origins of patriarchy or a universal description of its
manifestations.

Our book, *Envisioning Women in World History: Prehistory to 1500* CE,
addresses these issues from a global perspective. A comparative approach
to Women's History enables us to point out broad patterns in women's
experiences while acknowledging change across time and space. Women's
roles have been neither universal nor static, but their power within families, their sexual and reproductive rights, and their economic and political
influence have waxed and waned. Consequently, the meanings and manifestations of women's agency, or power, have also varied. Women have
not always been able to confront their oppression; indeed, the inequality
among genders may have even been embraced by the wealthiest women

1

in societies, who saw it as essential for maintaining their elite position. Over time, some urban societies allowed women more proactive roles in certain areas such as religion or economics. However, even in these circumstances, women never achieved full equality with men.

HISTORIOGRAPHY

From their inception in the 1960s, the disciplines of World and Comparative History have grown exponentially. In this age of globalization, universities, colleges, and high schools across the United States are increasingly recognizing the importance of these disciplines in raising awareness of diverse societies. In addition, over the past 40 years, Women's History has emerged as an area of serious historical research, generating interest in such fields as the history of sexuality, masculinity, and gender. However, within these growing disciplines, few scholars have attempted to "globalize women's history."[3] Cross-cultural studies of women's experiences have been at best minimal.

To remedy the situation, as early as 1984 the Organization of American Historians embarked on an ambitious project to integrate information available on non-Western women. The result was *Restoring Women to History*, Volumes 1–4, which was aimed at providing readers with a thematic historical overview of non-Western women's experiences. In 1995, world historians Sarah and Brady Hughes made an important contribution by integrating World and Women's History with their primary-source collection entitled *Women in World History*. In their first volume, these authors asserted that learning about women's experiences in the premodern world is a necessary prerequisite for understanding the modern constructions of femininity. Modestly labeling their work "an appetizer, though one which opens up a very promising banquet,"[4] they were truly the pioneers to "globalize women's history." In 2001, Peter Stearns published *Gender in History*, which provided an overview of a very large period. In writing this textbook, our goal is to provide undergraduate World History students with a synthetic and comparative historical analysis of patriarchal structures and women's experiences in several of the most representative premodern civilizations.

SOURCES

There is a ubiquitous problem for studying the premodern history of women—the nature of the sources. First, compared with later centuries, there are relatively few written sources—such as law codes, religious texts, letters, diaries, autobiographies, novels, and plays—authored by women before 1500 CE. Those that do exist are skewed, because they reflect the views of only an exclusive group of women in society. During the premodern period, writing was a skill accessible only to elite women or those who rebelled against patriarchal constraints by adopting an alternative lifestyle such as joining a Buddhist monastery, entering a Christian convent, or becoming a Sufi mystic (options that were typical mainly for the wealthiest in society). They offer us significant clues into upper-crust social relations, but these women's marginality dramatically influenced what they could and could not say. As a consequence, even surviving women's sources are filled with gaps and distortions.

For most regions of the world, our knowledge about ordinary women's lives before 1500 CE is even more limited. For example, there are no formal sources on the reactions of Aztec peasant women to the tribute system that ran their economy or the human sacrifices that their priests performed regularly. As some elite social practices such as *sati* (Gupta India), foot binding (Song China), or veiling (some communities in ancient Mesopotamia and the Islamic world) slowly percolated downward to include women from lower classes, we have no way of ascertaining their responses or resistance to the spread of such customs.

Therefore, faced with the paucity of women's and non-elite voices, scholars must examine those sources primarily authored by privileged men to help reconstruct the lives of premodern women. The biases of these authors are themselves evidence for male expectations about women in their respective societies. For example, fourth-century Athenian playwrights made their female characters speak, but the minds that composed the words were male. Other examples of such skewed but important primary sources are the *Laws of Manu* from the Gupta Empire in India, the Sharia from the Abbasid caliphate, or Confucius's Three Obediences from Classical China. Usually the ideal role advocated for women in these documents was one of passivity, controlled sexuality, and strict adherence to domesticity. Primarily aimed at the elite, these sources set the guidelines for women's behavior that women were expected to follow. Yet these were only ideals and did not represent real women's actions. In reality, we can conjecture that some elite women challenged the patriarchal constraints enforced on them. Others were content with their situation or even utilized the power structure to achieve a degree of authority.

An additional problem with the sources is the unrepresentative information about the accomplishments of those women who played a visible but secondary role to their famous husbands. For example, we know a lot more about Khadija and Aisha, the wives of Prophet Muhammad, or Zubaida, the wife of the Abbasid Caliph Harun-al-Rashid, than about the lives of female peasants or workers who lived during the same time periods. We can conjecture that these women received mention in formal sources authored by men because they were viewed as "ideal women" who complemented and did not threaten the powers of their husbands. Therefore, the invisibility of women (especially the lower classes) from formal sources poses a major challenge for studying the premodern era.

In the quest to fill this void, historians have begun collaborating with scholars in other disciplines such as archeology, anthropology, and sociology. For example, by analyzing sources as varied as archeological remains, poetry, folk tales, court records, sales deeds, bookkeeping records, paintings, inhumations, incantations, artifacts, and other examples of material culture, they are trying to weave together the lives of women before 1500 CE.

ORGANIZATION AND STRUCTURE

Analyzing the ebb and flow of women's status across cultures before 1500 CE is an ambitious task. To simplify the process we have selected seven different periods in early human history that are commonly taught in World History surveys. These are women's experience in (1) Eurasia before 1000 BCE, (2) the Ancient Mediterranean World, (3) the Gupta Empire and South and Southeast Asia, (4) the Maya and Aztec civilizations of Meso-America, (5) Tang and Song China, (6) the Abbasid caliphate, and (7) Western Europe during the Central and Late Middle Ages.

These seven chapters are arranged with common themes to highlight continuities. Each chapter begins with a general historical background so that students unfamiliar with a civilization's history can get an understanding of the political and social context that influenced gender relations and women's social status. Next, the chapters offer a comparative overview of women's social, religious, and economic contributions and their access to public power, if any. Because of its regional and thematic approach, each chapter can be read independently of others. Also, by providing thought-provoking comparative questions at the beginning of the chapters, we hope that this volume will prove intellectually stimulating for students and simultaneously allow instructors greater flexibility in creating different assignments.

QUESTIONS ASKED

The essence of patriarchy is the subordination of women's political, economic, and cultural roles to reproduction. As the following chapters will reveal, however, women's status was not monolithic but varied with societies' diverse family structures, their levels of militarization, their degree of state/empire formation, and class divisions. In some societies such as ancient Athens, Gupta India, and Song China, elite women's lives roughly resembled that of a typical patriarchy. However, within this model were groups, such as the Spartan and Southeast Asian women or Buddhist nuns, who successfully resisted the constraints enforced on them. The central question our book tries to address is what factors were responsible for heralding a difficult situation for some women while allowing others to acquire greater control over their lives across and within cultures?

In order to help resolve this central concern, we have woven our narrative around the following comparative questions: (1) What factors limited women's formal political power? (2) Why did the roles of women in the family take the shape they did in different societies? (3) How did women's access to economic independence provide them with avenues to autonomy in society? (4) Why was women's formal participation in religious ceremonies in many societies often different from their other public roles? (5) Why were the realities of women's lives often at odds with ideals authoritatively established in texts?

An inescapable phenomenon of World History has been the domination and oppression of one group over another. Applying de Beauvoir's argument to this fact means that any dominant group in society views the lesser as the "inessential" or "Other." With regard to the equation of the sexes, since historical time men have perceived women as the "Other," whereas they are the subject or "Self." De Beauvoir and Friedan wanted women to reclaim their "Self" and not just remain the passive "Other" in society. As will be seen throughout our book, this contest to gain visibility for women has been a long time coming.

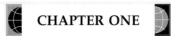 CHAPTER ONE

WOMEN IN EURASIA
BEFORE 1000 BCE

Women's fortunes on the whole declined between the appearance of the first human communities of hunter-gatherers (about 40,000 years ago) and the preeminence of urban centers established in Eurasia by 1000 BCE.* The first human societies were marked by flexible gender roles, little emphasis on the control of women's sexual conduct, an equal regard for both women and men's work, and a prominent role for female spirituality. But by the time cities developed, this situation had completely changed in some areas. Gender roles became rigid, with men usually controlling the political power of their states. Women's sexual morality often became an issue of public concern, with stringent laws enforcing a single woman's virginity or wife's fidelity to her husband. Much of the work considered appropriate for women moved out of the public view as their roles increasingly focused on domestic duties. The other work they did was frequently considered peripheral to their major tasks: the production of food and clothing, reproduction, and child care. Finally, creation myths of many early human societies suggest that prominent female deities were supplanted by masculine entities, and even the role of female cult leaders seems to have diminished.

We can see this reverse progress of women's lives in four different types of Eurasian communities that emerged before the year 1000 BCE:

Hunter-Gatherers The overwhelming majority of human history was experienced as hunter-gatherers, nomadic peoples who survived by hunting and gathering a wide variety of animals and plants. Evidence suggests the greatest amount of gender equality existed in these communities, but little from that era remains to us in the twenty-first century.

---

*CE and BCE, "Common Era" and "before Common Era," are chronologically equivalent to the abbreviations BC and AD.

Pastoralists and Villagers About 10,000 BCE some groups began to survive either by domesticating plants, or animals, or a combination of both. Those who continued to live a migratory existence but specialized in domesticating animals for survival were called pastoralists. Those who gave up nomadic lives and moved into permanent agricultural locations became the first villagers. While showing some degree of inequality between men and women, pastoralists and villagers tended to consider gender roles in a fairly flexible manner and held women's work in high regard.

Urban Dwellers The final category of women's experience is the primary focus of this book: urban dwellers, people who lived in city-based societies. The creation of Eurasian cities began as early as 3500 BCE and, in general, heralded a new degree of inequality for women.

These are the broadest economic trends in women's history, but it is critical to realize that these four types of communities—hunter-gatherers, pastoralists, villagers, and city dwellers—overlapped one another in time and often shared borders. Hunter-gatherers coexisted and interacted with pastoralists and villagers as well as urban dwellers. Thus, women's position differed greatly depending first on their society's ecology (their community's relationship with its environment and whether their surroundings could produce crops or support pasturing animals), and second, on whether they were urban dwellers.

Most of human history happened before 1000 BCE, but few humans living then left written records that modern historians can analyze. Written sources—codices (religious manuscripts), genealogies of kings, poems, and myths—were long considered by historians to be the only appropriate evidence to study the past. Thus most historians began the narrative of world history with urban civilizations because that was when written sources first appeared. That narrow view of what constituted appropriate evidence has been replaced by a more inclusive approach, which is aided by ground-breaking scientific techniques. The new methodology is driven by a determination to learn to "read" whatever clues early humans left behind. Historians now rely on disciplines such as archaeology, DNA analysis, forensic science, linguistics, and ethno-botany to examine the past. For example, archeologists use skeletal remains, burial sites, work spaces, garbage pits, and ruins of structures to illuminate the lives of early humans. For this most ancient period, history has become a detective story where we try to create a fuller picture based on specialists' careful work with a wide variety of evidence. Yet even when the analysis of written sources is augmented by other evidence, our picture is incomplete and changing all the time. Furthermore, countless stories of women who lived in the past will never be known or told. However, this chapter relies upon the best detective work of many disciplines to show how and why Eurasian women's lives changed with urbanization and militarization before 1000 BCE.

This chapter focuses on the earliest human communities that developed across Eurasia. This continent has historically been the most populated by humans and domesticated species of animals. Moreover, Eurasian history has benefited from a greater communication among civilizations than other regions. This was largely through the exchanges along the land and sea routes that connected the Tigris-Euphrates civilization of the area occupying modern Iraq to the other three Eurasian civilizations: across desert to northeastern Africa's Nile Valley, down the Persian Gulf and Indian Ocean coast to the mouth of the Indus Valley, and along the caravan trails that later became known as the silk roads to east Asia. Finally, the sources from Eurasia, scanty though they are for the years before 1000 BCE, give us more information than those from other regions of the world. We begin with a brief overview of hunter-gatherers and then discuss Eurasian villagers, pastoralists, and urban dwellers before 1000 BCE.

QUESTIONS FOR STUDENT ANALYSIS

1. What do we know about women's work and culture in hunter-gathering communities? How does this knowledge contrast with what historians have speculated about women's relative standing in these societies?

2. How did women's roles change when they became sedentary villagers? How does this contrast with the experience of female pastoralists? What factors account for the differences among these communities?

3. How did urbanization affect women's roles? Why did urbanization affect women so negatively?

4. To what extent can we see variety in the status of women in Eurasian urban communities that existed between 3500 and 1000 BCE?

WOMEN IN THE FIRST SOCIETIES: HUNTER-GATHERERS (BEFORE 10,000 BCE)

The hunter-gatherers of ancient Eurasia show no evidence of patriarchy— that is, the institutional domination of men over women. In fact, archaeological evidence suggests that women in these foraging communities were valued as much as men in social, economic, and religious realms. Nevertheless, this relative egalitarianism is a far cry from the mythical idyllic society that some hopeful historians suggest existed in early human history. While we lack sources for the universal supremacy of male-dominated societies, neither do we have any evidence for a time in which goddesses reigned supreme, or where women ruled over men on the basis of female potential for motherhood.

SOCIAL LIVES AND STATUS

Archaeological evidence and comparisons with modern hunter-gathering societies suggest that ancient hunter-gathering women enjoyed a higher status than those in other types of communities because of the large role they played in the survival of the band—usually a group of about 25 people, mostly non-blood relatives—who lived cooperatively together to survive. Cave art depicts women foraging for plants, suggesting that they may have been the primary plant gatherers. Since most people tended to survive with the nutrients and calories supplied by plants rather than animals, this made women's work invaluable to their communities. This in turn led to women's elevated position as a whole. The primary role of women as plant gatherers and the resulting high position they had in society can be seen in the modern example of the !Kung people of Africa: Meat supplies 30 percent of their calories; 70 percent comes from plants collected largely by women.

Historians have used similar evidence from ancient archaeological sites and comparisons to modern hunter-gathering societies to assemble a portrait of the social world of these women. Probably the starkest contrast between hunter-gathering communities and other lifestyles is the dominance of the social institution known as the band over that of the family. Bands moved from one temporary camp to another, operating together to forage for plants; hunt for animals; and share their food, water, and shelter.

While the leadership of bands may or may not have not been under men, some historians have suggested that matrifocal, or mother-centered communities, might have predominated, with women becoming the social center of many bands as they worked together to raise children. The life span of foraging women lasted only 25 to 30 years. They tended to space their children's births three to four years apart. (Mothers may have used lactation as an early type of birth control, nursing young children to suppress ovulation.) The transient and insecure nature of foraging existence made having too many children spaced closely together difficult. Fewer children meant that women's individual reproduction did not take precedence over other social roles. Furthermore, early mortality had the effect of leaving many children motherless, to be raised collectively by other relatives or band members. If the women of a band did play the predominant role in raising the community's children, they would have been involved in major decisions the band would have made, such as when and where to set up camp.

VALUATION OF WORK ROLES

Although women in hunter-gathering societies played a predominant role in gathering plants and in raising the children of their bands, gender roles for work as a whole were much more flexible than in other types of communities. Historians have deduced this from the archaeological evidence, which depicts animal hunting as a far less male-oriented occupation than the general stereotype of "man-the-hunter." Readers familiar with the most famous evidence from this period of human history can imagine the paintings depicting mammoths and bison that are preserved in the caves of modern western Eurasia. Since men would have been more likely to make the long excursions necessary to capture these creatures, many historians have concluded that men predominated in the task of large game-hunting.

However, when we look at other archaeological evidence we see a more rounded picture of who hunted and what animals were really most useful for the hunter-gathering bands. For instance, in modern Ukraine archaeologists discovered 20,000-year-old shelters that were constructed of mammoth bones. Examination of the bones of these shelters in close detail suggests that the communities who built them may have scavenged the bones of dead animals rather than actually hunting and killing the powerful beasts themselves. In fact, much archaeological evidence reveals that small-game hunting was of greater importance to early human communities than large animal hunting. Multitudes of rabbit skeletons found in ancient foraging sites (also in Ukraine) indicate that these creatures provided far more meat to these societies than did the flesh of larger animals. The ancient remains of easily maneuvered net snares suggest that rabbits and other small animals could just as easily have been caught by women, and even children, as by men. Additionally, we know that women played an important role in fishing in many hunter-gathering societies. Ancient burial sites from modern Scandinavia show women buried with fish bones and fishing hooks, revealing an association with women and fishing in that community. Other examples exist of women playing an important role as hunters on land and water in the earliest human societies.

Hunter-gathering women played a predominant role in other survival practices. Because women were the primary textile producers of the first settled village and pastoralist communities (later than 10,000 BCE), many historians have hypothesized that textile manufacturing played a similarly important role for women in earlier hunter-gathering societies. Historians do have rare evidence—cloth fragments—that textile production and basket weaving occurred as early as 27,000 years ago in western Eurasia. In a type of portable weaving called band weaving, cloth was made by weaving thin bands of plant fiber, stopping, rolling or unrolling the band, and restarting as needed when one was on the move. The final step was sewing the bands together to create a wider piece of cloth. Women also probably developed other tools for foragers' survival—skin bags for food collection, cloth slings for small-game hunting, or looms for weaving—but such organic materials are rarely preserved in the archaeological records. Given the general inventiveness of early humans, foraging women probably invented a type of digging stick to collect roots and tubers.

WOMEN IN RELIGION

To understand hunter-gathering culture and worldview, we need to project backward from what we know about more recent hunter-gatherers. Historians speculate that religion most likely took shape in animist beliefs and practices, wherein spirits are thought to dwell in living and inanimate objects. Some spirits are considered harmful, others not, and the separation between the natural and supernatural world is porous, sometimes transparent, or even non-existent. If animism was indeed the spiritual basis of foraging, then this helps historians analyze evidence of "Venus" figurines that appeared in a widespread area across Eurasia, from Spain to Russia, as early as 22,000 years ago. These are small statues of females whose wide hips and large breasts emphasize women's reproductive capabilities. Many more female sculptures have been found than male figures, although the latter exist. Some historians argue that these statues represent a widespread belief in a great Mother Goddess; others conjecture that they may represent a variety of fertility goddesses. Yet others suggest that perhaps the figurines were magical items used to assist women in becoming pregnant, or they represented spirits protecting the hearth. After all, many of these figurines have been found next to the hearth sites of hunter-gatherers. Some later village communities had rituals of protection around their homes that utilized figurines; therefore, some historians have conjectured that Venus figurines of hunter-gatherers might have served a similar function.

FIGURE 1-1   GODDESS FIGURINE FROM AUSTRIA
Hunter-gatherers may have created these figures to conjure their protective power or as aids to fertility.

Other evidence of female spirituality in hunter-gathering communities is provided by shamanism, which is a cultural practice still present in parts of northeastern Eurasia. Shamans were spiritual guides and held a high place in their communities. They were respected for their ability to transcend the boundaries between the invisible spirit-world and the everyday world visible to other humans. In later pastoral societies, some women have been identified as shamans based on analysis of their grave sites. Therefore historians have speculated that female shamans might also have played a role in the earliest hunter-gathering communities of northeastern Eurasia. Insofar as it is possible to estimate, the social, economic, and religious worlds of hunter-gathering women seem to have been marked by general equality with those of the men in their communities.

SOCIETIES THAT DOMESTICATED: THE FIRST WOMEN PASTORALISTS AND VILLAGERS (AFTER 10,000 BCE)

About 12,000 years ago humans entered a new historical era, that of the pastoralists and villagers. Hunting and gathering groups continued to flourish, but some people began to specialize in the domestication of animals; others settled in permanent communities to begin farming. Pastoralists and villagers slowly began to overtake parts of Eurasia and dominated that continent by 3500 BCE, as the first cities began to emerge.

The pastoralist herders tended to raise horses, camels, sheep, and goats on the steppes across central Eurasia. Around the Black Sea, groups of pastoralists raised horses as early as 4000 BCE; in many areas sheep herding also began.

Farming villages first grew in the less harsh climates of Eurasia: in the Fertile Crescent around modern Iraq, Turkey, and the eastern Mediterranean, where there was already a high diversity of plants with which the farmers could experiment. By 3500 BCE Nile Valley communities, linked to Eurasia by exchanges, also began farming in these centuries.

Pastoralists and villagers certainly experienced different lifestyles, but they nevertheless interacted with each other. Thus, pastoralists of the Tarim Basin in central Eurasia about 2000 BCE raised sheep and fabricated felt from wool, but they also foraged for plants and raised wheat they had carried from western Eurasian villages. Such pastoralists also made contact with the settled communities of northern India and used goat hair traded from India to make cashmere. The interaction between pastoralists and village dwellers caused a mutual exchange of knowledge between the societies, with both having access to domesticated plants and animals. Perhaps even as early as 5000 BCE, some pastoralists had developed the ability to milk animals and process milk into either cheese or yogurt, and later passed on that knowledge to villagers. By 3000 BCE, women of village communities in the Fertile Crescent also used sheep wool to spin and weave cloth.

What we notice about women's position in these societies is that it tended to be relatively high. Many village communities and pastoral bands continued to allow social traditions that elevated women's role in their communities, to value women's work as much as men's, and to observe religious traditions that placed female spirituality on a high level.

THE SOCIAL WORLD OF EURASIA'S FIRST VILLAGERS AND PASTORALISTS

In contrast with the bands of the hunter-gatherers, the villagers and pastoralists elevated the institution of family and made it the foundation of their societies. For pastoralists, the major social group consisted of parents and children. This type of community had fewer children than the villagers because the conditions of nomadic life were often unpredictable and difficult. Villagers were more successful at creating a food surplus, which allowed women to have more children. These women were more likely than their hunter-gathering sisters to live long enough to raise their offspring. With more children to tend to, women would have had to devote more of their time to nurturing their young.

Village communities did sometimes develop matrifocal, or mother-centered, communities—groups in which women played a large role in the leadership of families. For instance, one group, known to historians as the Linear Potter Culture of west central Eurasia (5500–4800 BCE), consisted of families that were headed by a maternal grandmother who organized her daughters and their husbands into longhouses where the extended family lived. Similar living arrangements appear in some southeast Italian communities that existed between 7000–4000 BCE, and in Japan, in the Jomon Era (2500–250 BCE), where women shellfish divers developed a strong oral tradition. Women played a large role in such communities, and there are still matrifocal organizations among women in some Japanese and Korean communities today.

However, not all village and pastoral communities were matrifocal. In fact, evidence suggests that between 4500 and 3500 BCE, many of these societies' families became patrifocal, or father-centered. In patrifocal communities, brides left their families to dwell with their husbands' families, whereas in matrifocal villages, if a woman's husband moved in with her natal family, then the relatives traced their kinship groups through a female line.

Some of the earliest evidence that male children were sometimes preferred over female comes from Eastern Eurasian village settlements. In some of these communities, grave sites show that fewer adult females existed than males, perhaps indicating that female infanticide was practiced. One oracle bone inscription corroborates this preference for boys:

> Diviner Gu practiced divination and inquired: "Will Fu Hao have an easy delivery when she gives birth to the child?" [After studying the omen] the king answered: "If she gives birth on the day *jiayin* it will be unlucky and she will give birth to a girl."[1]

Obviously, this evidence bodes poorly for the value of women in this society. The low value may have been based on the need for sons for ancestor worship in order to satisfy the living spirits of the dead: In some societies, only sons could carry out the essential rituals.

THE VALUE OF WORK: WOMEN'S OCCUPATIONS IN VILLAGE AND PASTORAL COMMUNITIES

The varied activities of village and pastoral women were critical to the existence of their communities. The labor of pastoralist women tended to be less restricted by gender roles than that of villagers because the nomadic lifestyle of pastoralists required less job specialization. Many aspects of nomadic people's lives could not be specifically "women's work," since adult men were regularly absent, according to the seasonal rhythms of summer pasturing or winter raiding. This meant that female labor was as valued as men's.

Pastoralist women played a predominant role in several areas besides child-bearing and rearing. Around 4000 BCE, women took a leading role in devising techniques for milking and processing milk, reaping four times the amount of energy from their herds than obtained by simply slaughtering the animal and eating the meat. Such procedures, while highly beneficial for their communities, were exceedingly time-consuming and, as they spread, led to a shift in women's position across Eurasia. For example, wherever the environment allowed large-scale herding with farming, men tended and milked the animals and women were relegated to milk processing. However, when forested regions (such as northwestern Eurasia) dictated small-scale herding, women continued to tend the animals and probably maintained a higher status since their jobs were similar to men's.

Pastoralist women rather than men tended to manufacture textiles and perhaps invented felt cloth production. Felt is made of great quantities of matted sheep's wool, which tangles naturally when pounded, heated, and dampened repeatedly—a labor-intensive process. But felt was ideal for nomadic women who raised large quantities of sheep, since felt production did not require a cumbersome loom. Pastoralists used felt widely for their tents, beds, rugs, clothing, saddles, and bags for carrying. As a consequence, felt production was a critical component of the pastoralist economy, as eventually was the production of rugs and of knotted, band, and loomed fabric. Pastoralist women's textile processing techniques spread to other parts of Eurasia.

Village women's labor tended to be more gender-specific than their pastoralist sisters' work. Nevertheless, the separation of work into "mostly female" versus "mostly male" occupations did not necessarily mean that village women's labor was valued less than men's. Women played a pioneering role in agricultural production. The transition to agricultural societies, beginning about 10,000 BCE, necessitated a great deal of experimentation with different varieties of plant species to see which sorts of crops could be counted on to grow when and where hunter-gatherers needed them. Working with digging sticks, women selected the seeds and plants that ensured group survival. When this led to hoe agriculture and settlement in villages, women's farming work would have been critical to their community's survival and highly regarded. Villages also depended on women's domestication of animals and fowl. All villagers—men, women, and children—worked together at harvest to ensure that families and communities would eat.

Village women also took up weaving, as did their pastoralist sisters. Unlike pastoralists, village women often used fiber plants, such as flax, hemp, and cotton, to weave cloth. This practice began about 7000 BCE in various parts of Eurasia. Spinning was almost always women's or girls' work, and enormous amounts of yarn were needed to make cloth. In southern Eurasia, women used horizontal looms, setting them outside their dwellings during the months that weather allowed. Women's weaving thus became a public activity; the more visible one's labor, the more it tends to be valued. Women also benefited from this type of weaving arrangement because they could easily assist one another in their tasks, perhaps reinforcing matrifocal arrangements. In the harsher climates of western Eurasia (modern Europe), women developed vertical looms that could be set up indoors.

One interesting and long-lived product of female weavers was silk, which historians speculate women first created in East Asia around 3500 BCE. Sericulture, the production of silk, became of critical importance to long-distance trading in Eurasia because the fabric was held in high regard across the continent, yet for thousands of years was manufactured only in its easternmost regions.

Village women took a primary role in fishing around the Caspian Sea and the Volga River around 9000 BCE, and in Jomon Japan about 5000 years later. In other parts of Eurasia, women were also associated with the manufacture of ceramics, a craft which makes food storage possible and cooking more efficient. Ancient Jomon women's thumb prints have been found on pottery, and in Minoan Crete about 3000 BCE, female shamans and healers in village communities were associated with the production of ceramics as well as the discovery of the curative qualities of certain plants—in other words, the creation of medicines.

WOMEN AND POWER IN PASTORAL AND VILLAGE COMMUNITIES

The pastoral and village communities that existed before the creation of the first urban centers around 3500 BCE did not belong to any larger political states, though in some villages, hereditary chiefdoms had developed.

Thus, trends that later allowed cities to develop written law codes, large-scale food planting with irrigation, or steep divisions between the ruling and non-ruling classes simply did not exist, nor did the inequalities regarding women's place in the public realm. We can see this in the way many village communities valued women's work, furnishing women's graves with the tools of their crafts or occupations. Even child rearing tended to be held in high esteem by village groups who wanted a reliable supply of labor to sustain their societies. These societies sometimes actually pressured women to have more children to increase the labor supply, and they valued women for their ability to foster population growth.

VILLAGE DEVELOPMENTS   By the time cities emerged, however, new factors began lessening village women's standing. First, patrifocal communities developed, which traced lineage through the male line, usually mandating that brides move out of their family homes to live with their new husbands. Hand-in-hand with this development was an increasing concentration of wealth into the control of a small group of villagers. When this happened, women's fortunes declined, because it became important for a richer family to retain wealth and prestige. Women's sexual morals were, therefore, more likely to be regulated, since establishing paternity was essential to keeping the family bloodline, and its reputation and property, intact. In village communities where land became more valued than labor, this tendency toward patrifocal families and greater stratification of wealth occurred frequently.

PASTORAL CHANGES   In many pastoral communities, there was relative equality of wealth and an absence of hereditary leadership before 1000 BCE. This lack of social stratification tended to promote women's status, because with no great interest in building up family fortune and prestige, communities felt no need to regulate women's morality in the name of ensuring the paternity of offspring or the reputation of a lineage. Pastoralist women were not only less regulated, but also more autonomous because of men's regular absence to raid or hunt.

On the other hand, women's influence in pastoral societies did lessen in two different circumstances. First, many pastoral communities that were influenced by the creation of the first cities after 3500 BCE became increasingly organized around raiding and military power; by 1000 B.C.E, hereditary leadership existed in some bands. This militarization among nomadic pastoralist peoples probably resulted in greater gender inequality, since formal warfare—which now conferred high status—was generally considered a man's occupation. Despite the tendency of militarization to lessen women's position in society, we do have evidence of women warriors in pastoral societies, perhaps naturally, since in pastoralist men's frequent absence, women defended their communities. Authors from ancient Greece and Persia commented that women of the Sauromatian and Saka pastoralists rode, hunted, and went to war. Some women apparently could not wed until they had killed an enemy. Archaeological researchers in the Black Sea area discovered later pastoralists' burials in which high-status women had armor, swords, daggers, and arrows. Finally, the fabulous legends of the women soldiers in the female-dominated Amazon societies, though undocumented, demonstrate an awareness of female pastoral fighters.

The second situation that led to lessening women's influence in pastoral societies (first documented in the Scythian groups of the Eurasian steppes around 1000 BCE) was a tendency to create a firmer division of labor and separate men's and women's work spaces. This had mixed results. It lessened pastoralist women's status, though it increased their autonomy. While pastoralist men dominated certain spheres, especially the increasingly important military and political matters, women were expected to control the home base, the mobile cart or tent. (Scythian women received a tent, called a *qionglu*, for their property upon marriage.) As we have already mentioned, when work is shared and interchangeable with men's, it tends to be noticed and esteemed, but when it is specified as outside the "public realm," the opposite holds true. Those politicized pastoral communities that followed the Scythian model of separating women and men's working spaces experienced a devaluation of women's labor. Yet generally pastoral communities maintained greater gender equality and autonomy for women into the modern era than did village or urban societies.

SHAMANS, CULT LEADERS, AND GODDESSES: RELIGION IN PASTORAL AND VILLAGE COMMUNITIES

Women in both pastoral and village communities played a prominent role in spiritual matters, although the nomadic life of pastoralists left fewer clues. Most pastoralist religion was organized around shamanism, which we have already discussed with hunter-gathering religion. In east central Eurasia, female shamans of an ancient pastoralist community were honored in their graves. One elderly individual, known as the "Cherchen woman," was interred around 2000 BCE. Her face was painted with yellow spirals, and she was buried with the materials of a healer. Another grave from about this time and place contained a woman who was buried with ephedra, a plant with medicinal and hallucinogenic properties. This shaman likely employed the plant in her practice.

Shamanism was also practiced in the settled communities, but another type of religious expression also developed in villages: cultic practices or religious rituals often officiated by people specifically selected for these duties. Across Eurasia, cultic practices were associated with many of women's productive activities, from farming to the making of textiles, ceramics, and even wine. Furthermore, village women held cultic positions that made them prominent players in a community's spirituality. Thus, the Minoan communities that dated from 2800 BCE on the Greek island of Crete painted murals and coffins showing women performing rituals and offering sacrifices.

FIGURE 1-2   MINOAN STATUETTE
Minoan women participated in many facets of Cretan life. This figure may be a priestess or a mother goddess.

Another component to women's religiosity that developed in village society was the worship of personified deities—gods and goddesses who held special powers over natural forces. Many of these deities were female. Although a society's worship of a powerful goddess did not necessarily translate into women's high status, the power of goddesses nevertheless reveals much about commonly held assumptions concerning female characteristics and the work women did for the community. For instance, in many Neolithic villages, earth goddesses abounded. The goddess Ishtar, of the Fertile Crescent, watched over grain storage, dairy, and wool. Also in this area, female goddesses had a strong association with water, perhaps indicating that gathering water was a woman's duty for these villagers. Thus, the goddess Nammu of the sea was said to have given birth to male and female deities, who in turn gave birth to all the other gods and goddesses. In eastern Eurasia, the goddess Nuwa was worshipped by villagers as the being who created all of humanity. Finally, the eastern Eurasian Goddess Xi Wang Mu was known as "Queen Mother of the West." Her first worshippers may have been villagers, but in time, her cult spread to urban and even pastoralist communities. Xi Wang Mu's powers were extraordinary, including the ability to grant immortality, protect from plague, and prophesy. The above examples show that across Eurasia the worship of goddesses reflected a respect for women's capacity for motherhood. Further, as we shall see, the introduction of urban communities often corresponded with a demotion of the powerful goddesses worshipped by villagers.

WOMEN IN THE FIRST URBAN COMMUNITIES (AFTER 3500 BCE)

The world's first cities emerged in Eurasia around 3500 BCE. Fostered by the spread of villages, the urban centers of this continent grew up along major river systems—an environment conducive to planting and harvesting crops with relatively predictable patterns. There were four major regions where urban civilizations developed: in the Fertile Crescent along the Tigris and Euphrates Rivers (also known as Mesopotamia, "the land between the two rivers"), along the Nile in Egypt, along the Indus River in modern Pakistan, and along the Yellow and Yangtze Rivers in China.

Eurasia's urban centers brought rapid changes in the organization of populations. Institutional patriarchy probably developed alongside the state, tribute extraction, social stratification, and slavery. The state, especially, was a political institution that organized, disciplined, and enslaved numerous inhabitants in order to provide security and order for itself. Law codes to promote universal standards of behavior, irrigation projects to ensure food supply, and extensive military defense were now possible and deemed necessary. Of course, in order to manage this type of society, institutional governments were needed, and the leaders who ran these growing states exercised a disproportionate share of power. State power transformed everything.

At the same time the world's first urban political institutions were taking shape, a disparity of wealth also grew in urban centers. Gaps between the haves and the have-nots of society appeared in heretofore unseen proportions. Slavery and the slave trade, essential to ancient Eurasian civilizations, are first in evidence. Some have argued that men's control and exchange of women's sexuality and reproductive capacity generally became the basis of private property in Mesopotamia between 3100 and 600 BCE. This affected not only female slaves and concubines but also the daughters of elite and free men. A bride's father, representing his family, exchanged her reproductive capacity for wealth and household goods and sometimes less tangible objects, such as status and/or influence. Sometimes payments were made in installments, and after a marriage, when her first child was born, the balance of bridewealth or dowry payments became due. This overall disparity in status, wealth, and power spelled a worsening of women's position.

Another explanation for the worsening of women's position and the emergence of patriarchy focuses on demography and technology, beginning with burgeoning populations of village communities, which, as discussed above, encouraged women's fertility to supply the needed workforce. Populous urban centers could no longer practice *hoe* agriculture, but often needed intensive *plow* agriculture to feed everyone. With more children, urban women had less time for heavier agricultural work and the long, intensive hours needed for cultivation. Women of plow-using cultures may have preferred and chosen to work around the house and to perform lighter agricultural work. This scenario resulted in a gradual loss of women's social power and prestige—sometimes through their own choices that made sense to them at the time, but that accelerated men's control over economic activity and social resources. Ultimately, then, when the communities began using plows and more laborious, intensive methods of cultivation (and the groups prospered materially), women's status changed.

Women's experience in the first urban centers was marked by a general devaluation of their social freedoms, a denial of their claims to the results of their labor, and sometimes even a reshaping of their religious expression. This decline did not affect all women's communities in the same way or at the same time. We notice this in the great variety of women's experiences across Eurasia in all four of the earliest urban areas.

WOMEN AND SOCIETY IN THE EARLIEST CIVILIZATIONS

Although some villages had begun to experience greater social stratification by 3500 BCE, the difference between the powerful and the powerless was not nearly as marked as it was in the earliest cities. The increased wealth possessed by a small proportion of the urban population led to a growing interest in keeping wealth and power within familial units. And it led in many ways to the constriction of women's lives, whether slave, concubine, free, or elite.

The social experience of many women was shaped by the flourishing Eurasian slave trade. In Mesopotamia as early as 2300 BCE, inscriptions for "slave girl" appear earlier than those translating as "slave male." Female slaves in Mesopotamia often originated as captives of raids and were more plentiful than male slaves. They also seem to have been valued more than male slaves. In Syria, the reward for the return of fleeing females was double that for male fugitive slaves. Enslaved women lived under a wide range of conditions, from the relative comfort of high-level slaves important in the domestic realm, such as concubines (unfree females purchased for reproduction) to female slaves used for their brute physical labor. Thus, although many enslaved women held very low positions in society, the status of some was not as low as slaves in other time periods. For instance, a second-generation slave was often valued more than one that had been recently captured. Furthermore, female slaves could upon occasion be freed from their servitude. In Babylon around 1750 BCE, slave concubines were frequently freed after the demise of their masters. Additionally, the children of freewomen and male slaves were considered to be of free status there. High slave mortality and these legal paths to slave freedom made slave raiding for new supplies a constant imperative.

The situation of free and elite women was shaped by family control. Ensuring the lineage of a family meant keeping ever-closer tabs on women's morality, which could include preserving a woman's virginity until marriage and ensuring that she had only her husband for a sexual partner. This would guarantee that the paternity of family members would be unquestioned. Even a woman's reputation could be of critical interest to her family. We see this in practices such as veiling and seclusion, which marked women's high familial social standing and reputation for chastity (meaning virginity when single and fidelity in marriage), and actually prevented her from any sexual contact with males other than her husband.

As mentioned above, the decrease in women's social influence did not strike equally in all places. For instance, little evidence points to women's morality being constrained in the cities of Harappa and Mohenjo Daro in the Indus River Valley around 2500 BCE. The thousands of written sources from this civilization have yet to be deciphered, and thus it would be hazardous to assume that women's social position never declined there, and yet archaeological evidence suggests that the gap between the haves and the have-nots might not have been terribly significant to the urban population. The façades of the residential buildings in those cities were relatively similar, even though some families possessed much larger storerooms than others. This evidence therefore suggests that maintaining a family's wealth and power, and the corresponding demotion that meant for women, was not as marked there. Coincidentally, no remains of defensive fortresses or other evidence of militarism has been found along the Indus River. Similarly, in the less urbanized Egyptian civilization, evidence suggests that women held positions of relative social equality and enjoyed freedom of movement unlike in other ancient societies. Given geographic barriers protecting them from warlike neighbors, Nile and Indus River civilizations were more militarily secure generally than civilizations in Mesopotamia and East Asia, and this may have resulted in fewer constraints on women.

INSIGHT FROM LAW CODES   We can see the inferior social position of urban women in law codes. Although legal texts from Mesopotamia often reflected social guidelines rather than actual practice, they nevertheless give critical insight to the way a society's most powerful people intended to govern. For example, in one Mesopotamian city in 2000 BCE, the murder of a woman was a capital offense. But by the time of Hammurabi (d. 1750 BCE), a Babylonian ruler and famous lawmaker in Mesopotamia, killing a common woman only resulted in a fine according to the law code. (There was a stronger punishment if an elite woman were the victim.)

We can also see the uneven treatment of urban women in the laws and practices surrounding marriage and divorce. For instance, wives' positions in Mesopotamia differed from city to city even within the same time frame. Whereas one law code from the urban civilization of Sumer made it legal for a new bride to refuse intercourse without punishment, later, a woman could be drowned if she refused to consummate her marriage. By 2500 BCE a law allowed a man to break his wife's teeth with a burnt brick if she disagreed with him. Divorce laws from Mesopotamian civilizations show that, although women experienced new inequities and constraints, they continued to enjoy some protections also. The cases compiled by the Babylonian ruler Hammurabi about 1700 BCE forbade women from divorcing, yet allowed men to terminate their marriages. Nevertheless, even Hammurabi's law code required divorced men to support their former spouses and any children they had together.

We can further understand the complexities of women's status in society by considering commonplace factors that tended to make the lives of ancient urban women either easier or more difficult. For instance, laws regulating divorce demonstrated the amount of control a woman had in her marriage. In Egypt, women had the right to initiate divorce, which was rare in ancient civilizations. A second factor that obviously affected a woman's social position was whether polygamy, the practice of having more than one wife, was the rule. Egyptian society was mostly monogamous, following the lead of the divine couple, Isis and Osiris. Kings were expected to have several wives. Similarly, in some areas of Mesopotamia around 1000 BCE, rulers had multiple wives and many concubines. Obviously, not all of these women were equally valued by their husbands. In the Shang civilization of ancient China after 1750 BCE, elites also practiced polygamy, and the first wives of the royal families there often had positions close to the ruler. Thus, Fu Hao (d. 1181 BCE), a first wife of royalty, actually managed large estates of land, supervised rituals, ran military ventures, and even governed her own town.

A third way to assess the social position of women is consideration of who controlled their marital arrangements. Throughout most of urban history it has been typical to view marriage primarily as a means of regulating procreation, transferring property, or making alliances: It was not to celebrate a romantic joining of two lovers, as it is commonly considered in modern society. Thus, in some early Mesopotamian cities, marriage even involved a written contract between the guardians of both husband and wife. It was not the contract that was particularly onerous for women, but rather the extent to which their participation was less important than men's. In one early Mesopotamian city in 3000 BCE, a prospective groom needed to ask the permission of the prospective bride's mother and father for her hand. Thus, the involvement of both parents was considered equally important. This law was revoked at a later period.

The degree of control that a husband had over his wife is yet another way to analyze a woman's place in her society. For instance, in some places it was perfectly legal for a man to injure his wife physically, as we read with the Mesopotamian example of the burnt brick. In the law code of Hammurabi, judges were encouraged to allow men to sell their wives and children into slavery in order to satisfy their outstanding debts. Many laws testify to the rights of a woman's family or husband to regulate her morality. Thus, in some Mesopotamian cities adultery, defined as a woman having intercourse with anyone but her husband, was punishable with death by drowning. Throughout the history of Mesopotamian civilization, however, men were allowed to have sexual relations with unmarried women. Such unequal treatment occurred in order to preserve the reputation of husbands and to ensure that the children of these men would be legitimate. In some areas of Mesopotamia, the tradition of veiling and secluding women began for similar purposes. As early as 2500 BCE, veiling perhaps began as a practice among elite women. It was thus not merely a tool to control morality, but was also a way to display the social status of wives. An example of veiling can be seen in a law code from the Assyrian Empire from about 1500 BCE, which states:

> Wives or [daughters as well as concubines] when [they go out] on the street, are to have their heads [covered]. The daughters . . . are to be veiled [and] their heads covered. . . . If she goes out into the street during the day, she is to be veiled.[2]

The fact that this code also dictated that prostitutes were forbidden from veiling demonstrates the elitism that accompanied such regulations. Guarding the virginity of unmarried women arose from the same motivations as did the practice of veiling. Thus, as Mesopotamian civilization developed, the unwed daughters of many powerful families were secluded as much to guarantee their lack of sexual contact with men as to display their family's social standing. This custom is first documented among the Assyrian kings in 1400–1000 BCE, whose female family members lived in seclusion in their palaces. The tendency to seclude elite women spread from there and became typical in many Mediterranean, Near Eastern, and Persian civilizations.

WOMEN'S LABOR IN EARLY URBAN SOCIETIES

The first cities witnessed a decline in the valuation of female labor and a constriction on the types of professions open to them, but the decrease in women's economic power was not as marked as that of their social freedoms. The labor of women—slaves and commoners in particular—continued to dominate the production of food, textiles, and ceramics, and some urban women exercised great control over financial assets and took up prominent occupations. Nevertheless, because the organization of cities promoted a great degree of job specialization, tasks increasingly became gender-based. In many urban areas, such as ancient Mesopotamia, "women's work" began to take on a particular focus around the home. Tending to young children, producing cloth, making pottery, and processing food typically fell under women's domain. These occupations, so critical to the function of a society, did not assume a particularly public role and thus were considered of less importance than "men's work." Although this had begun to occur in some villages around the time of the first cities (3500 BCE), the extent to which the domestication of women's labor happened in urban centers was much more marked. After all, many productive activities that men carried out were impossible for people without extensive training or the ability to spend large amounts of time away from home, such as metalworking, masonry, or glassmaking.

The increasing appreciation for male-oriented labor led to men earning more income and controlling more resources than women. Hand-in-hand with this tendency went an inclination to consider women of lesser value than men, even when they did the same jobs. This can be seen in some Mesopotamian areas that show wage gaps between male and female olive oil pressers. One document shows women pressers earning the equivalent of 50 liters of barley per month, while men received 300 liters. Another trend that occasionally caused a devaluation of women's labor was the appropriation of some female-oriented tasks by men. This could happen when an occupation was particularly profitable. For instance, the Mycenaean civilization, which conquered the Minoan peoples of Greece (1400 BCE), also supplanted the female control of the textile industry there. Mycenaean fabric production was no longer overseen by women, as it had been among the Minoans, but was rather under royal administration—which used female captives as laborers.

Despite these trends, much evidence exists to demonstrate the strong financial capabilities that some women of the world's first cities did possess. In the Indus Valley civilization of Mohenjo Daro, no decline of women's economic power is evident. In the Indus Valley, the fact that both women and men made pottery shows that at least some occupations that were considered women's work elsewhere, were not gender-oriented in the city of Harappa. Even in civilizations where labor tended to be divided according to male or female work, women could still exercise a high degree of control as managers or powerful merchants. For instance, the lucrative silk industry of Shang China (1766–1027 BCE) not only employed solely female workers, but was also frequently managed by elite women. Furthermore, in the Mesopotamian civilization of Sumer, the female family members of rulers and high officials oversaw vast households and their productive activity. The maintenance of royal farmland, fisheries, textile workshops, and laborers all fell under their authority. Thus, around 2400 BCE, two Sumerian royal wives named Dimitur and Baranamtrar were in charge of the administrative center of their city. Mesopotamian records dating from the period of Assyrian rule (1400–1000 BCE) give evidence of high-level merchant activity conducted by women. For example, a woman named Lamassi was involved in the long-distance trading of tin and fabric around the Eastern Mediterranean. She writes to her husband:

Kuluma is bringing you nine textiles; Idi-Suen three textiles; Ela refused
to accept textiles for transport; Idi-Suen refused to accept another five
textiles.[3]

Inheritance laws provide more evidence for the continued existence
of women's economic influence in early urban societies. Egyptian law
protected women's right to inherit property for thousands of years, unlike
other ancient civilizations, such as Mesopotamia, where that right was
eroding after 2000 BCE. In Babylon, the law code of Hammurabi (1700 BCE)
indicates that dowries, wealth that families gave their daughters when
they wed, were often under wives' control. In fact, this document mandated that fathers provided both sons and daughters with certain possessions when they married. Despite pressure to keep the bulk of a family's
fortune in the hands of male heirs, women could sometimes become the
main beneficiaries of familial interests. In the Eastern Mediterranean area
of modern Syria, a law from 1400 BCE stated that fathers could legally
change the sex of their daughters so that they might inherit the family's
property. She became "male and female," the legal son of her father, and
hence possessed the same ability to conduct business transactions and
maintain household customs that sons typically did, although she was
unable to control family property past her lifetime.[4] The male head of a
household could similarly make his widow into a widower according to
law. The rationale for changing the legal gender of a female inheritor was
to ensure that a family's estates would be kept intact, even when no male
family members existed that could inherit.

Women carried out a variety of other occupations, some gender-
specific and others not. In Mesopotamia and Egypt, evidence exists for
women working as scribes, bakers, prophets, and temple workers, none
of which were considered specifically women's work. On the other hand,
textile manufacturing was an occupation generally performed by women,
enslaved and free, even when it took place on a large scale and outside the
domain of households. Thus, evidence from 2200 BCE shows some Mesopotamian cities having large textile workshops that employed numerous
girls and adult women. Egyptian female spinners and weavers produced
a highly valued export and the primary exchange commodity. East Asian
women developed the art of sericulture to new heights upon the institution of the first cities there (during the Shang era, around 1750). Chinese
urban women learned to alter the cocoons of silk moths by "de-gumming"
them before the larvae could eat through the silk. As with the silk industry
begun by village-dwellers in earlier eras, sericulture was a labor-intensive
and highly profitable process. Silk was greatly sought after by elites across
Eurasia, both because of its beauty and its rarity: For thousands of years it
was produced only in China.

WOMEN AND URBAN POLITICS

Generally speaking, women were increasingly absent from political life in Eurasian cities. In Mesopotamia, from 3000–2000 BCE, women exercised more power than usually recognized, but by 1000 BCE political power passed to men. Early Sumerian queens had their own seals and occupied important positions, and dynastic tables from 2500 BCE list women's names. Royal women gave their sons legitimacy in succession. One Sumerian woman, Ku-Bau, consolidated the founding of the city of Kish, became a king, and reigned for 100 years according to the Sumerian King List. In later traditions, Ku-Bau is described as an "alewife," and her reign is blamed for Sargon's successful conquest of Kish around 2300 BCE. (No matter that the conquest occurred two generations after her rule.) The negative version of events was recorded in an era during which women's active role in society was frowned upon. Male kings became legendary heroes, but her reign was identified as an aberration and cause of misfortune. Royal and elite women in some cases had the independent authority to exchange gifts and letters with other royal wives in other city-states, playing an important diplomatic role, but later they lost that independent authority.

In Shang China, a first and favored wife might well function as a close official to the ruler. Fu Hao (1200–1181 BCE) was the powerful consort of Emperor Wu Ding. According to oracle bone inscriptions, she led military campaigns; oversaw landed estates; took charge of special rituals; and was the subject of many divinations concerning her illnesses, childbirth, and general well-being. Upon her death, women of a slightly less elite status than the royal consort were sacrificed as "accompaniers-in-death" and placed in Fu Hao's royal tomb.

In contrast, royal Egyptian women continued to have strong political influence. Four female pharaohs ruled in their own name. For example, the female Pharaoh Hatsheput (r. 1479–1458 BCE) was a highly successful ruler who strengthened Egypt's defenses and trade networks, initiated many construction projects, and enjoyed a stable, prosperous reign. To rule, she took male titles, dressed as a man (even wearing the ceremonial beard!), and proclaimed herself "king." These women were to some degree exceptions to the rule. In most Eurasian urban civilizations after 1000 BCE, women had increasingly less political visibility and were excluded from some public positions.

WOMEN IN URBAN RELIGIOUS CULTURE

Very often, the realm of female spirituality was the arena least affected by the growth of cities. Nonetheless, the involvement of urban women with the divine was, like the other aspects of women's lives, marked by regional variation. We can see the sustained value of female spirituality in the prominent role that goddesses continued to play in the world's first civilizations. For example, in the cities of the Indus Valley, many inhabitants prayed to goddesses who were connected to the role of agriculture and fertility. This is shown in the remains of ancient seals from this area. One depicts a tree growing from the womb of a woman or a goddess, and another shows a female deity appearing from a bush with worshippers in supplication before her. In ancient Mesopotamia, both male and female goddesses were associated with wine. The goddesses Nissaba and Ninlil came to be patronesses of writing, scribal arts, and accounting. The goddess Ishatur (earlier known as Ishtar in Mesopotamia) continued to be celebrated as a goddess of both motherhood and rivers and was seen as eternal virgin and sacred harlot. In Egypt, the most popular goddess was Isis, the ideal wife and mother. China's first civilizations revered "the First Silk Cultivator," and Shang royal wives made ritual sacrifices to her.

The continued prominence of women's involvement with religious matters can also be seen in the cultic functions they performed publicly as well as in the private rituals they conducted at home. Thus, in the Indus Valley city of Mohenjo Daro, a female bronze figurine that most historians interpret as a temple dancer gives evidence for female participation in urban religious rituals. Furthermore, an architectural structure from this urban center known as the "Great Bath," with many rooms off the courtyard, suggests that some women performed elaborate fertility rituals there and consecrated kings and priests. Later sources from this area discuss a practice of ritual cohabitation of female attendants with the men of the community in lotus ponds. These sources equated women with water deities known as *asparas,* who, although frequently considered harmful temptresses to men, perhaps represented a Mother Goddess in this early period. Women played an equally important role in temple rituals in Mesopotamian kingdoms before 2000 BCE. Thus, temple priestesses, often of royal blood, acted as intercessors between divine beings and mortals. One such was Enheduanna, priestess of the Temple of Ur and daughter of King Sargon of Sumer. Sometimes these rituals involved a "sacred marriage." In 2030 BCE, one priestess's poem shows the erotic nature of her spiritual duties:

> My sweet one, wash me with honey—
> In the bed that is filled with honey,
> Let us enjoy our love.
> Lion, let me give you my caresses,
> My sweet one, wash me with honey.[5]

Elite Egyptian women often became priestesses of Hatho, goddess of fertility, sexuality, and childbirth. Some priestesses controlled territory as virtual rulers, collecting taxes and spending resources. Egyptian women's relative equality to men is shown in the fact that both men and women of the elite could become gods after death. In China, although women were discouraged from holding religious offices after the Shang era, they nevertheless did perform private religious practices on a daily basis that often revolved around the acknowledgement of their family's ancestry. Domestic religious rituals were also important for women throughout the early history of Mesopotamia and the Indus Valley civilizations.

In some urban areas, however, there was a growing decline of the value of female spirituality. Goddesses were demoted in many civilizations in which men took over the most important agricultural tasks. Thus, in China the goddess Queen Mother of the West gradually lost her near-omnipotence. In Mesopotamia, many myths recounting the legendary battles between earth goddesses and sky thunder gods arose, suggesting a conflict between the growing power of the masculine deities and earlier village mother goddesses. In the eastern Mediterranean Mycenaean civilization (1400–1100 BCE), male gods such as Zeus and Apollo were put atop sanctuaries that had belonged to female divine beings, such as the Mountain Mother in the earlier Minoan period. In both early Chinese and Mesopotamian civilizations, the ability of women to take on important public religious offices was restricted as time progressed. For instance, by 1000 BCE, women throughout Mesopotamia no longer were permitted to take on cultic roles, such as priestesses. Furthermore, the first monotheistic religion, Judaism, had appeared there, and its Hebrew followers revered a single male god. In China during the Shang period (1766–1027 BCE), female shamanism declined as men took up the tasks of interceding between familial ancestors and their descendents. A belief that women could cause ancestral cults to become disrupted arose and was associated with a growing idea that women's sexual body fluids, such as menstrual blood and post-partum discharge, made them into "polluters." As such, they were deemed unfit to hold official religious positions.

CONCLUSION

Although the four different types of early human communities—hunting-gathering, village-dwelling, nomadic pastoral, and urban-based—that we have examined here did exist side by side in 1000 BCE, ultimately the organization of city-based civilizations prevailed. The lives of Eurasian foragers, nomadic pastoralists, and village-dwellers would be dominated by the organized political institution of the state that urbanization heralded.

The ultimate triumph of cities' influence on the lives of women around the world was far from complete in 1000 BCE. But the trends that would become typical for many women were already established in some of the major urban civilizations of Eurasia by that time, as well as in steppe nomadic pastoralism. The domestication of women's work, the concern over protecting women's sexual morality, and even a weakening of female spirituality would plague women in virtually every urban society after that date. Hand-in-hand with these trends was the nearly complete elimination of female authority in political affairs. In fact, most men and women were prevented from having a political voice until relatively recently in human history. Only a few men governed ancient Eurasian civilizations. This makes sense in light of the patrifocal communities that city life fostered.

Although these trends in women's social, economic, political, and religious worlds would continue for most of the urban civilizations that followed, they do not tell the whole story of women's experiences across the globe, particularly in pastoralist and stateless communities. We know less about such women, but we know that before 1000 BCE a special steppe dynamic developed among nomadic pastoralists that would influence later Eurasian civilizations such as Tang China. The practice of steppe patriarchy created different ideas about women, different experiences for women, and different male-female relations. Given the regular absence of men, women were not subordinate in the same way as they were in urban civilizations. Most pastoralist women enjoyed more power than did women in sedentary society, since they shared men's work and participated in all decisions but war. The division of labor among frontier nomadic peoples was much less pronounced than in settled urban society.

The following chapters will explore the nuances of women's situation in various societies and develop a more rounded picture of the forces that shaped women's lives and the ways in which women shaped the world around them.

CHAPTER TWO

WOMEN IN THE ANCIENT MEDITERRANEAN: CLASSICAL GREECE AND IMPERIAL ROME (CA. 500 BCE–500 CE)

The best-known societies of the ancient Mediterranean were the Classical Greek city-states and Imperial Rome. As shown in Chapter One, growing urbanization and the creation of states led to the demotion of women's status, and this trend continued in Greek and Roman societies. The traditions of patriarchy that surfaced in ancient Mesopotamian civilizations certainly continued in fifth-century Athens and Sparta and in the Roman world from 500 BCE to the late fourth century CE. Thus, "women's work" was separate from men's, and their marital and sexual arrangements were largely out of their hands. Men controlled most political affairs, and female spirituality often, but not always, took a secondary place to masculine ceremonies, deities, and rituals.

This chapter, however, examines how patriarchy shaped Classical Greece and Imperial Rome differently. The importance of women's contributions to their communities has always existed, but the degree to which their roles were valued in religious practices, social expectations, and political and economic influence has varied, along with women's ability to actively participate in these spheres. Regardless, women in ancient Greece and Rome received public acknowledgement only when their behavior championed patriarchal values. Indeed, it's likely that even the most famous and public of women supported traditional mores because, after all, the society that produced such ideas enabled these women to gain power.

Questions for Student Analysis

1. The democratic government of Classical Athens gave a great deal of freedom to men, whereas the militaristic government of Sparta set strict regulations on how men lived their lives. Nevertheless, in Athens women's lives were much more restricted than were the lives of their Spartan contemporaries. What about the political system of each society might have contributed to the relative power of women and men in Classical Athens and Sparta?

2. In what ways was the legal position of women in Classical Athens similar to that of Roman women during the early Republic? By the late Republic and Empire, what had changed about women's legal status in Rome?

3. How did the "ideal" Roman woman, as defined by men writing in the early Republic, continue to influence conceptions about female behavior in later eras?

4. How did the role of female deities differ in Classical Greece and Imperial Rome, and to what extent do you think these differences reflected the various positions of women in their respective societies?

Classical Greece: 500 BCE–338 BCE

Ancient Greece refers to any of the Greek-speaking cultures in the Mediterranean between the civilization that grew in Minoan Crete (as early as 3000 BCE) to the death of Alexander of Macedon in 323 BCE. The most famous era of ancient Greece, however, is the Classical period, from the fifth through the fourth centuries BCE, and it is this age upon which this chapter focuses. Furthermore, although there were numerous Greek states during this period, Athens shall be the focus here. This special emphasis is for two reasons: first, historians know much more about women from Classical Athens than other Greek states because of the abundance of sources from there. Second, although Athens was unique in the degree to which it was urbanized and democratized, many other Greek states appear to have shared at least some of its qualities. Ancient Sparta, however, was an exception to the rest of the Greek city-states.

THE FRUITS OF DEMOCRACY IN CLASSICAL ATHENS

One of the most significant attributes of the Classical Age is the fact that it witnessed the world's first known democracy in the city-state of Athens. Prior to the fifth century BCE, Athenian government had changed from an oligarchy (government made up of the wealthy), to rule by tyrants, and finally to an emerging democracy. By the mid-fifth century BCE, all citizen males between the ages of 18 and 59 were expected to vote on political matters. These men could also sit on a jury, be tried in court by their peers, and serve on the Council of Five Hundred—a body chosen annually by the free male citizens to enact legislation. Participatory government in Classical Athens was thus not dependent on wealth or noble lineage. Slaves, non-citizens, and women, however, were excluded from voting. As a result, the fraction of inhabitants that could play a role in government was probably less than 25 percent.

During the Classical era, or the "golden age" of Athenian society (ca. 500 BCE), great developments occurred in culture. The foundations of Western philosophy were established by famous thinkers such as Socrates, Plato, and Aristotle. Although their ideas and the degree to which they pursued knowledge were atypical of Greeks in general, they enabled later philosophers to build on their works. Theater was another development from this period, and the great tragedies and comedies of playwrights such as Aristophanes, Euripides, Sophocles, and Aeschylus are still performed to this day. Artistic developments in Classical Greece were admired and copied by the Romans, Syrians, North Africans, and Indians, and later by Italian Renaissance artists of the fifteenth and sixteenth centuries CE. The buildings on the Athenian Acropolis epitomize the Greek artists' ability to render marble into stately buildings, three-dimensional statues, and realistic action scenes.

An all-pervasive side of Greek life, as is the case with each of the societies discussed in this book, was religion. The Greeks worshipped many deities, and their gods and goddesses took on anthropomorphic (human-like) shapes. The most important deities were known as the Olympians, and they were thought to control almost all aspects of human life. Greeks offered prayers and sacrifices to their gods in order to obtain special favors such as safety in childbirth, success in war, or a good harvest. The purpose of prayer was not, therefore, to worship a deity for the deity's own sake, but rather to obtain something in a kind of quid pro quo arrangement. Greeks in the Classical Age were familiar with a large body of myths related to their gods and goddesses. They had a firm sense of morality, but it was not based on the example set by their deities. Thus, these myths do not make the Olympians out to be particularly ethical beings, but they do reveal how Greeks imagined the gods' role in the cosmos.

WOMEN AND ATHENIAN DEMOCRACY

For women who lived in Athens during the Classical era, the great political and cultural advances of their age would have been much less noticeable than the day-to-day restrictions on everything from physical movement to the legal standing that shaped their lives. In fact, the transition from rule by tyrants to democratic government in the fifth century BCE might actually have heralded misfortune for Athenian women. Scholars have speculated that Athenian women may have been freer before the Classical Age. Such freedoms were manifested in the work of the famous lesbian poetess Sappho, who charmed both men and women of the late seventh century BCE with her writings. "I cannot speak, my tongue sticks to my dry mouth, thin fire spreads beneath my skin," writes the poetess, whose words depicted a female's passionate attraction to a married woman.[1] The public visibility of Sappho represented an opening for women's voices that became impossible in Classical Athens. In fact, extant written sources from the Classical period were composed by men, a fact that makes our ultimate comprehension of how women understood their own lives impossible.

As participatory government for men grew, women's freedom declined. These trends were perhaps connected, because Athenian men feared that women would be objects of contention and sources of civil discord once legal power was distributed more equally among male citizens. Furthermore, lawgivers made many democratic reforms with a view to strengthening the economic independence of Athenian property-owning families. Such legislation often entailed limitation of women's ability to control their marriages and finances. Finally, Athenian democratic reforms caused restrictions to women's standing because of the growing emphasis on public versus private life.

As men's roles in Athenian society became focused around participation in civic affairs, women's absence from this arena was thrown into ever-sharper relief and even institutionalized. Women were seen as the anti-men, in a sense: those whose duties and character could be defined as the opposite of men's. This view transcended ideas about politics and defined ideas about women in all sorts of spheres, such as medicine and philosophy. Some of the most influential writings about women's role in reproduction argued that women played only a passive role in conception. Aristotle was the most famous progenitor of this idea, which lasted throughout the Middle Ages in Europe. Aristotle wrote, "A woman is as it were an infertile male; the female, in fact, is female on account of an inability of a sort."[2] As the playwright Aeschylus records, a woman is "not her offspring's parent, but nurse to the newly sown embryo. The male—who mounts—begets."[3] Therefore, as the political freedoms of men grew, the power and status of women decreased.

THE SOCIAL MILIEU

Set stages marked the life cycle of most ancient women: birth, marriage, and childbirth. Merely surviving childhood was a great feat for both male and female infants, but mostly for females. Due to the hazards of childbirth and the lack of sanitation, infant mortality might have been as high as 30–40 percent in the first year of life. Further challenges for girls lay in the fact that Greek families found them much more costly to raise than boys. This was because daughters were married off at a young age, often about 12, and thus would not have contributed to their family's financial situation. Furthermore, the practice of dowry (the custom of giving a financial package that would support the girl throughout her married life) was a commonplace, but providing this dowry was a hardship for many families. Since there was no economic advantage to raising girls, female infanticide by exposure—which entailed abandoning them in an unsafe outdoor area to die—was common. Although evidence for infanticide is scanty, studies have shown that the ratio of males to females living in Classical Athens was unnaturally weighted in favor of men. Evidence suggests that even after infancy, girls were regularly fed less nutritious food than boys.

Girls spent the period between birth and marriage preparing for their future roles in domesticated spheres. Until about age six, they mingled among boys their age, but after this they were taught jobs such as food preparation and cloth making. Girls of all classes remained uneducated, while boys who could afford to attend small private schools eventually did so. The extent to which this practice was an endemic part of Athenian society was expressed by a common fourth-century BCE adage that educating women was equivalent to giving weapons to a killer. Such sentiments illustrate the degree to which Greek society had changed since the late seventh century, when women such as Sappho wrote poetry for both men and women.

Females were expected to marry soon after the onset of puberty, around age 14, whereas men did not marry until age 30. Thus, the first 15 years of a bride's marriage stood in marked counterpoint to the men of her generation. Men would have been spending those years studying, socializing in the *gymnasium* (where free men met to exercise and discuss political affairs) and further learning how to conduct themselves in public life. These very separate lifestyles, combined with the discrepancy in age between husband and wife, necessarily led to a gap between the intellectual capabilities of the two. A man's feelings of condescension toward his wife were an established part of married life. The sentiment expressed by the character Hippolytus, in Euripides' fifth-century play, must have been a common one: "A clever woman, with more wit than becomes a woman, I abhor; I would not have such a woman in my house."[4]

Understandably, marriage was not an event to which a young woman necessarily looked forward. The male playwright Sophocles expresses sympathy toward the fate of women through his female character, Procne, who declares in a speech:

> Young women, in my opinion, have the sweetest existence known to mortals in their fathers' homes, for their innocence always keeps children safe and happy. But when we reach puberty and can understand, we are thrust out [into marriage] . . . forced to praise and to say that all is well.[5]

Women played no role in selecting their future husbands. A woman's guardian, or *kyrios* (usually her father until she married), handled all the negotiations with her future husband or his family. Perhaps to ensure that ties among extended families remained firm, marriage to close kin other than siblings was quite common. Grooms likely would have selected a bride in part because of her family lineage, but the size of her dowry was also a contributing factor. It was assumed that the purpose of a marriage was to beget children who would one day enhance the fortunes of the family within the Athenian state. Affection between spouses certainly might have occurred, but love—either erotic or romantic—was certainly not an expectation. In the words of Pseudo-Demosthenes (400 BCE): "We have mistresses for our enjoyment, concubines to serve our person, and wives for the bearing of legitimate offspring."[6] Men likely turned to prostitutes, slaves, concubines, or male lovers for sexual and romantic feelings rather than to their wives. That this practice might sometimes have inhibited the central purpose of the marriage is indicated by an Athenian law mandating that men have sexual intercourse with their wives three times a month.

Childbirth was, as in all ancient civilizations, an extremely dangerous event in a woman's life. The lack of modern standards of hygiene, medical knowledge of the female body, and ability to perform surgery contributed to a high mortality rate among birthing mothers. These risks were compounded by the very young age at which women began sexual relations in Classical Athens—about 14. These young women's bodies would not have finished maturing by that time. The median age of death for men and women in Classical Greece demonstrates the challenges of childbirth for women: One historian has estimated that it was 34.6 for women but 44.5 for men. In the play *Medea*, Euripides has the title character make this bold statement: "I'd rather stand three times in the front line than bear one child."[7] Historians estimate that Athenian women would have had to endure childbirth five or six times; besides the obvious danger to their health, the probability that mothers would have experienced the death of at least one child made a successful delivery cause for great celebration. If the baby was a boy, the birth was announced to the community-at-large by putting an olive crown outside the door of the newborn's house. If it was a girl, the door was hung with a tuft of wool, signaling her future duties as a spinner, wife, and mother.

By Western standards, wealthy Athenian women led extremely restrictive lives because they were expected to occupy different spaces than men. Even going to the market was considered a man's job, because it entailed crossing public space. The notion of what constituted public space even encroached into private homes. Women's quarters were kept distinct from men's—upstairs, if possible—in darkened, unsanitary rooms that contrasted sharply with the beautiful civic ornamentation of public spaces. Even when her husband invited male guests home for entertainment, a woman was not supposed to mingle in their company. "Whether or not there is anything blameworthy in a woman's conduct," says Euripides' character Andromache, "the very fact that she goes out of the house draws criticism."[8] The playwright Aeschylus wrote in the fifth century BCE, "Matters abroad are man's affair—let woman not advise thereon. Bide thou within and stir up no mischief."[9] Lead makeup, to make a woman's face look pale and untouched by the sun, was commonly used, and women were often portrayed veiled in artwork. Therefore, the ideal woman never left the house. Scholars have long debated the extent to which this forced seclusion was a fact of life versus an idealized standard, but it is likely that it was a reality for many women.

Confined within their own homes, wealthy Athenian women occupied themselves with household chores. Rearing children, preparing food, and wool working were tasks that took place inside the home. The fact that so much of women's work was out of public view demeaned the value of women's labor in the eyes of male society, contributing to a cycle of misogynistic thought that characterized women as lazy and parasitical. A fourth-century writer expressed the idea in these words: "Poor men! We . . . lead the life of slaves with our wives. We're not free. We can't say we don't pay a price for their dowries: bitterness and women's anger."[10]

On certain occasions such as funerals and religious festivals it was acceptable for women of all classes to broach their doorsteps. Women also traveled to each others' homes to help out during childbirth. Older women might have found fewer restrictions upon their movement, since it was thought that their honor was less likely to be compromised. On the whole, however, upper-class women led lives separated from male space.

A good number of Athenian women, however, did not have the financial independence or means to live secluded lives. Female slaves, noncitizen women, and poorer women would have had to spend some time in public spaces to earn a living to support their families. For example, there were grape-pickers, vegetable vendors, midwives, and prostitutes. Although historians lack a great deal of evidence about the daily activities of these women, archaeological evidence and some circumstantial textual evidence show that water wells were one area notorious for female gatherings. Most Athenian women probably led less segregated lives than male expectations for upper-class women stipulated.

As in the case of so many of the societies covered in this book, historians have no clue how Athenian women themselves perceived their civilization. Perhaps wealthy women felt proud to have been married to husbands who could afford to maintain wives who never entered public spaces, whose virtue would therefore never be questioned; wives who felt protected rather than demeaned by the strict restrictions placed upon them. Historians do know, however, why men thought that women needed to be treated as they were. Athenian men, like those of many other civilizations, thought that "proper" women must lead lives of outstanding virtue, particularly regarding their sexual behavior. Women, however, were considered to have weaker characters than men, characters that would easily bow to sexual temptation—thus, women needed to be confined, for their own sakes. These ideas had deep roots. Even in the seventh century while Sappho wrote, a male poet Seronides expressed the belief that a woman should be "exceptionally wise" in "cherishing her husband."[11] Although they should care for their husbands with unwavering loyalty, they should not enjoy sexual intercourse nor gossip about tawdry matters with other women.

Adultery was a public offense, whether a woman was raped or seduced, but because women were thought to be weaker and passive, the man was considered the guiltier party. His punishment could include death, large fines, or, if Aristophanes is to be believed, public humiliation by which a large radish would be inserted into his anus. The penalty for raping a married woman was less than for seducing her, since seduction would have meant that a woman's loyalties, not just her body, had been taken from a husband. Women also were punished for adultery, since cuckolded husbands were forced by law to divorce their spouses, which meant permanent disgrace and loss of her legitimate children to her husband. The gap between expectations of female virtue and women's actual experience was likely to have been large but, because of the confinement of women and the multitude of legitimate outlets for male sexuality, it is unlikely that female adultery was a common occurrence.

ACCESS TO POWER: THE POLITICAL, LEGAL, AND ECONOMIC MILIEU

Women were never enfranchised in Classical Greece, which is unsurprising when one considers the relatively recent enfranchisement of both men and women in modern democracies. The extent to which women lacked access to political power in Athenian society was noteworthy even for ancient civilizations, however. It went beyond women's inability to attend the assemblies, sit on juries, or act in the capacity of council members or generals—all privileges held by Athenian male citizens. Women were unable to operate "behind the throne," manipulating politics as wives of many powerful leaders have done in the past. This is because of the large number of male citizens who participated in the democracy, limiting the ability of individual women to shape politics.

In fact, in the entire history of Classical Athens, only one woman is notable for her influence on politics: the fifth-century foreigner Aspasia (who was from Miletus, another part of the ancient Greek world). Unlike other Athenian women, Aspasia was well educated, and her thoughts and advice were sought by leading men of the day. The philosopher Socrates was said to have learned about the art of rhetoric, for which he was famous, from Aspasia, and thought highly enough about her ideas for Socrates' student Plato to have remembered, and recorded, some of them. Reportedly, Aspasia gave her opinion on what sorts of characteristics people who arrange marriages should have and argued that men and women should each contribute to managing the household. Aspasia became the paramour of Pericles, army general and leading shaper of Athenian policy from 442 to 429 BCE. Pericles was criticized for being blinded by true affection for his consort. After divorcing his first wife, he took Aspasia as his lover. (He could not marry her because she was not Athenian-born.) According to Plutarch, Pericles kissed her when he left for the Agora and again when he returned—an event that was unusual enough that it warranted recording. Aspasia herself was widely condemned for having exercised too much control over Pericles in political affairs. She was blamed for having started a war between Athens and the Samians, another people from the Greek world, and was also put on trial for impiety. That Aspasia, as a foreign woman, was an anomaly hated for the power she wielded is apparent from a lead curse tablet that has survived with her name on it, as well as by the fact that Greek plays characterized her offensively.

In legal affairs, women's standing was low. Considered minors their whole lives under the law, legally they had no independent existence. Instead, throughout her life cycle, each female had a male guardian, or *kyrios*, who acted as her intermediary between public and private spaces. The kyrios was usually her father, then later her husband, and if she became a widow, her sons. The kyrios would speak for her in court, arrange her marriage, and negotiate her dowry. If a woman acquired any property, the kyrios controlled it and could dispose of or manage it without her consent. Exemplifying this absence from both legal and physical space is the fact that court proceedings were not supposed to mention women by name, but rather by their relation to men, as "wife of" or "mother of." Whereas both men and women had the legal right to initiate divorce, men were able to do so with impunity, simply turning their wives out (although they then relinquished control over their wives' dowries). Women needed their guardians to file a divorce case and, once divorced, gave up access to their children, who then became the property of their fathers. It was in fact extremely rare for a woman to seek divorce on her own initiative. More often, women who divorced their husbands were forced to do so by their fathers. At any time, a woman's father could legally end his daughter's marriage without her consent. In one Greek play, a daughter piteously attempts to stop her father from such an ambition:

> In the name of Hestia don't rob me of the husband to whom you have married me; the favour that I ask of you, father, is just. . . . If you refuse, you will be enforcing your will and I shall try to bear my fate properly and avoid disgrace.[12]

In fact, the most important manner in which women contributed to public life was by bearing Athenian male citizens. The role that a woman played in this was all the more emphasized after a law enacted in 451 or 450 BCE stated that, in order for an individual to claim citizenship, both parents must be Athenian citizens themselves. Women thus had the legal function of producing not just sons, but political beings. The female chorus in Aristophanes' play *Lysistrata* speaks for all women by announcing, "I have a share in public service. For I contribute men."[13]

As might be surmised, women's economic power in Classical Athens was very limited. It is true that women could own their own property, usually obtaining it through gifts, dowry, or inheritance. Most of a family's wealth, however, particularly its landed assets, was transmitted through male heirs, so the women would have possessed a relatively small amount. One exception to the usual inheritance patterns occurred when no sons were born to take over a family's lands. In such cases, the land was passed through a daughter to the grandsons. This system was called the *epiklerate* and did not entail a woman's possession of property per se; she was a conduit rather than an owner. The extent to which women were financially dependent is apparent from Athenian law, which stated that women could neither buy nor sell land. Women and minors were also restricted to negotiating commercial contracts valued at less than a *medimnus* (around a bushel) of barley.

Interestingly, the group of Athenian women who had most economic independence were the prostitutes. Prostitution, although legal, was not an option that most women would have found attractive. Most prostitutes had very little money indeed and were considered by male society to be improper and important only in terms of their function as objects of sexual pleasure for men. There were three tiers of prostitutes in Athens. The lowest-ranking group, called *pornai*, lived in brothels, where occupants were likely slaves of the brothel owner; these enslaved prostitutes would have had no choice in their line of work and would have made next to no money. Higher-ranking were free women who walked the streets, forced by law to wear diaphanous gowns dyed with saffron. These women were often foreigners and came to prostitution out of poverty. Although they might have survived, economically they remained impoverished. The smallest and most prestigious group were the famous *heterai,* "female companions," who made up the only substantial group of economically independent women in Athenian society. Heterai had more in common with modern Japanese geisha than with other ancient prostitutes. Often foreigners, they were well educated. Witty and intellectual conversation between heterai and men was both acceptable and sought after. (Aspasia was said to have been one of the heterai.) Heterai were thus not merely sexual partners, but entertaining companions for a select group of customers. Some heterai became brothel owners, managing the affairs of common prostitutes.

BEYOND SPECTATORS: WOMEN AND RELIGION IN CLASSICAL GREECE

Religion in Classical Greece was the only arena in which women played a public role, and not always a secondary one. Many women fulfilled roles that maintained the Greeks' special relationship with their gods and the earth. They did so both by participating in public rituals and assuming high offices such as priestesses. As such, they were able to have a more prominent position than women in some Mesopotamian societies who were barred from the priesthood. No matter how passive women were seen to be in other spheres, they played a fundamental role in maintaining the cohesion of the Greek family—the central institution that maintained the state's well-being. As such, they were indispensable participants in family rites that dealt with marriage, childbirth, and human fertility, for example, as well as those that dealt with the fertility of the earth.

The role that women played in Greek religion could be threatening to men, and society's unease with female power can be seen by the ways that it conceived of the most important goddesses in Classical Greece: Hestia, Aphrodite, Hera, Demeter, Athena, and Artemis. Of these, three were eternal virgins, and Hera was able to renew her virginity through a special ritual. In many Greek myths, it was the virgin goddesses who proved most helpful to mankind. For example, the virgin Athena played a critical role in helping the hero Odysseus on his long journey home. This pattern suggests that it was easier for Greek men to imagine their goddesses' power emanating from sources that were atypical for most women.

After all, although a girl had to be a virgin before marriage, most women were sexually active. Athena in particular had characteristics that separated her from mortal women: She was a warrior and was often depicted with her helmet and shield. The goddesses who were sexually active, and thus bearers of children, were often not portrayed as wise or beneficent as were their virginal counterparts. For example, Aphrodite was always getting into trouble with her unbridled lust for men. Of all the most significant goddesses who bore children, only Demeter, goddess of fertility, appeared to fulfill her maternal duties with consistent affection and love. Thus, a pattern emerges in which goddesses who had the greatest wisdom were the least likely to resemble real-life women, whereas those who best fulfilled the traditional feminine roles were the least helpful to humans.

Women's participation in public rituals manifested itself in several ways. Certain religious duties were usually performed by women. For example, if a woven garment or cloth needed to be made for a religious festival, women would make it. Often, women priestesses (rather than male priests) served female deities. Funerals were another area in which women played specific, and important, roles. Women ritually washed the corpse and publicly expressed grief by wailing and gesturing. Women—both slave and free—were able to participate in the Eleusinian Mysteries, secret rituals that paid homage to the goddess Demeter and her power over fertility.

One of the most significant Athenian rituals in which women partook was the festival called the Thesmophoria, also dedicated to Demeter and her powers over agricultural cultivation. Unlike the Eleusinian Mysteries, the Thesmophoria was only open to wives of Athenian citizens. For a space of three days, the Athenian women would move to the hill where the Assembly of citizens met, and there they usurped this public site from men. On the first day, the women proceeded to the hill, carrying sacred objects. On the second day, the women fasted, probably in commemoration of the myth that told how, after Demeter's daughter was kidnapped by the ruler of the underworld, the goddess mourned for her lost daughter during her absence. According to the story, Demeter's daughter eventually returned from the land of the dead, even though she had to return to her immortal husband for half the year. The period of her return was marked by a celebration on the last day of the festival, and it involved feasting and rituals that reinforced the fertile nature of the ground.

Priestesses were employed by 40 major religious cults in Classical Greece. Most of these were centered around female goddesses, such as the cult of Athena Polias, the patron deity of Athens itself. Priestesses of this cult all came from among famous and wealthy families, and the goddess's priestess was the only respectable Athenian woman who could have her name said out loud in public—thus giving her a masculine quality.

The most important exceptions to the tendency for women to serve goddesses rather than gods were for the shrines at Dodona and Delphi. The
gods of both these shrines employed priestesses as their spokespersons to
prognosticate and give advice on important state matters. Because of their
future-telling capabilities, these religious centers were known as oracu-
lar shrines. At Delphi, dedicated to the god Apollo, the priestess would
remain celibate while she lived at the shrine. Later sources stress that the
god's priestess came from a peasant family of humble origins. Thus, the
servant of the god was from both the powerless gender and family lines.
These facts belied her authority in the shrine. For, when consulted by visi-
tors who sought information, Apollo's priestess would go into a trance
and speak in the words of the god. Officials would consult the priestess at
Delphi on the highest state matters.

The women of Classical Greece also partook in private religious rituals and celebrations. Women prayed to deities for their various personal
needs. Artemis, for example, was the patron goddess of childbirth, and
Hera the goddess of marriage. A fourth-century Athenian source lists
the valuable dedications made by women to the divine being of Artemis
Brauronia, either in petition or as thanks for prayers granted. Some
women also engaged in witchcraft, as shown by archaeological evidence
from lead tablets with inscribed curses. One such curse dating from third-
or second-century BCE Athens has the woman Bitto state:

> I shall bind Sosiclea and her possessions and her actions and her
> thoughts. May she become hateful to her friends. . . . dedicated to the
> Maddener Furies [female avenging spirits from Greek mythology].[14]

The rare surviving evidence that details such religious practices of women
in Classical Greece reveals glimpses of the usually invisible world of
women's private lives.

SPARTA

No discussion of the Classical period would be complete without some
mention of Sparta, the great political rival of Athens. Unlike Athens, the
Spartan state was not urbanized and was certainly not democratic. Rather,
it was a military society whose wealth and social organization revolved
around its colonization policies. Sparta grew wealthy by conquering
neighboring lands and turning the inhabitants into forced laborers. These
laborers, called helots, performed the most important non-military jobs in
Spartan society: they farmed, mined, and did construction projects. Spartan citizens thus evolved into the helots' military overlords, maintaining
their prowess in war in part out of a desire to prevent their helot subjects
from revolting. A seventh-century law code developed strict proscriptions

on behavior, demonstrating the expectations for both men and women to maintain military superiority. Quite unusually, even by Ancient Greek standards, every Spartan citizen—male and female—partook in supporting the military capacity of their society, though women were not soldiers. Societal concern for the capacity to contribute shaped even an infant's first days, when, if the baby looked weak or deformed, whether male or female, it was left exposed to die. Boys lived with their mothers only until age seven, when they were shipped off to military camps, where they were raised to be disciplined fighters. Men would not leave their military group to live with their wives until age 30. Females, too, played a central role in supporting the militaristic society, not as soldiers but in other ways.

On the one hand, women from both Sparta and Athens fulfilled some of the same roles in their respective societies. Their role as child-bearers was of utmost importance in each civilization, and the daily life of many Spartan and Athenian women consisted of household management and child-rearing. These functions reveal only a surface-level similarity between women's culture in Athens and Sparta, however. Whereas Athenian women were producers of political citizens, Spartan women's progeny were destined to be warriors. Archaeological evidence illustrates the connection between maternal duties and warfare in Sparta by the fact that tombs with engravings were allowed only for men who had died in battle and women who had died giving birth. Whereas physical movement among Athenian women was supposed to be minimal, Spartan girls and women were encouraged to participate in public sporting contests, and some even became famous female charioteers. Such activities strengthened their bodies to enhance their childbearing abilities. Spartan mothers apparently embraced the rigorous demands that military life made upon their sons, endorsing the sons' role as soldiers whose duty was to make great sacrifices for the good of the state. One Spartan woman was said to have passed her son's shield over to him with the command to either return home victorious with it or to come back dead on top of it. Spartan women's lives differed from Athenian women's lives in other important ways. The age of marriage for both men and women in Sparta was 18, and thus the gap in physical and emotional development between spouses that characterized most Athenian marriages was absent. Whereas Athenian fathers exerted enormous control over their children—even as adults—Spartan fathers played a less prominent role. After all, they spent the first 12 or so years of their marriage away from their wives, visiting only occasionally for conjugal duties. Their children were thus likely to be unfamiliar with their fathers during the first years of their lives. Many boys, in particular, leaving home at age seven, would never have the chance to live with their fathers. The high esteem that Spartan women had as mothers transferred over to other aspects of their lives. They were not sequestered, and they had a great deal of access to economic power, unlike their Athenian contemporaries. Over time, women's relative independence was expressed by their control over Sparta's wealth: They owned about two-fifths of the landed estates in the fourth century BCE, a ratio certainly exceptional not only for Greek, but also for other ancient civilizations. Male writers from this century comment on the luxurious clothing and swift racehorses rich women purchased. It is a great paradox that the most democratic of all Greek societies had such restrictions of women's lives, while the most militaristic of these cultures allowed women the greatest freedoms.

Why would this have been so? Different societies in the Classical Greek world emphasized different social institutions. Athens, a flourishing democracy, allowed its male citizens a great deal of freedom, thus allowing property-owning families to vie for power and prestige, their efforts all the while supported by the state. Freedom for male citizens required the marginalization of women, especially upper-class women. After all, the respectability and financial status that all free Athenian families craved was only possible with a strident attention to maintaining wealth within a family and displaying hallmarks of power: in this case, leading to the seclusion of many women and the near-complete control over their marital lives. Ironically, in Sparta, a rural society based on colonization and military expansion, the imperatives of family property consolidation were less urgent than mobilizing both male and female citizens to rule conquered peoples. Because the contributions of Spartan women were considered so important to the state's success, Spartan women gained a more independent role. Patriarchy evolved differently in our two examples from Classical Greece, yet in both Athens and Sparta women were subservient to the needs of their families and society.

The next ancient Mediterranean civilization under discussion is the Roman Empire, which occupied a much more sprawling area and time period than did Classical Greece. Nevertheless, because the Greek world had such a huge influence on Rome, a comparison of the lives of women in these two societies can demonstrate important continuities within the Ancient Mediterranean world.

THE FOUNDATION OF ROME: THE REPUBLIC (510 BCE–29 BCE); THE EMPIRE (29 BCE–CA. 500 CE)

After Athens and Sparta were conquered by Philip of Macedon in 338 BCE, much of Greek culture was absorbed into the ruling classes that followed Philip and his son, Alexander the Great. Alexander and the succession of kings and queens who partitioned his empire after his death considered themselves heirs to ancient Greece. The area ruled for over 300 years by Alexander and his successors—from 338–31 BCE—is known as the Hellenistic world. During this time, rulers who traced their legitimacy to the reign of Alexander set up an elite society unto themselves that stretched from parts of the Italian peninsula to Egypt, the eastern Mediterranean, and even to the borders of India. Ruling elites spoke Greek, spent time in Greek-styled *gymnasia,* studied Classical Greek philosophers, and continued to worship Greek gods (albeit often they incorporated local religious deities into their practices). It is in this context that the subsequent development of the Roman world and the place of women in it must be understood.

The beginnings of Rome were relatively inauspicious. Centuries passed before the tiny city-state of Rome, traditionally thought to have been founded in 510 BCE, expanded to control the entire Italian peninsula. By the second century BCE, Rome had taken possession over both the Italian peninsula and much of the coastal Mediterranean, including the territories formerly encompassing Classical Greece. Part of the reason Roman expansion—slow but steady in these first centuries—was so successful is that the Romans were themselves first-rate borrowers. They copied the naval ships used by their enemies to build their own strong fleet. They borrowed the methods of organizing slaves most economically (and inhumanely) from an overseas empire. Most significantly, for our purposes, they consciously took elements of Greek civilization to build up their own culture. The borrowings from ancient Greece can most notably be seen in Roman religion, which adopted wholesale the Greek pantheon of deities, changing their names to Roman ones (Vesta instead of Hestia, Juno instead of Hera) but leaving their mythology and functions more or less intact. The ways that prayer and morality operated in Greece—prayer being a way to obtain one's desires from the gods, whose lives did not reflect the moral expectations of mortal society—remained the same in Rome. High culture, too, was modeled on the Greek civilization. A solid Roman education included not only the Greek language, but also a thorough understanding of the most important philosophers and naturalistic artistic traditions of Athens's golden age. And, of course, many expectations about female virtue and behavior were also imported from Greece.

The periods of Roman history focused on here are the Republic (510–29 BCE) and Empire, or Imperial era (29 BCE–ca. 500 CE). During this millennium, the Roman world's expanse varied, but at its maximum stretched for thousands of miles beyond the Mediterranean Sea, encompassing Britain, Spain, modern France and Germany, Italy, Greece, Turkey, Egypt, North Africa, and the Mediterranean's east coast. The Mediterranean itself was sometimes called *mare nostrum,* "our sea," by the Romans, whose economy, religion, culture, and government touched all shores of this body of water. It is therefore important to recognize that the lives of women differed enormously across this expanse. Although the lifestyles of Roman aristocratic women were unusually homogenous, there were notable exceptions in some localities. And lower down the social scale, the ways women lived varied even more, according to diverse local customs. Thus, in Egypt, women's status on the whole tended to be higher than in other areas, because of long-standing local tradition. In Britain, the lives of many lower-class Roman women might have been virtually indistinguishable from their non-Roman neighbors.

Another reason that women's lives changed during the several centuries under discussion is because of the dynamic political upheavals in Rome. Prior to 29 BCE, Rome's government had been a republic, governed by an elected body of male officials, the most important of whom were senators. Although in theory the Republican centuries gave a political voice to a wider body of people than the Imperial period that followed, in fact, the senate was usually controlled by men of the wealthiest social strata. Nevertheless, Roman common men had a number of freedoms in the Republic. They often ran for minor political offices, and they were able to represent themselves and argue their cases in court. Men and women of all social ranks benefited from government's programs, such as road-building or civic games and festivals, but most sources suggest that the lives of women were more restricted during the early Republic than they were later on. As the Republican centuries drew to a close, the stability of the government was challenged by a number of insurrectionists, would-be tyrants, and various political factions. Underlying this instability was the Roman government's inability to handle the changes that came with military conquest and political expansion. How would the new territories be taxed? Who should be able to obtain citizenship status? How should the new wealth brought about by conquest be distributed?

These questions, if not solved, ceased to be a matter of great political debate with the ascension of Caesar Augustus to power in 29 BCE. Eventually, Augustus took on the title of emperor and was the sole leader in Rome in almost all but name. For even though Augustus managed the bulk of the Roman treasury, was leader of the Roman armies, and controlled legislation in his reign, he maintained the illusion that he was sharing power with the old Roman senate. As long as he and his successors maintained this ruse—allowing the senate to ratify his laws, avoiding undo displays of power—the wealthy senatorial class, exhausted and weakened through years of civil war, acquiesced to his demands. Some of the emperors that followed Augustus were extremely talented and effective leaders, and some were psychopaths. All of them, however, ruled under the legacy created by the first Roman emperor.

WOMEN'S LIVES IN ROMAN SOCIETY: IDEALS AND REALITIES

Just as Augustus ushered in an age that saw a gap between the reality of Roman political power and the idealization of Rome's political structure, the Roman world also witnessed an ever-growing fissure between the expectations of female behavior and the realities of women's lives. During the early Republic (510 BCE–ca. 170 BCE), an image of the "ideal" Roman woman developed that endured for centuries. While this paragon likely never had many real-life counterparts, even Romans would have considered the feminine ideal outdated by the late Republic and Imperial eras. Nevertheless, this model served as a reference point for later writings throughout Roman history, so an understanding of what it entailed is necessary. The ideal woman, as developed in the early Republic, was someone who devoted her whole being to the greater glory of her family and the Roman state. Since the Roman family was dominated by one leading man, his wife was expected to bring him honor through her reputation, as well as her ability to rear devoted children and supervise a household.

The Roman ideal left women a wider range of freedoms than existed for the women of Classical Greece. As one Republican leader wrote, comparing the two societies, "For what Roman would be ashamed to bring his wife to a social gathering? Or to let his family's mother have the primary rooms in the house or let her move about freely? The Greek tradition differs altogether."[15] Nevertheless, despite the lack of sequestering, the ideal Roman woman was expected to obey her husband in all matters and to do so in the interests of the state. The example of the noblewoman Lucretia will suffice to illustrate.

Lucretia was the wife of a well-known Roman aristocrat who was part of a group that wanted to transfer political power from rulers called tyrants to the elite class that would govern during the Republic. Because of her great virtue and beauty, she attracted the lustful attentions of the reigning tyrant's son. One evening, as she sat alone dutifully spinning wool, her admirer entered her home and threatened to rape her. When Lucretia prepared to scream to drive him away, he told her that if she resisted, he would kill her, strip her body, and put the murdered body of a naked male slave beside her. This would give anyone who found the bodies the idea that Lucretia had been having an affair with the slave. Not wanting this, poor Lucretia kept silent and was raped by her attacker. Later that evening, when her husband returned with his retinue, he found Lucretia poised with a knife above her breast. She explained what had happened and prepared to kill herself. Even though her husband begged her to stop, saying that she was blameless for the rape, Lucretia committed suicide. Her parting words get at the moral of this story: "I am innocent of fault, but I will take my punishment. Never shall Lucretia provide a precedent for unchaste women to escape what they deserve."[16] Lucretia was a legendary rather than historical figure, but her behavior was esteemed by Roman men throughout their history. Obviously, maintaining one's honor—having no extramarital intercourse (even to the point of accepting blame for being raped)—was seen as critical to maintaining the stability of the Roman family. Furthermore, her personal interests were subordinated to those of the Roman state. The self-immolation of this woman went hand-in-hand with the esteem in which Romans held her: Death was the price of glory. This ideal of the Roman woman remained constant throughout the Roman world, but as time went on, the ideal matched women's lives less and less, despite the attempts of some male leaders to preserve it.

THE LIVES AND LIVELIHOODS OF RICH
AND POOR WOMEN IN ROME

How did Roman society operate for women? As in Athens, during the early Republic (510 BCE–ca. 170 BCE), the Roman family structure imposed severe circumscriptions on women. The head of the household, the *pater familias,* was given the legal right to discipline his other family members, to arrange their finances, and to manage their daily lives. If a father believed one of his children or his wife had committed a crime or done wrong, it was his responsibility to make them atone. Thus, he had power over life and death of his family members. Even though he had incentive not to abuse this power, since doing that might mean the depletion of his family's well-being, Roman records suggest that the judgments of the pater familias could be harsh indeed by today's standards. One writer told of a young woman named Horatia, whose father had engaged her to be married to a family with whom he later came to blows. During a fight between the two families, most of her brothers died, along with her future spouse. When Horatia grieved for her fiancé's death, her remaining brother stabbed her, saying, "Thus perish every Roman woman who mourns an enemy."[17] Horatia's father supported his son's sororicide.

During the early Republic, a woman was overseen throughout her life by a guardian, much as had been the case in Classical Greece. The extent to which a woman was thought to belong to her father can be seen with naming patterns. Women often received feminine forms of their father's first name, a tradition that continued long after the *pater familias* had lost absolute control over his family. When a girl married, it was to a man her father had chosen. At that time, guardianship (*manus*) might pass to the husband. In another arrangement, the pater familias retained guardianship over his daughter even after she married. Women's lives during the early Republic were also limited by the fact that only men could initiate divorce.

By about 170 BCE, many of these traditional limitations on women had changed. The pater familias no longer had power of life and death over his family, for example. Furthermore, he could no longer pass judgment on his family members for civil crimes. These things were now the prerogative of the state, and the shift was a positive one for Roman women's freedoms. Thus, even though women were still legally bound to be under the control (manus) of a guardian until the reign of Emperor Diocletian (r. 285–305 CE), the actual power of their keepers waned considerably. Marriage patterns demonstrate this. By the late Republic, women most often were married without transferring their manus to their husbands, which technically left legal control to the members of their biological families. In fact, continuity of parental guardianship usually gave women more freedom, since they were beyond the daily control of their overseers. A woman whose guardian was displeasing to her could arrange to have another male family member step in his place. Women of the later Republic and Empire were free to shop in the marketplace, visit with friends, or participate in or attend religious festivals as they wished. Women without great wealth took on a great variety of jobs. Those who could afford education for their children supervised their learning, especially in the early years. Compared with Classical Athens, then, Roman women of the Late Republic and Imperial era led freer lives.

There were, however, similarities in some of the basic life patterns among girls from Classical Athens and Imperial Rome. To begin with, death in infancy was common because of poor medical care. Furthermore, in both civilizations girl children were not as esteemed as boys, and many infant girls were put to death through exposure. One Egyptian Roman wrote to his wife at the end of the first century BCE, "If you have the baby before I return, if it is a boy, let it live; if it is a girl, expose it."[18] The legality of female exposure stemmed from the ancient Law of Romulus, which stated that a man had to raise all his sons, but only his first-born daughter. The preference for males was also manifested by the state in the amount of money or food it supplied indigent children. When Augustus distributed goods for needy youths, he stipulated that only boys 11 years old and younger were qualified to receive them. Finally, both rich and poor women died young in these ancient Mediterranean societies—the life span for women was likely the same as in Classical Athens.

As usual for early civilizations, the women whose lives historians know best were the rich. These Roman matrons retained early Republican role models (memorializing women such as Lucretia), but their lives conformed little to these expectations. Marriage arrangements, especially

FIGURE 2-1   TERRACOTTA RELIEF FROM THE TOMB OF SCRIBONIA ATTICE, MID-SECOND CENTURY CE
Roman women used the services of a midwife (often a professional) to aid in childbirth (ca. 150 CE).

for the first-time bride, certainly remained undesirable by today's standards. Augustus had set the minimum age for a citizen girl to marry at 12, and the likelihood in reality was that she was married by 15, although poorer women married in their late teens. A woman's parents continued to arrange the marriage, even though technically both bride and groom had to agree to the arrangements. A young girl's ability to decline her parents' wishes seems unlikely. One first-century BCE poet addressed the following to an engaged young girl:

> It is not right to reject the man to whom your father and mother gave you. You must obey them. Your virginity is not entirely yours. One-third of it belongs to your father, one-third to your mother, and only one-third to yourself. Don't fight against your parents. . . .[19]

Probably such sentiments were common. At least Roman girls were closer to the age of their fiancés than girls in Classical Athens: Augustus declared that citizen boys could marry by age 14. Obviously, the slighter discrepancy in years also meant that newlyweds might be more compatible in maturity. Another benefit to marriage during the late Republic and

Empire was of course a woman's lack of accountability to her husband because of the popularity of marrying without the guardianship of her spouse. Finally, some women were able to negotiate or at least play a role in establishing their marriages. Because young widows and divorcees were quite common, many women had more than one marital partner. In second marriages women were much more likely to exercise choice than in first ones. For example, the famous statesman Cicero's daughter, Tullia, selected her husband-to-be with her mother's help while her father was away. Cicero was displeased with the new groom, but made no attempt to break apart the marriage.

Both women and men easily obtained divorces during the Imperial era, even though it was far more common for men to initiate them. Common causes of break-ups among the very elite included a desire to make better political alliances with new brides. Infertility was also a typical reason that a man left his wife, since producing children was considered a critical component of marriage. Real affection was nevertheless a factor in many Roman marriages and sometimes could override even other motives. In the late Republic, one Roman statesman wrote a eulogy for his wife Turia that expressed real fondness for her. Although Turia lived up to the ideal Roman matron in terms of her loyalty, her sense of duty, and her selflessness toward her husband, she failed in the important task of bearing children. Turia apparently suggested that her husband divorce her so that he could produce legitimate heirs, but he abruptly refused, out of love for her.

Many Roman marriages were not as close, and adultery appears to have been common in the late Republic and Empire. As in the case of Classical Athens, men who had sexual relations with prostitutes or concubines were not considered adulterers, whereas any woman who had intercourse outside of marriage was guilty of this crime. Both men and women could be divorced for adultery, although legally only a woman was punishable by the state. At least some Romans thought that the inequalities regarding adultery were unfair. As the third-century CE writer Ulpian wrote, "It is very unjust for a husband to require from a wife a level of morality that he does not himself achieve."[20] Regardless of the punishment, clearly many Roman women had intercourse outside of marriage. A prime example includes Augustus's own daughter, whom he sent into exile because of her promiscuous ways.

The typical Roman matron spent much of her life engaged with the tasks of birthing and raising children, managing her house, and weaving. Despite the fact that women were supposed to produce children, both contraception and abortion were common. Because of the state of medicine, however, these methods could have limited success. Beyond acidic douches, one form of birth control suggested that a woman should have a cold beverage and sneeze after having sexual intercourse to avoid pregnancy.

Once children were born, their mothers would see to their education. Young upper-class girls could go to elementary schools, where they might learn to read Greek and Latin, but they did not follow their brothers onto higher studies outside the home. Educated women were held in esteem. For instance, the Roman lady Cornelia, who lived in the late Republic, was praised for her fluency with the lyre (a small harplike musical instrument), her interest in philosophy, and her knowledge of geometry and literature. Even though the degree to which Cornelia was educated was unusual, the fact that she was applauded for her intellectual capabilities was not. Although very few original literary compositions exist as testimony of Roman women's intellectual ambitions, evidence shows that such works were written. Some love poetry remains, for example, by Sulpicia. Nevertheless, to many Roman men, a woman's education was important only insomuch as it displayed her good breeding. Pliny the Younger's praise for the intellectual activity of his wife (focused, as it was, on his work) shows this to be the case:

> She has even, because of her affection for me, taken an interest in literature. She has copies of my books, she reads them over and over again, and even learns them by heart. . . . She even sets my poems to music and sings them, to the accompaniment of a lyre. . . .[21]

Only the upper-class women of Imperial Rome received an education as preparation for marriage. Relatively little is known about poorer women. Slaves, who made up as much as a third of the population, were not allowed to enter into legal marriages. If their masters allowed, they might make an informal partnership but were subject to their masters' whims, and couples could be sold apart from each other. Slaves who worked in their masters' homes were sometimes able to earn a small salary and eventually buy their freedom. These former slaves, called freedmen and freedwomen, often took pride in their ability to formally marry. Tombstone inscriptions attest to the longevity of these marriages, and it is likely that mutual attraction played a strong role in forming the partnerships. Since by law children received the social status of their mother, it was more important for slave families to purchase her freedom before her husband's. Indeed, more slave women were freed than slave men. No doubt there were many other impoverished free Roman women about whom nothing is known. Some indigent women would have been prostitutes, and some were even forced to become gladiators.

FROM DIVINE MORTALS TO PIOUS GODDESSES:
ROMAN WOMEN AND RELIGION

Although the deities and mythology of Classical Greece were well-known, Roman society, and especially women, developed their own interpretation of Greek religion and its prescriptions for women's behavior. Whereas in Athens virginal goddesses were more helpful to humankind than the sexually active goddesses, and the Greek Hera was primarily a jealous, revenge-seeking wife, sexually active goddesses could be very helpful to Romans. The Roman goddess Juno, Hera's counterpart, was celebrated in temple architecture as the patroness of marriage and childbirth. The fact that helpful Roman goddesses could be sexually active shows that beneficent female deities possessed more attributes of typical women than did their Greek sisters.

One of the central goddesses for Roman women (and men, for that matter) wasn't even a part of the Greek pantheon. This was the Egyptian goddess Isis, whose popularity peaked in the second century CE. The popularity of her cult during the Roman Empire testifies to the continuing propensity of Romans to borrow from other societies and adapt whatever was taken to the contours of Roman civilization. The Roman cult of Isis demonstrates the extent to which goddess worship in Rome could reflect the status of women there. Unlike the Roman state-sponsored cults, which focused on the connections between the gods and goddesses and the prosperity of Rome, Isis was the leading figure of one of several mystery cults that grew in popularity throughout the Empire. Mystery cults focused on the well-being of an individual rather than of a group and promised help from a deity to the worshippers in the form of guidance or prosperity on this earth, or, by the third century CE, even life after death. The cult of Isis was open both to men and women, but her power was viewed as distinctly feminine, and her cult promoted a degree of equality between genders. A second-century CE Egyptian hymn records that Isis "made the power of women equal to that of men."[22]

The most important religion to originate from the Roman Empire was of course Christianity, which initially had much in common with other mystery cults, including a personal god who required adherence to a distinct moral code and who promised his worshippers guidance in this life and happiness in a life after death. On the other hand, Christianity differed from mystery cults in important ways. First, its founding figure Jesus (d. ca. 30 CE) was a historical person, and second, it began as a splinter sect of the monotheistic Judaism and therefore included much from this older faith. Female followers of Christ existed from the lifetime of Jesus, and in the earliest centuries of the new religion, writings concerning proper behavior for both women and men emphasized extreme asceticism (denial of worldly comforts). For example, Christians reading the words of St. Paul in the first century would have heard him emphasizing the virtues of celibacy, stressing that a life without sexual relations was the holiest life possible. This message would have made sense to many early Christians, who thought that the world was going to end soon and that Christ would return within their lifetimes, but it was certainly at odds with mainstream Roman culture. In these early centuries, women who embraced Christianity sometimes had access to public approbation that they would not have otherwise had. The Christian woman Perpetua, a martyr from north Africa who was put to death by the Roman government for practicing her religion in 203 CE, achieved great fame in her local community because of her unwavering faith, and eventually, her unflinching acceptance of death.

As Christianity gained popularity in the later third and particularly in the early fourth century (the religion was legalized by Emperor Constantine in 313 CE), more upper-class women began to practice the new religion. During this time, wealthy women who gave away all their possessions and took up ascetic roles achieved prominence in the church. As the religion became more institutionalized in later centuries, however, the special privileges that women gained by converting waned. Although some Christian women in western Europe maintained high profiles—and these were very often the richest, most well-connected individuals—these became more and more exceptional from the late fifth century onward.

Although the Christian writer Paul notes the existence of female preachers, as the church grew more organized it eliminated women from positions of authority. On the other hand, pagan Roman women could hold priestly offices. Whereas in Greece, priestesses almost always only served goddesses, in Rome such women had a wider variety of roles. In Rome, holding a priestly title transcended religious status and could also signify one's general importance to society. Roman inscriptions testify to this particular function of priestess. In second-century Asia Minor, Plancia Magna of Perge was given several titles, among them "both first and sole public priestess of the mother of the gods."[23] Plancia had endowed the city of Perge with an enormous entrance gate, replete with numerous costly statues, and the inscription was made by the city's grateful inhabitants in part to remember Plancia for her donation. Priestesses could also serve cults specifically dedicated to the Roman state.

Other ways through which Roman women were involved with religion—or with the supernatural—included private worship, festivals, and the use of magic. None of these arenas was the domain of women alone. Women throughout Rome would have believed in a plethora of deities that could give them assistance if prayed to and sacrificed to correctly.

Thus, Vesta was not just a state goddess, but a divine being whom women would have worshipped in private altars within their homes. The Roman world was regulated by the rhythm of its sacred holidays, which combined community bonding and festivity with piety. The February holiday called Lupercalia, for example, was extremely popular. In fact, long after Christianity dominated the Roman world, Lupercalia was still celebrated. Pope Gelasius I (d. 496 CE) even attempted to gloss over the pagan aspects of this celebration by declaring the day the Festival of the Purification of the Virgin Mary. During the holiday, young men would run through the streets and chase anyone in their way with strips of goat hides. Women who hoped for fertility and good childbirth would intentionally stand in the young men's way, since it was thought that getting lashed would help them in their endeavors.

WOMEN'S ACCESS TO POLITICAL AND ECONOMIC POWER IN IMPERIAL ROME

Although Roman women were legally barred from holding political offices, they were more involved with state power than were their Classical Greek counterparts. Evidence shows how some women pursued power independently of male assistance, while others wrangled their way into positions of political influence by becoming powerful behind the scenes. Some authoritative women were praised by Roman male writers; others were harshly condemned for overstepping the boundaries of acceptable female behavior. Often the praise or criticism stemmed from the biases of the authors: Those who agreed with a woman's particular political position praised her leadership, and those who disagreed did not. When Roman writers criticized women they did so in a particular fashion, characterizing them as selfish, masculine, or manipulative. For instance, the late Republican Sempronia, who helped the conspirator Catiline in a failed plot to overthrow the Roman government, was described as having "masculine daring and boldness," as well as other traits that "lead to moral dissipation."[24]

A prime example of such evil women was Cleopatra of Egypt, who allied herself with the Roman statesman Mark Antony in a war against Octavian (who was later to reign as Emperor Augustus). Her intelligence and charisma were widely known and accepted by the Roman writers, who nevertheless condemned her in their writings. As one author put it:

> Her beauty, as it is recorded, was not in and of itself incomparable, not such as to strike those who saw her. But conversation with her attracted attention, and her appearance combined with the persuasiveness of her talk, and her demeanor which somehow was diffused to others produced something stimulating. . . .[25]

Such writers, however, also abrasively described the Egyptian leader as a manipulative, conniving person who used her wiles to control Antony (who had been popular among some Romans) and turn him into a fawning pawn. By doing this, the blame for Antony's eventual revolt against Octavian was shifted to Cleopatra. The contemporary poet Virgil encapsulated elements of this relationship in his work *The Aeneid* by creating the tragic Queen Dido, who used her beauty and charm in a failed attempt to lure the hero Aeneas from his true destiny of serving Rome.

Alternatively, the characteristics of powerful women praised by Roman authors also tended to fit into patterns. For example, since the earliest days of Rome, women who took on a leadership role were cast in the capacity of peacemakers by later writers. One early famous legend about the foundation of Rome demonstrates this. The leader Romulus, one of the supposed founders of Rome, lacked enough women to populate his city. To remedy this situation, he attacked a nearby community whose people were called the Sabines. Romulus and his men successfully carted off the Sabine women, raping them and then taking them as wives. When, about a year later, the Sabine men retaliated and attacked the Romans, the Sabine brides took to the battlefield and held their new babies up to the fighting men. Unwilling to slaughter their blood relatives, the Sabines made peace with the Romans.

The role of women as "preventors of war" might trace its roots to the fact that very often Roman marriages were arranged for the purpose of alliance building. The reputation of Octavia demonstrates this. Octavia, the sister of Octavian, was newly widowed. As part of a deal between Octavian and his rival Antony, Octavia was given in marriage to Antony. Roman writers characterized her as a peace-loving contributor to the political alliance of the two most powerful Roman leaders. When Antony divorced Octavia, precipitating a civil war between the two men, Octavia was said to have fled from Antony's house in tears because she was so dismayed that she might be the cause of war.

A third acceptable model for powerful women was as legitimizers of men's political authority. Roman emperors especially utilized this particular role, since throughout Imperial history the strongest links between emperors and their successors were often through female connections. For example, the emperor Claudius claimed legitimacy to the throne through his grandmother Livia, his mother Antonia Minor, and his older brother Germanicus. Claudius emphasized his female lineage because these women were related to illustrious ancestors.

Women who did achieve a political voice did not always fall within the usual accepted stereotypes of "masculine manipulator" or "virtuous connection-builder" discussed above. Women of all social levels occasionally managed to promote their views. Voices of women from the lower social ranks can be found in the graffiti inscriptions discovered in the ruins of the Italian city of Pompeii. In the first century CE, political campaigns were spread in part through such graffiti, and women's names have been found endorsing certain political candidates. One such marking reads, "Epidia, not without Cosmus, asks you to vote for Marcus Samellius for aedile [a low-level office]."[26] A better-known Roman matron named Cornelia, from the late Republic, encouraged her two sons in their endeavors to bring political reforms to fruition. Although she did so from behind the scenes, she was nevertheless known for her political acumen. At one point, she even turned down a marriage offer from King Ptolemy of Egypt— a man who had obviously recognized her diplomatic value. Records also reveal instances of women gathering and speaking out publicly on issues they felt the male population had ignored. The late Republican Hortensia gave a well-known speech in 42 BCE in which she publicly argued that a tax that had been unfairly levied on women's private property should be remitted; she ultimately succeeded in having the tax repealed.

Amid the inner court circles navigated by the emperor, women also pursued political influence. Too many examples exist of this to be listed here, but two will demonstrate the point. Augustus's wife Livia was thought to have given such astute advice to her husband that Augustus took notes on what she said and studied them. Even the concubines of emperors could wield political power. Caenis was Emperor Vespasian's lover. Vespasian enjoyed her presence so much that she became very wealthy, and people who wanted favors from the emperor sought her help.

Even more significant to women's power in Imperial Rome than having a political voice was having economic strength. Rome as a whole became very wealthy during the Republic, partly as a result of territorial expansion, and women began to reap a share of this wealth by the late Republic and the Imperial era. Overall, there was a growing tendency for wealthy women to control their finances independently of their husbands or guardians. For example, more and more women were able to make their own wills during the Imperial era, something they could seldom accomplish during the Republic. Furthermore, women obtained control of their own dowries, which had not occurred in earlier times. This was true despite the fact that, legally, the pater familias continued to control all property of his family. Nevertheless, the third-century legal writer Ulpian argued that a woman without a guardian could sue to reclaim her dowry. This suggests an eventual awareness that a woman's dowry might belong to her, rather than to her biological family.

What did Roman men think about the growing population of wealthy women? The Voconian Law of 169 BCE suggests an early fear of women's economic independence. It decreed that it was illegal for a man in the wealthiest social classes to bequeath over half his estate to his daughter. At the same time, however, Roman men who married wealthy older women did gain the benefit of a higher reputation in society. Clearly, though, by the Imperial era, the ability of women to control their own estates conjured less surprise among Roman men. The growth of independently wealthy women, which began during the late Republic, reveals much about the relative position of Roman women in these centuries, since access to wealth is one of the surest indicators of social equality, and exclusion from it indicates inequality.

The End of the Ancient Mediterranean World

The western half of the Roman Empire collapsed in the mid-fifth century, its political integrity eaten away by both internal and external strife. The Roman military became increasingly independent from the control of the emperors, leading to widespread infighting and internal plotting among political rivals. At the same time, groups of people whom Romans called barbarians—assimilated into traditional Roman culture to varying degrees—fought against the central state. The resources emperors needed to control both army and military dissipated, and widespread economic chaos ensued. The collapse of the western half of the Roman Empire (the eastern half continued until the middle of the fifteenth century) affected areas differently, and the impact of the fall on women was equally varied. Roman Britain, for example, collapsed swiftly in the fifth and sixth centuries, whereas the area approximating modern southern France maintained the Roman infrastructure and even tax systems for hundreds of years. Women's lives had never been homogenous, but now they were even more disparate. The common aristocratic culture of the Imperial era was slowly fading away, and the lives of poorer women have left little evidence of change. Rome's fall left an enormous wake—the Roman Empire had been the first time western Europeans had been exposed to such a unified state, with all the security and problems that it entailed. In the centuries to follow, western Eurasian leaders would live under the shadow of the broken empire, unable to imitate its successes completely, yet bound to gauge their endeavors by using it as a standard.

Conclusion

In the ancient Mediterranean, patriarchy had different faces, as women's autonomy in families and societies and access to their wealth and religious power diminished or grew. In Classical Greece, the society of

Athens developed democracy for men, while women's public roles and economic independence were restricted. The two events were connected in part because of beliefs that expanding political power to all male citizens would cause social strife unless women's lives were carefully curtailed. Although Athenian women managed to maintain important roles in religious spheres, their ability to own property, to form relationships with other adults, and even to appear in public was strictly limited. The civilization of Sparta, however, proved to be different for women. Ironically, although it circumscribed the lives of its male citizens by dictating that every man would serve the state in a military capacity, in many ways Spartan women had more freedoms and economic power than their Athenian sisters. In ancient Rome, the transition to Empire oversaw the erosion of the strict feminine ideals formulated in the early Republic. These ideals, which had meant, in theory and practice, the limitation of women's independence in marriage, access to economic power, and educational potential, were still theoretically important throughout the late Republic and Empire. Nevertheless, by the time of the first century CE, these ideals were reversed: Women were able to initiate divorce, control their own finances, and aspire to participate in Roman public culture to a degree unknown before. The harsher restrictions of earlier forms of Mediterranean patriarchy had fallen away by the end of the Classical period.

CHAPTER THREE

THE HERITAGE OF THE GUPTA EMPIRE: INDIA AND SOUTHEAST ASIA (CA. 320 BCE–1500 CE)

Her hair is disheveled, her eyes red and fierce, she has fangs and a long lolling tongue, her lips are often smeared with blood, her breasts are long and pendulous, her stomach is sunken, and her figure is generally gaunt. She is naked but for several characteristic ornaments: a necklace of skulls or freshly cut heads, a girdle of severed arms, and infant corpses as earrings. She is usually said to have four arms. In her upper left hand she holds a bloodied cleaver, in her lower left, a freshly cut human head; her upper right hand makes the sign "fear not," and her lower right hand, the sign of one who confers boons. . . . (Kinsley, 1996)[1]

. . . Deprived of her consort a woman cannot live, thou canst not doubt this truth where I am concerned. . . . O thou of pure soul [Rama], I shall remain sinless by following piously in the steps of my consort, for a husband is a God. . . . O Raghava [Rama] thou knowest I am truly pure and I have been bound to thee in supreme love. . . . The husband is a God to the woman, he is her family, and her spiritual preceptor, therefore even at the price of her life, she must seek to please her lord [husband]. (Kinsley, 1986)[2]

These two dichotomous images epitomize Hinduism's ability to reconcile with extremes and give us insight into two distinctive constructs of femininity in premodern India. The first quote provides a terrifying image of the goddess Kali. *The Devi-Mahatyma* ("Glorifications of the Goddess"), an important Sanskrit text of the Classical period (320–500 CE), refers to Kali's orgiastic dancing, which brought death and destruction of evil from the cosmic universe. She symbolized erotic passion, violence, frenzied motion, change, and empowerment. Both men and women belonging to the *Shakti* tradition (those within the Hindu tradition who believed in the divine being feminine) worshipped her.

On the opposite spectrum we have Sita, the heroine of the Sanskrit epic *Ramayana* (ca. 200 BCE), who in the second quote implores her husband, Rama (a reincarnation of Vishnu, the Hindu Preserver God), to believe in her faithfulness to him. She represents the paragon of femininity, wifely devotion, ascetic sexuality (sexuality controlled by her husband), and self-denial. These attitudes about female gender, shaped through centuries within India, continued to exert important and sometimes conflicting influences throughout the period examined in this chapter.

As in other regions during the premodern world, the problem confronting the cross-cultural study of women is the absence of women's voices telling us about their own experiences. This means we have to rely on the religious and secular literature of the time authored principally by the elite men of society, and in the case of India it was the *Brahmins* (priests) who constituted the highest caste or social division in society. These records indicate that premodern India was a patriarchal, patrilineal society. Within this patriarchal structure, however, women's power and status changed dramatically from the Vedic period (ca. 1500–500 BCE) to end of the premodern world, about 1500 CE. Primary sources portray Vedic women as playing a complementary role in family matters and religious ceremonies. By the end of the Vedic period (ca. 500 BCE) as the Brahmins increased their power and Indian society became increasingly stratified with the intensification of the caste system, women's familial and religious influence entered a period of gradual decline.

Though the Buddha challenged the dominance of the Brahmins and the inequalities fostered by the caste system, he accepted many of the female stereotypes of his time. Still, a group of determined Buddhist nuns used the egalitarian implications of their religion to carve out an unprecedented amount of autonomy. Hindu women, however, were unable to turn back the rising patriarchal and sexist tide, especially after the transcribing of the *Laws of Manu*, (ca. 200–400 CE), which placed several restrictions on them. This phenomenon was also linked to the broader political, economic, religious, and social changes that occurred in India from the end of the Vedic period (500 BCE) to the reign of the Guptas (ca. 320–500 CE). Consequently, women lost much of the economic, religious, and legal rights they had enjoyed during the Vedic period.

It was during the Gupta period that religion found an ally in trade and commerce to spread Indian cultural traditions to Southeast Asia. Historians are divided on the exact nature of the impact of this cultural diffusion on Southeast Asian women. Sources reveal that Southeast Asia, like India, was a patriarchal society. However, women enjoyed relative economic autonomy uncommon to most societies in the premodern world. This economic empowerment translated to greater freedoms for women in the institutions of family, marriage, and religion. For example, Southeast Asian women were attracted to Buddhism because of its message of inclusiveness and spiritual equality. Although the ruling elites adopted many features of Hinduism, including the *Laws of Manu*, to legitimize their authority, the prescriptions laid out for the treatment of women were ignored. When we compare Southeast Asian women with Indian women throughout the Gupta period, we find reason to believe that they enjoyed numerous economic, legal, and social privileges unknown to Indian women.

QUESTIONS FOR STUDENT ANALYSIS

1. Some historians have argued that religion can be a contributing factor to the development of patriarchy. How would you analyze this statement with reference to the development of Hinduism in Gupta India?

2. To what extent did a woman's ability to control wealth shape her social status in Southeast Asia and Gupta India?

3. Compare and contrast the development of the concept of the "ideal woman" in Classical Athens, the Roman Republic, and Gupta India.

4. Was there anything inherent about the social and political dynamics in Classical Athens and India that contributed to deterioration of woman's status?

HISTORICAL OVERVIEW: VEDIC PERIOD TO GUPTA PERIOD (CA. 1500 BCE–500 CE)

POLITICAL HISTORY

Sources reveal a fragmented political situation and presence of great socioeconomic and religious pluralism in premodern India. Despite this continuous fragmentation, perhaps the clearest way to understand the political history of this time period would be through the traditional periodization of the major consolidated monarchies. Therefore, chronologically speaking, the history of premodern India can be broadly divided into the following time periods: the Aryan or Vedic age (ca. 1500 BCE–ca. 500 BCE), the era of the Mauryan empire (ca. 320–180 BCE) followed by the period referred to as "dark ages"(ca. 180 BCE–ca. 320 CE), the Classical period encompassing the reign of the Gupta rulers (ca. 320 CE to 500 CE), and the post-Classical period.

Of the many migrations India witnessed over the course of its history, perhaps the greatest impact was that of the arrival of the Aryans in about 1500 BCE. These pastoral nomads, probably originating in the Caspian Sea/Black Sea area, brought with them into the Indian subcontinent an Indo-European language. This later evolved into Sanskrit, the classical language of ancient India, and is the basis of many contemporary languages spoken throughout North India today. The Aryans also brought the fourfold divisions in society commonly referred to as the caste system and a polytheistic religion that later developed into Hinduism.

Under the Mauryas (ca. 320–180 BCE), India witnessed for the first time the development of a centralized empire, encompassing a vast territory. Buddhism, the newly emerging, heterodox religion, was transformed into a major religious force because of the royal patronage of King Ashoka (r. 268–231 BCE). The death of Ashoka and the eventual decline of the Mauryan empire was followed by a 500-year period that many historians describe as India's "dark ages." During these centuries, India fell prey to outside invasions. Therefore different conceptions of community, economy, and social structure confronted one another, and the resolution of these conflicts contributed to the distinctive qualities of the Gupta age.

Historians concur that the two centuries of Gupta rule and influence were India's golden age, comparable to that of Classical Greece. As in Greece, the Gupta era was known for its cultural brilliance and its leaders' centralized political power. The Gupta rulers brought all of North India under their control and allowed certain distant kingdoms to coexist as tributary states. Compared to that of the Mauryas, the territorial area that they governed directly was much smaller but more effectively administered.

The cultural achievements of this period are undeniable. The Gupta rulers, along with locally powerful officials and a growing mercantile community, patronized scholars and artists. There was a resurgence of Sanskrit literature, drama, and poetry. The great Sanskrit playwright Kalidasa (popularly referred to as "India's Shakespeare") composed his two classic works, *Shakuntala* and *Meghaduta* (The Cloud Messenger) during this period. In addition to Sanskrit, authors also wrote in Pali, a derivative of Sanskrit. Important scholarly works on astronomy, medicine, mathematics, and science also appeared during this golden age.

ORIGINS OF THE CASTE SYSTEM (CA. 1500 BCE–500 BCE)

Much of our information on the Aryan migration and settlement (called the Vedic period) is based on the *Vedas* or Books of Knowledge. There are four of them—*Rig, Sama, Yajur,* and *Atharva*—of which the oldest is the *Rig Veda,* comprising 1,017 hymns, written in Sanskrit. These Vedic collections are complemented by the *Brahmanas,* devoted to explanation of the hymns and their ritual application, and the *Samhitas,* hymns in praise of various Aryan deities.

From these sources we know that the Aryans brought with them a hierarchical structuring of society that divided people into four overarching *varna*s or castes: the *Brahmins* (priests), *Kshatriyas* (warriors), *Vaishyas* (traders), and the *Sudras* (peasants). The Sanskrit word *varna* or "color" suggests that this functional division had a racial basis, at least insofar as the lighter Aryans were distinguished from the darker indigenous population (referred to as the *dasas* or *dravidians*). More recently, historians have argued that this division of society was to ensure the Aryans' political, economic, and social dominance over the dasas. In a very unstable time, Aryans believed that social order would prevail if the different castes adhered to their respective caste duties.

FROM VEDIC RELIGION TO POPULAR HINDUISM (CA. 1500 BCE–500 CE)

The Aryans' social system was justified by the *Purushasukta,* or Hymn of the Sacrifice of the Primeval Being, in the *Rig Veda* and thereby became irrevocably entwined with the Aryans' Vedic religion (named for their *Vedas* or religious texts), which was essentially polytheistic and animistic. By about 1000 BCE the structural elements of the caste system were in place. Caste status became hereditary. The three upper castes were regarded as twice-born because they were allowed to undergo the donning of the sacred-thread ceremony. This was an initiation ceremony symbolizing two things: the passage from adolescence to adulthood and the person's ritual birth—which conferred eligibility to study the Vedas.

The epicenter of Aryan worship was the different sacrifices dedicated to the Aryan Gods: Indra (War God), Varuna (Sky God), and Agni (Fire God). The Brahmins dominated the caste system based on the acceptance of their claims that they had unique access to sacred power, which emanated from their performance of these sacrificial rites.

Over time, the four main castes were further divided into a mesh of *jatis* or subcastes. The Brahmins' notion of purity pollution[3] also became deeply entrenched within the system, causing it to become very rigid. They laid down strict rules to prevent social mobility and interaction between the three upper, or twice-born, castes and the *Sudras* (the lowest caste, regarded as ritually impure). For example, intercaste and interracial marriages were strictly prohibited. Caste limited people more than politics did. Unlike Greece or Rome, everybody identified first with his or her caste, not with the state. Eventually a fifth caste was added, known as the "untouchables" or "outcastes." It included those who performed menial jobs considered to be ritually unclean or impure.

The sacrificial excesses in the Vedic religion, along with the rise of a mercantile class and economic changes, facilitated the rise of the new religion, Buddhism (ca. 563–483 BCE). It challenged the authority of the Brahmins and the violence involved in sacrificial rituals by preaching personal salvation and rejecting the caste hierarchy.

Centuries later, during the Gupta era (320–500 CE), the Vedic religion regained its ascendancy over Buddhism by transforming itself into what came to be known as Hinduism. Four important aspects of Hinduism crystallized during this time: (1) *bhakti* or devotional worship became popular, as opposed to the primacy of sacrificial rituals; (2) the four legitimate goals of a Hindu man became more pronounced: *kama* (seeking pleasure), *artha* (accumulation of wealth), *dharma* (following one's caste duty), and *moksha* (quest for liberation from the transmigratory cycle); (3) the Hindu Trinity, comprising Brahma (Creator God), Vishnu (Preserver God), and Shiva (Destroyer God) was created; and (d) practicing Hindus were divided into three sects: *Vaishnavas* (followers of Vishnu), *Shaivas* (those who believed in the supremacy of Shiva), and *Shakti* worshippers (those who regarded the divine as feminine). Brahmins continued to assert their role in rituals despite the popularity of Buddhism. They received patronage, frequently in the form of land grants and court positions, not only from the Gupta rulers, but also from high-level administrators and wealthy landlords.

Not only was there a resurgence and redefining of Hindu religious authority during this period, but major systems of Hindu philosophy were also articulated. For example, the *Vedanta* (a philosophical treatise) that developed the teachings of the *Upanishads* (a compilation of more than 100 mystical dialogues between teachers and disciples questioning the very foundations of the Vedic religion) posed a powerful, attractive alternative vision to Buddhism for those Hindus critical of Brahminical dominance. Technically speaking, Hinduism and Buddhism were rivals, but Gupta rulers patronized Buddhist academic centers of learning at Taxila in northwest India and Nalanda in the Ganges Valley in exchange for political loyalty from Buddhists.

VEDIC PERIOD (CA. 1500 BCE–500 BCE)

The Vedas suggest that Aryan society, although patriarchal and hierarchical, fostered a certain respect and appreciation of women. The Vedic corpus linked the complementary roles of males and females to the well-being of society and universe. This notion was reflected in various religious symbols, like the "divine couples" (iconographic representations of the different Aryan gods with their consorts) and the concept of *ardhangini* or *dampati* (man and woman, respectively, as joint owners of a household and property). Because sacrifices played an integral part in Vedic worship, the presence and participation of a wife at a sacrifice was a prerequisite at all religious rituals. Such activity presupposed a substantial education for the wife. One Vedic text says: "An unmarried young learned daughter should be married to a bridegroom who is learned like her."[4] Therefore educating girls before they were married was the responsibility of parents.

Further, evidence shows that as many as 20 women seers composed Vedic hymns. Ghosha, Lopamudra, Visvavara, Apala, Indrani, and Sachi are frequently mentioned in the *Rig Veda,* among others. Unfortunately not much is known about the personal lives of these women. Other examples show that there were women scholars who were not afraid to engage leading male Vedic scholars in public intellectual dialogue. One such exemplary woman scholar was Gargi Vachaknavi. Known far and wide for her intellectual abilities, she challenged a leading male Vedic scholar, Yajnavalkya, in a public debate around 600 BCE. Thus we find that during this period, both men and women from the three upper castes had access to learning the religious literature. Women were allowed to wear the sacred thread (the symbol of ritual purity for the three upper castes) and officiate at certain Vedic rituals or act as priestesses. This indicates that women played a prominent and public role in Vedic religion.

Marriage took place when the girl reached puberty—and sometimes to the man of her choice, although her father and especially her mother had a veto. The Vedas do not give us detailed accounts of the different forms of marriages prevalent at this time, but there are hymns extolling *swayamvara,* self-choice marriages. Monogamy seems to have been the general rule, though phrases like "Indra among his wives"[5] and "triumph over my rival wives"[6] in Vedic hymns indicate that polygamy existed among the elite and was a reflection of social status. In Vedic society, marriage was not mandatory for a woman. If she chose not to be married, she could live in her parents' house without public censure or choose to become a *brahmacharin* (an ascetic). Daughters inherited property from their fathers and, after marriage, became joint owners of the household and property along with their husbands. That physical seclusion was not practiced in Vedic times is evident from the fact that upper-caste girls and women moved freely in public and attended social gatherings. Widows were expected to remarry, and it was common practice.

Scholarship from the past two decades indicates that the status of women in the Vedic period was high compared with the subsequent Classical period. As shown in Chapter One, prehistoric societies were marked by relatively egalitarian economic and social organization. There was a sexual division of labor, but both men and women shared in the decision-making process. Women were revered for their procreative power. Around 1500–1000 BCE, as the Aryans were making the transition from nomadic pastoralists to agriculturists, their society evolved into a patriarchal one. Still the Aryans recognized the complementary roles of women and men in society and especially in religion.

THE CHANGING STATUS OF HINDU WOMEN

By the end of the Vedic period, however, significant changes occurred in the status of women who belonged to the three upper castes. This was linked to key economic, political, social, and religious developments occurring in late Vedic society (ca. 1000–500 BCE). We know that the oppression of women worsened as private property began to be accumulated by men. As individual family units emerged, the responsibility of raising children shifted solely to women. Consequently this led to limitations on women's public roles. In India, as the Aryans migrated farther into the heartland of the Indo-Gangetic Plain and adopted a sedentary agricultural lifestyle, conflicts arose relating to land disputes, control over resources, and inheritance. Villages were split into private land holdings, and communal ownership declined. Competition in trade intensified, and an element of insecurity and uncertainty pervaded society. In these trying times, social and legal institutions were needed to safeguard one's property and establish harmony in society. The institutions of marriage and family became crucial in determining a legitimate heir and perpetuating patrilineal descent. This prompted men's need to control women's physical mobility and sexuality.

During this time other important changes were taking place in politics and religion that also affected the status of women. Autonomous village communities were replaced by stable monarchies that excluded women from exercising any political ambitions. As the Vedic religion underwent changes, the ritual status of women altered as well. The ideas embodied in the *Atharva Veda* (the last of the four texts) had a direct bearing on this changing attitude, stating that "a woman was unclean below her navel."[7] The notion of transmigration and ceremonial purity saw women as impure, particularly during their menstrual cycle, pregnancy, and childbirth. Therefore, women were relegated to the position of a *sudra* (the lowest, ritually impure caste). They were barred from learning the Vedas and increasingly excluded from participating in public rituals and sacrifices beside their husbands. Conducting sacrifices and rituals became the sole preserve of the male Brahmin priests, leading to the emergence of *brahmanical* patriarchy. From this time onward, a woman was socialized into *stri-dharma* (the ideal of wifely fidelity), as opposed to *dampati* (a joint owner of a household and property), and her social worth was measured in terms of her ability to bear a male son. Their once-public religious role was gradually relegated to the household, where they could partake in several private rituals. A high-caste Hindu man's status now became irrevocably linked with his ability to control his wives or daughters and protect their honor. Respectable women were those under the protection of a man.

A definite double standard of sexual behavior emerged. Respectability was legislated by the Brahmins, and women maintained theirs at the cost of self-expression and freedom. These developments seem to have climaxed during the Gupta period (ca. 320 CE–500 CE). Although the Gupta period is regarded as the golden age of Indian culture, the status of upper-caste Hindu women deteriorated considerably and the disparity between men and women intensified.

GUPTA PERIOD (CA. 320 CE–500 CE)

Around 200 CE to 400 CE, a whole new genre of sociolegal treatises concerned with the ideal nature of Hindu society emerged. These were the *Law Books,* of which the *Manusmriti* or *Laws of Manu* give us valuable insight into the prescriptive role of women during the Gupta period. In a time when the excesses of the Vedic religion and caste hierarchy were being challenged by Buddhism, the primary aim of these laws was to preserve social order by reinforcing brahmanical hegemony. Therefore, the laws sanctioned familial control of women and ensured the perpetuation of a patriarchal society. The code treated the sexuality of women as positive and even auspicious as long as it was properly channeled, that is, through marriage and bearing of male children. Just as in ancient Athens, the laws deemed the female body, once revered for its procreative power, to be just a "vessel for the male seed" and regarded it as impure and polluting. Thereafter, the ideals spelled out in this work had a great influence on the development of Hindu tradition.

FAMILY LIFE

Let us try to reconstruct the life of a Hindu woman by analyzing the *Laws of Manu.* Although Brahmins intended these laws to be universally applied, they actually most often would have shaped the lives of upper-caste women. Because of the lack of sources we have no way of knowing the extent to which the laws might have affected ordinary Hindu women, but we can speculate that they may reflect the general tendency toward a decline in women's status during this period. As in most premodern societies, a Hindu woman's life during the Gupta period was marked by distinct stages: childhood, virginal adolescence, marriage, motherhood, widowhood, and death.

DAUGHTERS: CHILDHOOD, ADOLESCENCE, AND MARRIAGE   As in other patriarchal cultures discussed in this book, the birth of a daughter was not as heralded as was that of a son. Often there was a complete absence of the festivities that marked the birth of a boy. The *Laws of Manu* stressed that all embryos are essentially male and that the birth of a daughter was the result of weak semen. Therefore it cautioned all pregnant women to protect themselves from evil ones. The universal desire to have sons gave rise to elaborate prenatal ceremonies. A ritual especially instituted for avoiding the birth of a daughter constituted simply throwing grass upward while repeating a special mantra. The need for sons was emphasized at every step. In the *Brahmanas* is a story of mythical King Harish Chandra, who had a hundred wives but no sons. The Brahmins of his court revealed to him the need to produce a son by stating that a son was a "boat of salvation, a light in the highest heaven . . . but a daughter a misery."[8] Girls were considered a liability rather than an asset.

The early lives of females must have depended on the social status of their families. Affluent families socialized their daughters to *stri-dharma* (an ideal of wifely fidelity) so that they could become good, obedient, efficient housewives. Girls would often play indoors with other girls. Music, dancing, and playing hide-and-seek were common forms of entertainment. By the Gupta period, prepubescent marriages had become more common. Girls as young as eight years old were married off to men double and even sometimes three times their age. The *Laws of Manu* state:

> A thirty-year old man should marry a twelve-year-old girl who charms
> his heart, and a man of twenty-four an eight-year-old girl; and if duty is
> threatened, [he should marry] in haste.[9]

This reduction of marriage age seems to correlate with certain developing trends. First, there was tremendous social pressure on families to preserve family honor by protecting a girl's virginity before marriage in order to ensure patrilineal descent. Second, it was perceived that young brides could be more easily socialized to remain docile and loyal to their husbands and in-laws, even in abusive situations. Some historians suggest that child marriages indirectly reflect the high maternal mortality rates as adolescent girls gave birth too frequently for their young bodies. This situation was paralleled in Classical Greece and the Roman Republic.

The *Laws of Manu* document eight forms of marriage: *Brahma, Daiva, Prjapatya, Arsha, Gandharva, Asura, Paishacha,* and *Rakshasa*.[10] The highest and ideal form was Brahma. The most important aspect of this form of marriage was the *Kanyadan,* or the gift of a virgin daughter by a father to an eligible groom. Just as in Classical Greece, a Hindu woman in this ideal form of marriage did not have any say in the choice of her partner. Her father arranged it. Even though spiritually extolled in the *Laws of Manu,* Brahma was in reality a transaction that took place between the father and the groom, ensuring the transference of a daughter from the hands of her father to her husband. It reiterated the notion mentioned in the *Laws of Manu* that a woman could not be independent at any time during her life cycle. Similar to the Three Obediences in Confucian China, or the Laws of

Guardianship in Classical Greece and Republican Rome, the *Laws of Manu* clearly stated that a woman was dependent on her father until marriage. Next she belonged to her husband, and when widowed, she became the responsibility of her sons.

> In childhood a woman should be under her father's control, in youth under her husband's, and when her husband is dead, under her sons'. She should not have independence.[11]

Such attitudes reflect fear of women who played such a central role in procreation and the further tightening of patriarchal control over women's life cycle. The *Laws of Manu* considered Gandharva—a love marriage, when a couple chose each other out of mutual physical attraction—of low rank and spiritually unacceptable. There are several examples of Gandharva marriages in Indo-Aryan literature, but these were generally not common in Gupta society. Unlike in modern Western society, marriages were not based on romantic love, but were contracts between two families.

The *Laws of Manu* also defined what constituted femininity in the Gupta period. The "beauty myth," as modern feminist Naomi Wolf calls it in her book by that name, is omnipresent in contemporary society. It consists of the belief that femininity is equated with beauty. Similar ideas and myths about femininity and beauty affected the lives of Indian women—not only during the Classical period, but continuously through-out premodern and into modern times. For example, the *Laws of Manu* pointed out that an eligible bride needed to "have smooth limbs," possess a "graceful gait like a swan," and be "free from all bodily defects."[12] Further, if "a wife is not radiant with beauty she will not attract her husband" and if she fails to attract her husband "no children will be born."[13] In the Gupta period, such ideas of beauty suggested that a woman's physical appearance affected her ability to have healthy children.

Further, the Brahmins' fear of women's uncontrolled sexuality became the driving force for making marriages mandatory for girls. Without mar-riage, a woman could not be absolved from the transmigratory cycle. It was better for a father to get his daughters married to unworthy, unat-tractive men than let them remain single. One notices the double stan-dards here. Women were critically judged for attractiveness and rejected when they lacked it. Men's sexuality, on the other hand, was described in positive terms, and the laws admonished girls for rejecting a marriage proposal based on the physical traits of men, for "women do not care for beauty [in a man] nor is their attention fixed on age. It is enough that he is a man [and] they give themselves to the handsome and to the ugly."[14]

WIVES   The *Laws of Manu* clearly outlined the duties of wives. From an early age, a woman was taught that her welfare was secondary to that of her marital family. A good wife was subservient and docile to her in-laws and husband, and she had no independent existence. The *Kamasutra* (a handbook dealing with methods to acquire pleasure) has chapters directed to elite women advising them not only in the art of making love, but also how to be a good hostess, worthy conversationalist, and perfect housewife. Usually the daughters of upper-caste families would undergo this training from older female relatives or governesses. All dutiful wives wore the red dot that symbolized not only her marital status but also her ability to bring prosperity to her marital family. In addition, a wife was expected to fast regularly for the longevity of her husband and to wear gold jewelry (such as earrings, necklaces, bangles, and toe-rings) that were all feminine fertility symbols. If a man died before his wife (which was often the case), she was blamed for bringing bad karma upon her marital family by her in-laws. The *Laws of Manu* stated, "a virtuous wife should constantly serve her husband like a god"[15] "A good wife," according to the laws, was "not born but made."[16] Men were advised to keep a tight control over their wives, because they "are like leeches, even if daily gratified with ornaments, dresses, and food, they never cease to extort a man. A small leech merely sucks the blood while the other (wife) draws the wealth, property, flesh, energy, strength, and happiness of a man."[17] The laws warned that if she were "allowed to have her own way, she becomes uncontrollable like a disease." The language is clearly misogynist, and it reflected the Brahmins' view of society. Another verse that reflects this attitude states: "The bed and the seat, jewelry, lust, anger, crookedness, a malicious nature, and bad conduct are what *Manu* assigned to women."[18] The *Laws of Manu* stated, "a husband must be constantly worshipped as a god by a faithful wife . . . if a wife obeys her husband, she will for that reason alone be exalted in heaven."[19] Thus a woman's hope of salvation also came to depend on how well she adhered to this wifely ideal. A woman could not initiate a divorce, although if she was involved in an abusive relationship, she could return to her marital family and stay under the protection of her brothers. It was believed that the ritual of *Saptapadi* (going round the sacred fire seven times during the marriage ceremony) sealed the union between man and wife for seven generations.

Female protagonists from religious and secular literature provided models for wives. Two of the most influential were Sita and Parvati. As we saw in the introductory paragraphs, Sita, the heroine of the Sanskrit epic *Ramayana*, was regarded as the ideal wife. She was extolled for her chastity, loyalty, faithfulness, and obedience to her husband, Rama (the incarnation of Vishnu). She also symbolized ascetic sexuality, sexuality controlled by her husband. When Rama was banished from his kingdom for 14 years by the evil manipulations of an old nurse and his stepmother, Sita was

FIGURE 3-1   ROCK WALL PAINTING, SRI LANKA, CA. SIXTH CENTURY CE
The goddesses in this painting wear the preferred personal adornments of upper-class
women during the Gupta period. Many ornaments were considered beneficial to the
woman's fertility.

persistent in her efforts to accompany Rama wherever he went. Her beauty
made her the prey of Ravana, the evil 10-headed demon king of Sri Lanka,
who disguised himself as a beggar and approached Sita. The sweet, unsus-
pecting Sita defied orders by her husband and brother-in-law and crossed
the protective ring drawn around the courtyard in order to give alms to
the mendicant. Ravana revealed his true self and took Sita captive. When
Rama finally rescued her, he wanted her to prove her faithfulness. Sita
performed the ultimate test of walking across fire to prove her fidelity to
her husband. Even today Sita is hailed as an ideal wife because she was
a paragon of femininity and wifely perfections. She had no independent
existence and perfectly fit the model promoted by the *Laws of Manu*.

The other popular ideal was Parvati, the consort of Shiva. She was
extolled for her intense devotion to her husband as she went to the
extreme of killing herself, after her father insulted Shiva by not extending
a formal invitation to him. In the other Sanskrit epic, the *Mahabharata*, an
example of an extremely devoted wife was Gandhari, who was married to

the blind King Dhritarashtra. From the day she married him to her death, she placed a bandage over her eyes so that she might be able to relate to what her husband was going through.

As in other cultures, in India we find women protagonists who were atypical and considered to be dangerous for undermining the feminine ideal and challenging the traditional model. One character was Draupadi, the main female protagonist of the *Mahabharata*. Draupadi was an educated woman who eventually was asked to marry the five inseparable Pandava brothers (who represented the five elements of nature). She was very much involved in decision-making processes and was frequently consulted by the brothers before they undertook any venture. Unlike Sita, her existence did not revolve around her five husbands.

MOTHERHOOD   In the life cycle of a Hindu woman of whatever caste or class, motherhood was of crucial importance. By becoming a mother of a son she gained social approval. As extended families were the norm in Gupta society, a newly married couple did not establish their own home but usually lived in the household of the groom's parents. Once a newly married woman moved into her in-laws' house (an event that usually occurred after puberty), she was expected to get pregnant. If she failed to conceive by the second or third year of her marriage, she was subjected to subtle and often not-so-subtle pressures from her husband's female relatives, especially her mother-in-law. If she was the oldest daughter-in-law, the birth of a son was particularly desired for the perpetuation of the family lineage and for giving moral sanction to the marriage. Once a young woman announced her pregnancy, everybody sighed in relief and waited anxiously for the arrival of a male child. A woman's life was transformed by the birth of a child, preferably male.

As in other cultures discussed in this book, childbirth was a dangerous, painful, and frightening experience for women. The two significant features associated with childbirth were modesty and pollution. Modesty prescribed that a woman should deliver in silence, try to suppress her pain, and not expose her condition to the male members of her family. Similar to Athenian women, most Hindu women would have to endure childbirth five to six times during her lifetime. Once a woman was in labor, she was shifted to a birthing chamber that was exclusively a female domain, where no men or children were allowed. Nobody could touch or come near the mother or newborn until they were ritually cleansed, which was generally after a month for the upper castes and less for the lower castes.[20]

WIDOWHOOD   Child-marriages produced many girl widows. Until the Gupta period, widows were allowed to remarry but, as the Gupta period emerged, the lot of Hindu widows became more and more restricted.

The *Laws of Manu* clearly indicated that a widow had no legal position in society and was considered unlucky. Basically if she did not commit *sati* (a unique custom of self-immolation in the funeral pyre of her husband), a widow led a life of austerity. In practice this meant the widow's head was shaved and she was expected to sleep on the ground, eat one meal a day, wear only white clothes, wear no jewelry, refrain from any forms of celebrations, and not attend happy social gatherings, like births or marriages.

The origins of sati are still shrouded in controversy. Like foot binding in Song China, this practice has been viewed by Westerners as an "exotic" custom. The first instance of recorded sati dates back to about 316 BCE in the Mauryan period, when the wife of Indian general Meteus committed sati after her husband was killed in a battle fighting the Greeks. After Alexander's invasion, Greek travelers who came to India observed this custom among the Kathai tribe in Punjab. Diodorus, who visited India in the first century BCE, made the following comments:

> . . . They passed a law ordaining that a wife, unless she was pregnant or had already borne children, should be burnt along with her husband, and that if she did not choose to obey the law, she should remain a widow to the end of her life, and be forever excommunicated from the sacrifices and other solemnities as being an impious person.[21]

How this custom became an alternative outside the Punjab region for Hindu widows not wanting to lead an austere life is still not clear. The first mention of a Hindu goddess performing this custom is Parvati, also called Sati, the consort of Shiva discussed above. Despite the fact that sati appears in Hindu mythology in the self-immolation of the goddess Parvati, historians have pointed out that belief in this myth did not set the precedent for this custom.

Recent scholarship indicates that the tradition evolved over a period of time. Anand Yang argues that this practice was not exclusive to the upper castes as was previously believed, but that women of lower castes also practiced sati. One of the religious justifications given for this practice was that the woman who performed *sati* would bring 35 million years of bliss to her natal and marital family. Usually a "sati stone" was constructed at the site of the ritual and often became a pilgrimage site and place of worship. The increasing popularity of sati throughout the Gupta period was due to the importance of protecting family honor and to a widow's desire to bring social recognition to the marital family. The practice became popular with the lower classes because it brought financial relief to the marital family: The male members no longer had to take care of the widow. The *Laws of Manu* did not condone sati, but neither did they offer any way out for widows. Instead, the laws categorically disapproved of widow remarriage:

The appointment of widows is never sanctioned in the Vedic verses about marriage, nor is remarriage of widows mentioned in the marriage rules.[22]

From the Vedic to the end of the Mauryan period, the practice of levirate marriages—widows re-marrying brothers-in-law—was common. It was especially recommended if the husband had died without a male heir. This practice, common in other ancient societies such as some Mesopotamian civilizations and the early Islamic Arabian communities, actually offered protection for widows. During the Gupta period, this custom was strictly prohibited by the *Laws of Manu*, which equated the life of a widow without sons to that of a servant and stressed that so long as widows remained chaste they would receive salvation. "A virtuous wife who after the death of her husband constantly remains chaste, reaches heaven, though she may have no son, just like those chaste men."[23]

ECONOMIC ACTIVITIES

The diversity in women's participation in economic activities in India is comparable to that in the ancient Mediterranean world. During the Gupta period, women's work was largely dependent on the caste and social status of her family. Though information on women's economic activities during this time period is scanty, by analyzing the secular literature—compilations of popular stories and folk tales—one can conjecture what ordinary women's economic lives were like. One such compilation is J. A. B. van Buitenen's *Tales of Ancient India.* From the various short stories we learn that women from the lower classes worked at such activities as farm cultivation, spinning, pottery making, painting, basket weaving, and embroidery.

Indian wool, silk, and cotton textiles were in great demand in the Mediterranean world. Though little is known about cultivation of silkworms in India at this time, this tedious job may have been women's, as it was in early Chinese civilization. Women probably worked in cotton fields cultivating and harvesting the crops, while others spun silk or cotton thread and embroidered the final cloth. Both men and women were often employed in weaving and dying Indian cloth commercially. Whatever their work, it was impossible for women of the lower classes to sequester themselves. They needed to work for their daily sustenance, unlike upper-caste women.

We have some evidence to indicate that physical seclusion was practiced among upper-caste women, just as it was in Classical Athens. This practice seems to have been related to the fact that family honor was irrevocably linked with female chastity. As a consequence, women from the three upper castes were disallowed from participating in public economic activities. However, we can speculate that, just like elite Greek women, they must have embroidered, spun cotton, or tailored garments for family use within the confines of their homes.

By the Gupta period, dasis (women slaves) were no longer employed in heavy agricultural work. Instead sudra, lower-caste peasant women, performed this labor. Women belonging to the three upper castes could become dasis. The recruitment pattern was common in other ancient societies. They were enslaved either through captivity, being given as gifts, or being given as default payment of debt. As the caste system became more rigid and upper-caste women practiced physical seclusion, dasis now fulfilled a large number of onerous domestic duties, such as fetching water, pounding grain, washing clothes and dishes, and cleaning the house. In many instances they acted as wet-nurses. Over time, dasis became a common addition to upper-caste families, relieving elite women from performing arduous domestic chores. They were preferred over sudra women (untouchables), who were considered to be ritually impure.

A profession that defied class and caste boundaries and allowed women to control their own sexuality as well as earn a living independently of men was prostitution. The *Kamasutra* ("The Book on the Art of Love"), compiled around 400 CE by a Brahmin named Vatsyayana, is an amazing handbook directed to men and women for the fulfillment of *Kama*, or love—one of the four legitimate goals of a Hindu man. In its blunt treatment of sexuality, it is unique in the Classical world. From this work we get a candid picture of prostitution during the Gupta period. The *Kamasutra* clearly distinguished between the roles of a wife and a courtesan. The wife's duty was to stay at home and take care of the family, while men sought cultural companionship in a *ganika,* or courtesan (who held higher social standing than a *veshya,* an ordinary prostitute meant for a commoner). The ganika played a role comparable to the heterai of classical Athens or the geisha of Japan. She was an accomplished musician, dancer, actress, singer, and excellent conversationalist. She was expected to possess beauty, poise, elegance, and social grace. Despite her considerable talents, though, she could never hope to gain the legitimate status of a wife, even if she produced a male child. Courtesans received patronage from wealthy merchants, high administrators, and even kings. There are examples to indicate that some affluent courtesans lived in palatial houses and controlled a whole enterprise consisting of male bodyguards, numerous servants, and maids. Women from all castes and classes were attracted to this profession.

Courtesans were widely respected during the Classical Gupta period, and we see examples of both admired and reviled courtesans in popular literature. A classic play is from Sudraka's *Mricchkatika* ("The Little Clay Cart"). A courtesan named Vasantasena was in love with Charudatta, the Brahmin hero. She sacrificed her ornaments to save her lover from a wrongful lawsuit. In the end her position is validated when her lover marries her and takes her home to meet his first wife. It would appear from the play that wives often envied the freedom, beauty, and splendor of the courtesans, and the courtesans envied the wives' respectability. That courtesans enjoyed a high position in Indian society is also evident from the fact that they enjoyed a degree of legal protection from the state. If a courtesan was cheated or physically abused by a client, then the perpetrator was punished severely. The attention paid to them was probably conditioned by the fact that an important source of state revenue came from the taxes paid by courtesans. Prostitution was not considered to be a crime or sin and was treated like another trade. The *Kamasutra* says:

> A courtesan of a pleasant disposition beautiful and otherwise attractive, who mastered the arts has the right to a seat of honor among men. She will be honored by the king and praised by the learned and all will seek her favors and treat her with considerations.[24]

The *veshya*, on the other hand, was a common prostitute, not refined, and usually was not amply remunerated like the courtesans. Theoretically speaking, the *Laws of Manu* forbade Brahmins from seeing prostitutes and imposed punishments on those who did. However, as another historian observes, " . . . the secular attitude differed very greatly from the religious ideal, and here it was the secular view which prevailed."[25] One reason for this was that the Brahmins who were promoters of the *Laws of Manu* became involved with development of the institution of *devdasis*—the temple dancers.

The custom of devdasis, comparable to vestal virgins in Rome, was predominant in Southern India. In times of famine, poor parents sold their beautiful virgin daughters to temple priests for a nominal sum of money. These young girls spent their entire life in the temple complex, singing and dancing during religious ceremonies, offering food and flowers to the deities and, after reaching puberty, providing sexual favors to temple priests. Like courtesans, they were drawn from all classes and castes, but unlike them, devdasis did not have any legal protection, could not control their wages, and were completely at the mercy of temple priests. Often they were treated badly and abused; their wages could be confiscated by corrupt priests.

An important indication of the economic position of Indian women in the Classical Gupta era is their loss of property rights. In order to ensure strict patrilineal descent, women could no longer inherit any property other than the *stridhan*, the gifts given to her by her natal family at the time of marriage. Comparable to the dowry of other ancient civilizations, the stridhan often consisted of her jewelry, which she kept under her personal control, often in a locked box. Historians argue that dowry was given to ensure the daughter's well-being in her marital family.[26] In cases of emergency, she could be asked to part temporarily with the jewelry so it could be pawned or sold. Her marital family was obligated to compensate for this loan of her property or return it to her after the need was over. The *Laws of Manu* state:

> A wife, a son, and a slave, these three are traditionally said to have no property; whatever property they acquire belongs to the man to whom they belong.[27]

However, these injunctions were not universally followed throughout India. There were certain tribal areas, such as the Nayars, where matrilineal descent was popular. In the province of Bengal, widows were allowed to inherit some property of their husbands. Overall, however, during the Gupta period, the legal rights of Hindu women greatly diminished. The limitation of women's ability to control wealth was common to a number of Classical societies, including Greece and the Roman Republic, where a similar emphasis on patrilineal descent also provided the rationale.

WOMEN'S ACCESS TO POLITICAL POWER

The *Kamasutra* has a chapter outlining the duties of kings and how they should rule the country. An important duty of the state was to maintain social harmony by regulating the caste system. Since the caste system mandated upper-caste women's familial roles, theoretically they were excluded from formal participation in politics. However, as we will see, women did not ordinarily exercise power themselves, but as representatives of their families, especially minor sons, they might exercise influence as indirect power.

An exception to the rule occurred during the very foundation of the Gupta Empire. Some historians argue that the founder of the Gupta empire, Chandra Gupta I (r. 320–330 CE) came from an obscure background, but his marriage to the powerful Licchavi princess Kumaradevi gave him much-needed access to power. The Licchavis had a distinguished pedigree. The importance Chandra Gupta attached to his marriage is evident from the coins minted during his reign. It included both the king and queen's names, suggesting perhaps that Chandra Gupta wanted people to recognize Kumaradevi as a co-ruler. Samudra Gupta, their son, equally recognized the political significance of having the powerful Licchavis on his side. In the coins minted during his reign, he refers to himself as the son of a Licchavi princess and not the son of Chandra Gupta.

We have no evidence of other women rulers during this time period. However, from the two epics the *Ramayana* and the *Mahabharata*, we get examples of legendary queen mothers who played behind-the-scene roles in order to ensure the throne for their sons. From this we can extrapolate that some women exercised indirect political power. Such women were seen in a negative light and generally regarded as interfering with what was supposedly a male domain.

One such example is Rama's stepmother, Queen Kaikeyi, the second wife of King Dasratha. Influenced by an evil maid, she decides to remind the king of a boon that he had granted her for saving his life. As the king was getting ready to hand over the throne to Rama, his eldest son, Queen Kaikeyi tells the king that she wants her son Bharata to be crowned instead. The king was bound by his promise to then banish Rama for 14 years to the forest and make Bharata, his second son, the king. However, Bharata, being a loyal brother, is embarrassed by his mother's antics and requests Rama to return to the kingdom. When he doesn't, Bharata uses his brother's slippers as symbols of his power.

The *Mahabharata* also has examples of many women, especially mothers, who went to great lengths to secure positions for their sons. Kunti, the mother of the five Pandava brothers, is consulted on every major mission that the brothers undertake, especially on the eve of the Battle of Kurushetra to regain land that had been illegally confiscated by their hundred evil cousins, the Kauravas. In Kalidasa's play by that name, Shakuntala travels far and wide to take her son back to his father, the prince, to claim the throne for him.

These literary sources confirm that India had influential women who defied male censure to exercise informal power. Rather than imagining these exceptional women as any type of proto-feminists, we should see them as products of their time, in a society that valued men's political roles and denied women's. Thus, women like Shakuntala and Kunti exercise great influence but only on behalf of their sons, not to gain rulership themselves. We can conjecture that women's access to formal power was largely nonexistent in India, just as it was in Imperial Rome and Classical Greece.

WOMEN IN RELIGIOUS CULTURE

THE DIVINE AS FEMININE: GODDESSES AND THE *SHAKTI* TRADITION   One of the great ambiguities of feminine ideals one encounters while examining the status of women in Classical India is that of goddess worship. In a strictly patriarchal society like India, the worship of goddesses did not translate into the elevated status of women. An important religious work in Sanskrit, the *Devi-Mahatyma* (ca. 500 CE) provides valuable insights into the *shakti* tradition (the divine being worshipped as the feminine) during the Gupta period. Followers of this tradition believed that Devi (a supreme goddess) was the primary embodiment of shakti—cosmic power. She was the creator of the universe and controlled the three gods of the Hindu Trinity: Brahma (Creator God), Vishnu (Preserver God), and Shiva (Destroyer God). In times of need, Devi manifested herself in two different forms: the terrifying Kali and the beautiful Durga.

From the *Devi-Mahatyma,* we get to know about the origins of the goddess Durga. The story goes that the male gods of the Hindu pantheon were being tormented by Mahisa, a vicious buffalo demon. In order to defeat him, the gods unanimously decided to combine their powers and create one supremely powerful and beautiful female: the goddess Durga. Hindu iconography depicts Durga seated on a lion with eight arms, each holding a different weapon vanquishing Mahisa. Historian David Kinsley points out that ". . . this beautiful young woman who slays demons . . . who exists independent from male protection or guidance represents a vision of feminine that challenges the stereotyped view of women found in traditional Hindu Law books."[28] This anomalous myth can be explained as originating from the relatively egalitarian era of the Indus Valley civilization (ca. 3000 BCE–1500 BCE).

Of all the Hindu goddesses, perhaps Kali intrigues Westerners the most. Rita Gross points out that the traits Kali represents are liberating for modern women around the world. Of her many qualities, perhaps it is "her universal range of activity" and her "explicit sexuality" that has prompted feminist research on her.[29] Some have compared her symbolically to Greek goddesses Demeter or Artemis, but there is none like her elsewhere in the premodern world in terms of the way she is depicted in iconography. There are many versions of the origins of Kali. One popular story suggests that she was actually created from the brows of Durga to help her destroy two demons. Whatever her origins, Kali "is always black or dark, is usually naked and has long disheveled hair. . . . She is usually shown on the battlefield, where she is a furious combatant who gets drunk on the hot blood of her victims., . . ."[30] In some areas of India, Kali was worshipped as an independent deity and not linked to any male deity. When she was associated with a male god, David Kinsley points out, "it is almost always Shiva. As his consort, wife or associate, Kali often plays the role of inciting him to wild behavior."[31] He goes on to say that the "iconographic representations of Kali and Shiva nearly always show Kali as dominant. She is usually standing or dancing on Shiva's prone body, and when the two are depicted in sexual intercourse, she is shown above him."[32]

Therefore, Kali is the embodiment of all those traits the patriarchal *Laws of Manu* tried to repress in an ideal woman: untamed sexual energy, passion, and empowerment. Kali was at first commonly worshipped by those considered to be on the fringes of society. After the Gupta period, she became the central goddess of Tantric Hindus: those who believed in the ideology "that reality is the result and expression of the symbiotic interaction of male and female."[33] In other words, Tantrics believed that true worship of the divine could be achieved through sexual intercourse between a male and female. Tantric Hinduism was at first popular in the eastern part of India and then gradually spread to other areas. Why Kali became the central goddess of Tantrics is not known. As a goddess with untamed energy threatening the stability and order of the universe, she projected female power in its dangerous form and was therefore an antithesis to what the *Laws of Manu* had prescribed for women. Perhaps it was this aspect that made her feared and revered by both men and women.

WOMEN IN BUDDHISM   During the Gupta period, Buddhism, with its message of personal salvation and democratic ideals, was a popular, unconventional religion that attracted both male and female converts, especially from the lowest castes. As discussed earlier, the Vedic religion made significant adjustments to try to regain preeminence after Buddhism's challenge. Let us try to analyze the status of women in Buddhism and understand why it proved to be a popular alternative to Hinduism.

The *Three Pitakas* and the *Jatakas* are important primary sources that help historians reconstruct the early history of Buddhism in India. These records were first transmitted orally and then finally written down in the Pali language. From these sources, we know that the historical Buddha was born Gautama Siddhartha around 563 BCE in Kapilavastu, which is situated in modern-day Nepal. His father, Suddhodhana, was a prince of the Sakya tribe. Siddhartha led a very sheltered existence, but recognized the suffering and pain of life by witnessing the Four Sights: illness, old age, death, and asceticism. Leaving his material life behind, Siddhartha wandered around for six years, practicing extreme asceticism. Unable to find the cause of suffering, he decided to sit and meditate under a Bodhi tree. On the forty-ninth day, he reached enlightenment and became known as the Buddha. At Deer Park, Sarnath, near Varanasi in North India, he delivered his first sermon, called the Sermon of the Turning of the Wheel, which enunciated the Four Noble Truths and the Eightfold Path: the basic teachings of Buddhism.

The Buddha attacked the inequalities of the caste system, the violence involved in ritual sacrifices, and the dominance of the Brahmins. He taught a middle way between asceticism and a life of moderation and moral responsibility. Despite the alterations to the later Vedic religion, his views about the role of women in society mirrored some key Vedic beliefs. Early sources suggest that Buddha's advice to young girls was to conform to their familial roles, that is, to marry and practice the virtues of an ideal wife: loyalty and obedience to husband and in-laws, obedience

**FIGURE 3-2   SCULPTURE FROM BUDDHIST TEMPLE AT
KARLI, FIRST CENTURY CE**
This sculpture shows the ideal Buddhist married couple, as it
emphasizes that they are in perfect harmony with each other.

to all elders, and a focus on housekeeping. "To whatever husbands, your
parents shall give you in marriage, you will honor, revere, esteem. . . ."
"Women," the Buddha is believed to have told his friend Ananda, "are
uncontrollable . . . envious . . . greedy . . . weak in wisdom. A woman's
heart is haunted by jealousy and sensuality. . . ."[34] However, we have no
way of verifying whether these were the original views expressed by the
Buddha himself or words later incorporated by monastic men who compiled these canons. The Buddhist canons reiterated that women were subordinate to men, they were inherently sinful by nature, and their sexuality

needed to be controlled because they were a source of contamination to men. As in later Vedic religion, arranged marriages were extolled.

The Buddha, however, departed from the later Vedic religion's treatment of women in some aspects. For example, unlike Hindu practice, widows and divorced women were allowed to remarry, and love matches were not spiritually looked down upon. The Buddha asserted that in spiritual matters men and women were equal. Even though the Buddha himself had left behind his wife and infant son when he went on his journey to attain enlightenment, he recognized the importance of the role women played as procreators for the perpetuation of society. It was this inclusiveness that gave women a sense of self-worth and freedom and attracted them to this new religion.

By analyzing secular Buddhist accounts, we know that lay women played an important role in the rise of Buddhism, just as they did in the nascent Christianity. They provided the much-needed economic support to sustain the newly emerging religion. These women mostly came from affluent merchant families and were hailed for their intelligence, generosity, and organizational skills. For example, Vishaka, a matriarch of a prominent merchant family, was an ardent supporter of monastic orders and her generosity is extolled in Buddhist canons. Many of these rich benefactresses were also affluent courtesans. They were very much a part of society, women of independent means earning a legitimate income. Perhaps one of the most famous courtesans mentioned in Buddhist literature is Ambapali. The Buddha stayed with her when he visited Veshali and later engaged her in an ecclesiastical debate. Ambapali was so impressed with the Buddha that she renounced her material life and became a nun. There were several other courtesans in Buddhist canons who gave up their profession to become nuns.

In an often-repeated story, it was Buddha's aunt and foster mother, Mahaprajapati Gautami, as well as his friend Ananda, who persuaded him to allow women to join the *sangha*—the monastic order of monks and nuns. Some historians have argued that the Buddha's initial hesitation was because of his fear of undermining the importance attached to women's role as procreators. The acceptance of women in the sangha was indeed a revolutionary step, considering the severe limitations that Brahmin orthodoxy placed on them. The Buddha, however, laid down eight cardinal rules that all nuns had to follow. If one analyzes these eight rules, it shows that nuns had to defer to monks. "She shall with her hands folded in prayerful attitude, rise to greet him and bow down to him."[35] In addition to these cardinal rules, nuns also had to abide by the *Rules of Pratimoksha*. The ordination process was made more difficult for nuns than for monks, and their lives were closely regulated. Therefore, women being ordained into the sangha found themselves bound by a far greater number of rules and regulations than their male counterparts.

An extensive body of literature known as *Theri-Gatha* ("Psalms of Nuns") was authored by as many as 73 nuns. Based on this valuable source, historians have pointed out that joining the order of nuns allowed women uncommon opportunities, including access to higher spiritual education. It especially provided an alternative to women who wanted to dissociate themselves from the familial role. In some cases women joined the order after repeated failed marriages or to relieve their natal family from the burden of paying dowries. For example, Ishidasi joined the order after three disappointing marriages. Others joined to pursue philanthropy or an acetic life of spiritual devotion.

Nuns were punished for showing any romantic or sexual interest toward a monk. "A nun who, moved by desire, touches, strokes, takes hold of, or presses up against a man, . . . anywhere between his neck and his knees—she is expelled and no longer allowed to be part of the community."[36] This renunciation of sexuality was not too high a price for many women. The willingness of some women to contend with such a lifestyle was a testimony to their desire to find an alternative way of life. Women from different socioeconomic backgrounds became nuns. Examples of women from royalty abound. One such notable example was Sanghamitra, the daughter of King Ashoka. She traveled to Sri Lanka to spread Buddhism. From Chinese Buddhist pilgrim's accounts, we learn that nuns lived simple lives and were engaged in scholarly work.

The Buddhist belief in transmigration means that individuals are born again and again to endure pain until they reach perfection and are released from this cycle. The most virtuous way one could hope to achieve this enlightenment was by practicing family life. Even though Buddha allowed women to become nuns, he had done so grudgingly. He always maintained a preference of lay women over nuns. Nancy Falk has argued that "the Hindu *dharma's* values percolated through into popular Buddhist expectations as well. Buddhists, like Hindus, honored fecund housewives especially if they were pious lay women."[37] She suggests that, "many Buddhists, like Hindus, also preferred to see women at the hearth rather than on the road or within a monastery's walls."[38] She points out, however, that given this preference, the relationship between lay women and the nuns was one of peaceful coexistence because the monks and nuns depended on these rich benefactresses for economic sustenance.

After the death of Buddha, Buddhism split into two main branches over doctrinal differences: *Mahayana* and *Hinayana* Buddhism. The question of whether a man is spiritually superior to a woman was widely debated in Mahayana Buddhism. Mahayana Buddhism relegated nuns to a subordinate position, but opened the debate over whether a woman could become a *bodhisattva*.[39] (that is, reach enlightened existence—become a Buddha-to-be).

Vajrayana or Tantric Buddhism (borrowing heavily from Tantric Hinduism) developed around 300 CE and exalted the female power.[40] Vajrayana Buddhists believed that both men and women could achieve nirvana or enlightenment through the intensive study and practice of eight different forms of yoga or meditation. This was usually taught under the supervision of a *guru* or teacher. Unlike other branches of Buddhism, recent scholarship has shown that women practiced and taught tantric meditations just as freely as men did. Tantric *yoginis* (women practitioners) have left behind their experiences, which form a valuable primary source to get a better understanding of their lives. From them, we know that the majority of them became yoginis after their marriages dissolved. These stories point to initial feelings of isolation being replaced by sense of spiritual fulfillment after adjusting to life as a yogini. Tantric Buddhism recognized women bodhisattvas. As a consequence of this, there were several female bodhisattvas in the Tantric pantheon. Tara is perhaps most commonly known to Westerners, and she was worshipped by both men and women.[41]

WOMEN THROUGHOUT SOUTHEAST ASIA (CA. 300 CE–1500 CE)

During the Gupta period, trade and commerce helped to spread Hindu and Buddhist cultural traditions to other areas of Southeast Asia. Archeological evidence and merchants' accounts point to the thriving trade that existed between South Asia and the Mediterranean world. The latter's enormous wealth generated a great demand for exotic goods from Asia, especially India. Indian merchants went to countries of Southeast Asia—Myanmar, Thailand, Cambodia, Vietnam, and the various islands of Indonesia—to establish trading centers. As Indian expatriates they played an important role in cultural diffusion.

On the other hand, Buddhist monks and Brahmins were often invited to Southeast Asia to help establish and consolidate the power of kings as state formation began there around 250 CE. For example, legend has it that the kingdom of Funan (ca. 250 CE–560 CE), situated along the Mekong Delta region of modern South Vietnam and Cambodia, resulted from a marital alliance between a Brahmin and a local princess. Two additional kingdoms in premodern Southeast Asia that were once under Funan hegemony but established independent states with strong Hindu and Buddhist cultural elements were the kingdoms of Srivijaya at Palembang in Sumatra, Indonesia, (ca. 670 CE–1025 CE) and Angkor in Cambodia (ca. 889 CE–1431 CE).

Historians look at epigraphic records, traders' accounts, and archeology to argue that the trade contacts between India and Southeast Asia allowed for certain Indian cultural traditions to be exported to Southeast Asia. Exports included the Sanskrit language; the Indian epics the *Ramayana* and the *Mahabharata*; and Hindu and Buddhist sculpture, painting, and temple architectural styles. The world-famous temple complexes of Angkor-Wat in Cambodia and Borobodur and Prambanan in Java are standing testimonies to the borrowing of Hindu and Buddhist temple architectural and sculptural styles from India. However, unlike Buddhism, which was more universal in its message, Hinduism, with all its complexities, did not aggressively seek converts in Southeast Asia and remained an influential force primarily among the royalty and elites of society. The ruling elites adopted Sanskrit, Hindu ideas of polity, the sociolegal treatises collectively called the *Dharmasastras* (to which the *Laws of Manu* belonged), worship of Vishnu or Shiva, and other cultural traditions. Thus historians now refute previous claims that "Indianization" of Southeast Asia was the product of military conquest and proceeded in a uniform manner. Rather they argue that it was through "maritime trade, not by conquest or colonization . . . "[42] that Indian cultural diffusion occurred, and it molded and adapted itself to suit local needs. This ensured that "Southeast Asia retained its distinctiveness even while borrowing numerous elements"[43] from India.

In this section, we will briefly examine the status of women in Southeast Asia and try to analyze what impact the spread of Indian cultural influences had on their lives. A major problem for this early period is the paucity of sources from Southeast Asian women. When one tries to reconstruct their lives, it is clear that the *Laws of Manu* were hailed in Burma, Thailand, Cambodia, Java, and Bali as "defining documents of the natural order, which kings were obliged to uphold. They were copied, translated, and incorporated into local law codes, with stricter adherence to the original text in Burma and Siam [Thailand] and a stronger tendency to adapt to local needs in Java."[44] If that was the case, how much influence did these laws have on the status of women in Southeast Asia? Some historians have suggested that "the women of Southeast Asia were the most fortunate," when compared with all the premodern cultures.[45] What were some of the privileges they enjoyed and what contributed to them? This section will try to analyze these central questions.

ECONOMIC AUTONOMY

Anthony Reid describes Southeast Asian society as a patriarchal system within which gender roles were uniquely defined. For the most part there was no competition between the sexes, as they were involved in different economic activities. Unlike women in India, Southeast Asian women were valued and productive members of society. The common belief was "the more daughters a man has, the richer he is."[46] They were revered for their reproductive ability. There is no evidence of physical seclusion, as both elite and ordinary women actively participated in economic activities. Examples of economic activities that women were actively engaged in were weaving, farm cultivation, vegetable growing, and pottery making. Since documentary evidence is scanty for the earlier period, by looking at Chinese and Western travelers' accounts from the thirteenth to fourteenth century CE, we can conjecture that women traders from elite and ordinary classes were involved not only in domestic trade, but also in the long-distance spice trade. Women traders from Cochin China (part of modern South Vietnam) and Aceh controlled their own wages, conducted negotiations, made business deals, and were actively involved in all aspects of trade. In Bali and Batavia (Java), women could own slaves.[47]

Unlike the women of the Mediterranean world and India, Southeast Asian women inherited an equal share of property, including land from their fathers, which they continued to control after their marriage. Thomas Kirsh, in his analysis of kingship and genealogical claims among the ancient Khmers of Cambodia, points out the presence of matrilineal descent among the royalty. He argues that matrilineality was an ideal that all kings believed they needed to adhere to because it was considered sacred and was in contrast to the ordinary pattern of inheritance, where both daughters and sons got an equal share from fathers.

Another major difference between Southeast Asian women and women from the Mediterranean world and India was that they could demand a bride-price from the prospective bridegroom. Bride-price can be viewed as compensation to the bride's family for the loss of the woman's labor. The bride-price varied according to the social status of the bride's family. It could be paid in livestock or land (among farmers) or in money (among the mercantile classes). Similar arrangements were also prevalent among many peoples in Africa. Some sociologists equate male payment of bride-price to women enjoying relatively high status in society.

OTHER FAMILIAL AND SOCIAL PRIVILEGES

This relative economic autonomy that Southeast Asian women enjoyed gave them access to privileges uncommon in other cultures in the premodern world. For example, women throughout Southeast Asia exercised considerable control over their sexuality. They married at a later age, usually between the ages of 15 and 21. Prepuberty marriages or even marriages between the ages of 12 and 14 were unheard of. Since women married at a later age, virginity was not a prerequisite for brides. In some areas of Southeast Asia like Pegu or the kingdom of Siam, priests performed special rituals to break the hymens of virgin girls to prepare them for marriage. Premarital sexual relationships were commonplace among Southeast Asian women. Women chose their own lovers and husbands and regularly practiced birth control by taking herbal concoctions. Since most women were involved in some form of economic activity, abortion was not uncommon, especially among women involved in farm cultivation who could not afford to spend time being pregnant.

The best example to show that women in Southeast Asia demanded sexual pleasure from men and were not just passive recipients was the custom of inserting pins, wheels, spurs, or even metal studs on the penises of men. Believed to enhance the sexual pleasure of women, this was a very common practice among all the classes throughout Southeast Asia. The most graphic description of this painful custom comes from a European observer, Pigafetta, who visited the Southern Philippines soon after 1500 CE:

> The males, large and small, have their penis pierced from one side to the other near the head with a gold or tin bolt as large as a goose quill. In both ends of the same bolt some have what resembles a spur, with points upon the ends; others are like the head of a cart nail. . . . They say that their women wish it so, and that if they did otherwise they would not have communication with them. . . .[48]

A variation of this custom prevalent in the kingdom of Siam (modern Thailand) was the insertion of small balls or bells under the loose skin of the penis. A Chinese commentator noted:

> When a man has attained his twentieth year, they take the skin which surrounds the membrum virile, and with a fine knife . . . they open it up and insert a dozen tin beads inside the skin; they close it up and protect it with medicinal herbs. . . . The beads look like a cluster of grapes. . . . If it is the King . . . or a great chief or a wealthy man, they use gold to make hollow beads, inside which a grain of sand is placed. . . . They make a tinkling sound, and this is regarded as beautiful.[49]

It was not until the arrival of Islam and Christianity that this practice was finally suppressed. Men were expected to dress elaborately, paying special attention to hair, jewelry, and physique. "After his meal a man would put on his sarong and he would undo it twelve or thirteen times until he had it to his liking."[50] Besides hair styling, filing and blackening of teeth were an important facet of daily life for men once they had reached puberty. Generally they kept long hair, tattooed their bodies, and blackened their teeth regularly by chewing betel or coloring teeth with dyes. Unlike in India or the Mediterranean world, the onus was on men to make themselves attractive to women.

Economic independence strengthened a woman's right to initiate divorce if she was not sexually or emotionally satisfied in the relationship.

Cambodian and Javanese women especially were not tolerant about their husbands' absences for long periods of time. If Javanese men were away from their wives for " the space of seven months," then their wives had the right to initiate a divorce.[51] Monogamous marriages were the general rule, though polygamy was practiced by the royalty and elite, among whom it was a reflection of social status. For example, the king of Angkor had a harem consisting of 4,000 to 5,000 women. Concubinage or temporary marriage was preferred over prostitution in Southeast Asia, where it was a common phenomenon, especially after the arrival of foreign male traders at the end of the period. From the above discussion, we can conclude that the *Laws of Manu* and the treatment of women they embodied did not have a major impact on the status of Southeast Asian women.

CONCLUSION

Women's lives in premodern cultures were rooted in their particular historical contexts. Nevertheless, we can draw broad comparisons between the lives of women in the ancient Mediterranean world and India. Whereas we mostly see similarities among women's lives in Classical Athens and Gupta India, more contrasts appear between women of Imperial Rome and their counterparts in Classical India.

First, the institutions of family and marriage were central to both Classical Athens and India. These institutions explicitly emphasized the dominance of husbands over wives and fostered many inequalities between men and women. In both societies, elite men mandated women's familial roles. The system of arranged marriages in which young girls were married to older men chosen by their natal families was a feature common to both. The custom of giving dowry for the well-being of a daughter was practiced in both Classical Athens and Gupta India. As is common in patriarchal, patrilineal societies, the purpose of marriages in both these civilizations was to ensure patrilineal descent by producing a male heir. Therefore there was a distinct preference for male child over a female. Due to the difference in ages and education between husbands and wives, in both societies, men sought cultural companionship in courtesans. Women also lost their right to initiate a divorce in both the areas.

Second, we notice that in both Athens and Gupta India, religion became an ingredient for patriarchy. For example, the worship of goddesses in both societies did not automatically translate into women's elevated status in society. In Gupta India, especially, women were regarded as polluting during their menstrual cycle, pregnancy, and childbirth and consequently were excluded from playing more prominent roles in public rituals. Both Athenian and Indian women continued to play a central role in private rituals and socializing young children into religion.

Third, in both societies, we notice great diversity in women's participation in economy. Restrictions placed on elite women's physical mobility excluded them from actively participating in public economic activities. However, it was different for women belonging to the lower classes. They needed to work for their daily sustenance. Another important change common to both societies was that women lost the right to inherit land. There were exceptions—for example, Spartan women could independently own land.

Fourth, in both we notice the lack of women's access to exercise formal power. In Athens, the introduction of participatory government excluded women from exercising even the indirect influence that was possible in India. Thus we notice significant similarities between the statuses of women in these two world areas.

An important difference existed in the political milieu between Classical India and the Roman Republic and Empire. Centralizing forces in Indian politics led to the gradual decrease of power for women. This trend is reflected clearly in Gupta India, where we notice a dramatic decline in the status of women. Women lost much of their legal, political, social, and economic rights, whereas the reverse occurred in Rome during the late Republic and Imperial eras, when harsh restrictions imposed on women had started to fade.

As Indian cultural influences spread to Southeast Asia, the strong patriarchal impositions did not implant themselves in society. We can speculate that women's status remained relatively elevated in Southeast Asia, despite the selective borrowings of Hinduism, particularly among the elites. Aspects of Hinduism that were most likely to be adopted included the trappings of Gupta power but not the inner workings of patriarchal gender dynamics. Indeed women in this region continued to embrace Buddhism because of its more inclusive message. We can also speculate that in Southeast Asia during a pivotal era, with little competition for resources or dominance, women continued to enjoy relative independence in making their own decisions in choice of marriage partners, of economic activities, and even of exploring their sexuality without fear of public censure.

 CHAPTER FOUR

WOMEN IN TANG AND SONG CHINA (618–1279 CE)

Chinese women's status declined from the Tang to the Song era with the emergence of a more restrictive form of patriarchy that was based on Han Confucianism (206 BCE–220 CE). The Confucian Three Obediences was the foundation of Han Chinese patriarchy: Daughters obey their fathers, wives obey their husbands, and widows obey their sons. This fundamental Chinese cultural tradition provided the main guide for behavior in the family and the state as well as a sense of coherence to Chinese society. As this dominant cultural tradition emerged in the Han era, a powerful unified Han Chinese state was created, which sustained itself with an elaborate bureaucratic system. Military and political life, from which women were excluded, were the main paths to high status and prestige for men. Patriarchs headed extended families and male ancestors were honored. Confucianism emphasized that the only way for women to achieve honor in society was by fulfilling their familial roles as wives and mothers.

However, both internal and external changes combined to weaken patriarchy by the Tang era (618–907 CE). New outlets appeared for women to achieve honor, because of political chaos, nomadic incursions and frontier cultural influence, and the consolidation of Buddhism and Daoism as organized religions. Tang Chinese rulers and elites adopted nomadic steppe practices in politics, culture, and attitudes, which contributed to greater freedoms for Tang women than what had been before, or what would appear later.

The Song era (960–1279 CE), with its strong Neo-Confucian culture—which reasserted select Confucian values and practices, such as the Three Obediences—restored and reestablished a firm patriarchy. Rejecting the influence of nomadic pastoralists north of the Yangtze River and the pastoralists' conquest of that region in the twelfth century, Neo-Confucian government servitors hoped to return to an emphasis on social order and political hierarchy. Southern Neo-Confucian culture came to dominate China, putting more constraints on women, rejecting Tang gender relations, and opposing Buddhist women's monastic power. In reaction to the subtle increase in power and independence women had gained during the Tang and early Song eras, Neo-Confucianists emphasized segregating the sexes and subordinating women to men in family life, productive work, religious practices, and public life. The tradition of the Song ornamental wife became crystallized, and ultimately a tenacious form of Chinese patriarchy emerged that lasted into the twentieth century.

However, Song women were partners in constructing the Chinese Neo-Confucian social order. They were indispensable to that order in their fulfillment of family roles as daughters, wives, mothers, and mothers-in-law (producing offspring, assisting in-laws, worshipping husbands' ancestors, and managing the "inner quarters" of the home). Equally crucial for sustaining Chinese patriarchal order, but often forgotten, were concubines and purchased women (also producing male offspring for the patriline—that is, the family line of their master, the patriarch). Song women managed to achieve some measure of power, even as they contributed to the stronger patriarchy that constrained them.

Most of what we can imagine about Song Chinese women's experience focuses on elite women, because Neo-Confucian writers largely concentrated on the elite. Ultimately, however, it is clear that Chinese women of all classes came under increasing constraints. Women's weaving and other productive work were devalued, whereas their role in the reproduction of the family took precedence. Alternate paths of becoming Buddhist or Daoist nuns were closed off, as were public roles for women. Furthermore, the most oppressive Chinese elite practices, including foot binding and the cult of widow chastity, originated in the Song era and spread widely to women of all classes in later dynasties.

QUESTIONS FOR STUDENT ANALYSIS

1. How did the changing ideals about the ideal female actually affect Tang and Song-era women's lives in family, work, religious, and public life?

2. What were the stages of women's lives in a Song Neo-Confucian family, and how were they similar to and different from those of women of other civilizations you have read about?

3. How were the productive roles and work conditions of Chinese women similar to and different from the work of women of other civilizations?

4. What roles did religions such as Daoism and Buddhism offer to women that a family's ancestor cult could not? What similarities do you see between the appeal of religious asceticism for women in China and other civilizations, such as western Europe and Southeast Asia?

Overview of China under the Tang and Song Dynasties

When the Han empire crumbled in 220 CE, several centuries of political chaos, great uncertainty, and cultural change ensued. Confucianism, which had been the foundation of the Han imperial system and social order, lost its monopoly over elite education. The Sui and Tang Dynasties (581–618 CE and 618–907 CE) reunified China and set it on a path of imperial expansion. But political reunification was more easily accomplished than the cultural unity of a past age.

The Tang dynasty especially was a time of conquest, religious and cultural influx, and a strong military elite. The empire conquered vast territories in Central Asia and expanded China's western borders. China's military might was at its apex. Ushering in a highly cosmopolitan era, Tang rulers practiced religious toleration and encouraged merchants to trade with India and Byzantium. Chinese religious practices blended ancestor worship, Buddhism, and Daoism (a longstanding and many-faceted tradition emphasizing unity, harmony, and a link between people and nature) very comfortably. Diverse outsiders thronged to the Tang court where exoticism (the fervent admiration of foreign practices, ideas, and goods) flourished. The northern Tang aristocratic elite was descended from Chinese who had lived under and intermarried with Turkic-speaking steppe peoples and thus developed a culture influenced by steppe practices. In steppe society, among pastoral nomads, power was less centralized, and hereditary chiefdoms ruled loosely. Given the frequent absence of men, women were less regulated and more autonomous than women in settled Chinese society, and labor was less restricted by gender roles.

The Tang elite and imperial family led lives of luxury and opulence. They protected their status and maintained the social order through practices of exclusion. Social and government service status (a position in bureaucratic service) came only through descent. Elite marriage practices and family rituals were forbidden to commoners. In 907 CE, decades of leadership crises, scandals, frontier attacks, and general instability brought down the Tang dynasty.

The Song dynasty came to power in 960 CE and set China on a different path. The economy began to shift geographically. Before 800 CE the northern plains were the heartland, but in the ninth century, the rich potential of the southern Yangtze River rice lands grew in importance. A trend from subsistence to commercialization appeared. Towns and cities, which had been administrative centers earlier, became centers of production and consumption during the Song dynasty. Much of rural China came to be tied in a web of interregional commerce. Economic prosperity meant that boundaries between older social categories of scholar, peasant, merchant, and artisan became permeable.

An educated, southern elite displaced the northern hereditary aristocracy as the governing class of China. The new political elite came to their positions through merit, rising through the Confucian exam system. Elite families intermarried and came to dominate the exam system. They practiced inclusion and wanted to build a social order that was ranked, but open to all. They hoped to bind the whole population into a shared orthodox culture. To do so, they developed Neo-Confucianism—a reassertion of many classical Confucian values and practices. Developing a new form of civility, Neo-Confucianism drew commoners into its ruling culture. Neo-Confucian family rituals were intended to tie people together through the male family lines (patrilines) and common ancestors of patriarchs, whether diverse family members were rich or poor, educated or uneducated. Neo-Confucians opposed rival beliefs from foreign cultures, such as Buddhism, which had grown very popular. Furthermore, in the eyes of southerners, ever since the fall of the Han dynasty, alien rule over the northern Chinese heartland had barbarized north China, letting steppe culture permeate the region. The Tang dynasty came to be remembered as an era dominated by a northern frontier culture, and the Song dynasty saw itself as a southern, more civilized, culture.

By the twelfth century, the Song dynasty was threatened by nomadic pastoralist neighbors to the north. Enormous carnage and dislocation attended these upheavals. In 1127 CE, hundreds of thousands of people, including twenty thousand high officials, tens of thousands of office staff, and four hundred thousand military families moved south. During the twelfth and thirteenth centuries CE, different steppe peoples killed or drove off Chinese from their northern farmlands, converting the acreage to pasture. The imperial court shifted its center to the more secure southern part of China. In this context, elite families lost faith in the state and worked to create a stable order locally in families and communities.

In this later Song era, even more outsiders were allowed to compete in state exams, and the educated class expanded. The educated leadership justified their place by their cultural expertise in practices that encouraged social harmony and cultural conformity. Finally in 1279 CE, the Southern Song dynasty fell to the nomadic pastoralist Mongols, who created, at Chinese expense, the greatest Eurasian empire to date.

A CHANGING FEMALE IDEAL

As in the Mediterranean world and Gupta India, ideals for Chinese women shaped their experience and varied across time and space. In the classical era of the Han Empire, these ideals about womanhood had been articulated by Confucian writers. Prescriptive texts had set out the doctrine of Three Obediences: women's submission to their fathers and mothers as girls, to their husbands as wives, and to their sons as widows. Around the end of the first century CE, Ban Zhao, a woman Confucian writer and model of widowly rectitude herself, wrote *Admonitions for Women* to instruct her daughter as to the proper conduct of wives. For example, she wrote "The husband is heaven. How could one not serve him?"[1]

After the Han dynasty fell, the influence of steppe culture on northern China created different ideas about women. In 589 CE Mr. Yan, an official from the south, contrasted a typical southern wife (submissive and sacrificing for her husband's displays of wealth) with a northern wife (demanding, extravagant, and sometimes critical of her husband). "North of the Yellow River . . . the traditional niceties are seldom observed. . . ."[2] The northern female type described by Mr. Yan showed the influence of a steppe dynamic that rulers of the Tabgach (a pastoral nomadic frontier people) had introduced into northern Chinese culture. Tabgach women, like women in other nomadic societies, were expected to know how to tend the herds and hunt, because the men left them in charge when they went to battle. Northern tribal women were expected to share men's work and participate in all decisions but war. Northern women in general were less regulated and more autonomous than Han women had been.

Daoism joined Eurasian frontier currents to reshape the female ideal in Tang China. Daoists, believing in the principles of yin/yang, saw men and women's differences complementing each other harmoniously, a view not overly constraining for women. Indeed, in this time there was no uniform model worked out by male writers. Beauty and talent, commemorated by poets, were ideals for which to strive. Elite women were believed to be able to handle legal affairs and business, as well as to represent their own interests at court. Wealthy women were expected to be important consumers of exotica—appealing, foreign commodities from other regions across Eurasia such as Central Asian, Turkish, and Persian fashions. Elite women were expected to play polo and perform whirling dances for recreation and ride horseback with great ease—sometimes bareheaded and dressed in men's riding clothes and boots.

The one Tang writer to set out a clear female ideal for Tang society blended Confucianism and frontier influence. Around 730 CE Lady Zheng, an elite court woman, wrote *Book of Filial Piety for Women*, an advice book modeled on the Confucian classic *The Book of Filial Piety*

FIGURE 4-1 TANG WOMAN ON POLO PONY
Tang Chinese woman riding a polo pony around 750 CE. (An artistic rendering
of a Terracotta figure.)

[for men]. Perhaps showing her northern roots, she advised that a wife
should admonish her husband if he slipped into incorrect ways. In Lady
Zheng's vision, a wife set an example of rectitude and virtue, and her
husband enthusiastically copied it. She also argued that filial piety (reverence for family) was the supreme virtue for all women, but there were
different ways of expressing filial piety for women of different classes.
Noble ladies should show restraint, "observe the diligent toil of others
and understand their viewpoints . . . [and not be] great in status but little
in virtue." Women of common families were enjoined to "follow the way
of the wife . . . "[3] by putting others first and themselves last in order to
serve their parents-in-law. Producing textiles and clothing were acts of
filial piety for common women. Thus, there was no monolithic view of
the ideal Tang woman.

With the rise of the Song dynasty and its southern ideal, Neo-
Confucianism spread to the whole empire, resolving the cultural conflict

between north and south. In particular, the freedom of Tang women evaporated, to be replaced by the strict ideals expounded by the works of Neo-Confucian writers. Ideals for women changed, partly because ideals of manhood shifted. In the Tang era, aristocratic men had excelled in hunting, war, and physically demanding activities, much like the steppe warriors, and, as we have seen, women were also encouraged to be assertive, physically active, and mobile. By the Song era, the ideal of manhood had shifted away from the warrior aristocrat. The Song Chinese elite male distinguished himself from others by being a "scholar/servitor": one educated in Confucian classics and who served in the imperial bureaucracy. The scholar/servitor defined himself in contrast to China's northern rivals, the warrior Turks and Mongols. Expectations about female beauty also softened: The aesthetic ideal was a languishing flower upon which the educated man could gaze and about whom he could write a poem. According to the foremost specialist on Song women, "The desire to see women as delicate and small probably had something to do with the gradual spread of foot binding during the Song." Women with tiny bound feet would naturally move about less, sit more, stay home, get less exercise, and become the more languid ideal, which would enhance and contrast with the image of even scholar/servitor men as "larger, harder and more active."[4]

Song writers believed that there were important natural differences between all men and women. Unlike Daoists, Neo-Confucian writers saw male/female differences in a hierarchy, with males dominant, females submitting. Social morality meant that these differences should always be observed and respected. The ideal female embraced marriage as a sacred and central harmonious institution because it illustrated the distinctions between male and female. The most famous eleventh-century Neo-Confucian writer, Sima Guang, wrote, "The boy leads the girl, the girl follows the boy; the duty of husbands to be resolute and wives to be docile begins with this."[5] Separation of males and females was also seen as a sign of respectability essential for public morality. One prosperous family's regulations explained, "Males and females must not share toilets or baths to forestall any suspicion. Males and females must not take or receive from each other directly. This is the expectation of propriety."[6] Separate spheres offered women a degree of dignity, freedom, and security impossible in mixed company. As in Classical Greece and Gupta India, the ideal for elite Song women was seclusion.

Ultimately, Song-era ideals and expectations for women were complex. On the one hand, women, like men, were seen as able to learn, to be intelligent and morally responsible individuals. Legal wives had dignified roles as partners of husbands. In this view, elite women functioned as "inner helpers" to their husbands and were able to exercise managerial abilities to see that their family thrived. On the other hand, women were seen as morally inferior to men, their nature evil, and their existence a threat to the social order; thus their strict control and confinement was necessary. In this vein, writers discouraged female literacy and education and emphasized unconditional obedience. Ideal wives would forget the wealth of their natal family and serve devotedly the poorer families into which they married. Chaste women would have but one husband, and widowhood would be a test for women. Such Song Neo-Confucian views would intensify into an obsession with female chastity after the Song era, when widow suicide would be advocated as an ideal! In later periods of overwhelming historical turmoil (the centuries of foreign rule by Mongols [1279–1368 CE] and Manchus [1644–1912 CE]), when values became insecure and families felt a heightened need to control and subordinate women, patriarchal culture thus turned to more restrictive ideals—the darker side of Neo-Confucianism—and these ideals came to confine Chinese women for centuries.

Thus, Neo-Confucian male writers asserted and attempted to play out their role as guides for all classes of society. How closely women of different classes followed these guides is a difficult question to answer. Elite women conformed more closely than common women, who needed to work. However, the civil service exam system opened up government service to all men who could excel, trained them, and sent them around the empire; thus Neo-Confucian ideals about women spread through regions and classes.

WOMEN IN FAMILY LIFE

The family life of Chinese women became more constrained during the Song dynasty. As in the Mediterranean world and Gupta India, Song Chinese women's social lives followed distinct stages of family life under the control of a patriarchal father, husband, or master. Whether as daughters, daughters-in-law, wives, mothers, or widows, women responded to incentives and rewards, negotiated their place in the Song family system, and thereby played a role in reshaping it. The status and advantages that elite women gained in their families were often achieved at the expense of lower-class or younger women.

Families became more central. Thus, Neo-Confucian writers of this era began to write about propriety in families in order to provide order and unity to Song society. They created and reemphasized rituals of family and kinship, including ancestral rites; mourning obligations; patterns of difference and authority; the ritual "daily courtesies" of morning greeting, paying respect, and bidding goodnight; as well as life-cycle ceremonies (coming of age, marriage, funeral). In fact, from brothels to Buddhist and Daoist convents, all social institutions sought to take on the rituals and qualities of the family.

Women were perceived as vital to the fate of families in general. Some male Song writers, such as Yuan Cai (1140–1195 CE), blamed women for family discord; others saw them as central to strong families. "When family members drift apart, the culprit is always women." "Discord arises in families mostly when women provoke their husbands and peers with words!"[7] On the other hand, another male Song writer, Cheng Liang (1143–1194 CE) wrote that relationships made through women were a critical resource when families were in trouble. Women were not passive instruments in relationships, but responsible for rescuing orphaned relatives, arranging marriages, and keeping ties with wives' natal families and powerful ancestors.

DAUGHTER

An unmarried daughter had a temporary position in her natal family. She was by definition virginal ("a person who had remained inside her room"), and much of her early life was spent preparing for marriage and joining her husband's family, where she would serve and reproduce for the rest of her life. However, female children's family position changed subtly from the Tang to Song era. Daughters during the Tang era, married or not, could inherit if all male siblings had died, but Song daughters commonly claimed inheritance rights only in the form of dowry. In the Song era, it became more acceptable for a family to adopt a male heir than to pass property to daughters or any females.

The education of daughters became a controversial topic by the Song era. In the second century CE, Ban Zhao had pronounced, "Women make better wives if they are literate." In the eleventh century CE, Sima Guang wrote,

> People who do not study, do not know ritual and morality, . . . cannot distinguish good and bad, right and wrong. . . . Thus, everyone must study. How are males and females different in this regard?[8]

The Neo-Confucian Guang admired Ban Zhao and admitted the value of some education for women. However, he warned, "Nowadays some people teach their daughters to write songs and poems and play popular music; these are entirely inappropriate activities."[9] Such knowledge would render elite daughters too much like courtesans, so girls learned how to read, but not how to write. The main thrust of their early learning was how to deport themselves as females and wives in their husbands'

FIGURE 4-2   FOOTBINDING SLIPPERS KNOWN AS "LOTUS SLIPPERS"
Shoes such as these were increasingly worn by elite and aspiring women in the Song period, indicative of the increasingly passive role they were to play in society. Note the embroidered blue bird, perhaps meant to be the Queen Mother's messenger. Shoes are 5.5 inches long and 2.5 inches across the heel.

family. At age 10, girls were instructed "in compliance and obedience, and the principal household tasks":

> Breeding silkworms, weaving, sewing and cooking are the proper duties of a woman. . . . [Such] instruction lets a girl learn the hardships through which food and clothing are obtained so that she will not dare to be extravagant.[10]

Beyond a Neo-Confucian education, foot binding became a rite of passage for increasing numbers of young girls between 900 and 1300 CE. This practice was initially restricted to courtesans and entertainers, but in the Song era spread to elite women, and still later, to other social groups. Foot binding came to be seen as a means to a better life for daughters of all classes, for only the tiniest feet could lure the best catches in the marriage alliance game. The practice—consisting of repeatedly breaking, bending back, and binding daughters' young feet and toes—was inspired by a new aesthetic that had developed during the Song era in which a female's tiny feet enhanced her attractiveness. By the 1300s CE, elite families were ashamed not to bind their daughters' feet.

WIFE AND DAUGHTER-IN-LAW

Once she reached 22 years of age, a young woman's life was shaped by the institution of patrilocal marriage, as she left her natal home to become a stranger in a new house. But first, she endured marriage negotiations—cumbersome, but nonetheless, of the highest importance to both families involved. A young woman's value, first to her birth family and then to her husband's family, rested in the fact that she would be instrumental in their survival and prosperity. A daughter's father aimed to win a desirable son-in-law in the competitive marriage market and thus improve his own status and that of his family. For the prospective groom's family, marriage meant joining two families to the service of the man's ancestors and continuing *his* line of descendants. In this way, marriage rooted families in the order of the cosmos. Little about marriage arrangements was romantic, especially marriage finance. Dowries of wives grew in value as the elite service class expanded. A generous dowry enhanced the status of a bride entering a family. In the Tang era a groom's betrothal gifts (bridewealth) given to the future bride were certain to be returned as dowry, which ultimately went to the husband's line. But in the Song era, concerns that a bride might not bring enough wealth with her could have negative consequences for her. Neo-Confucian writers explained, "When parents-in-law have been deceived they will maltreat the daughter-in-law as a way to vent their fury. Fearing this, parents who love their daughter put together a generous dowry in hopes of pleasing her parents-in-law."[11]

Though some Neo-Confucian writers warned that wives should have no control over their dowries or other property, this advice was not heeded until after the Song dynasty fell. Other writers celebrated wives who willingly used their dowries for larger family purposes. For example, a young woman from a rich official family married a man who passed the exams at 17. She felt uncomfortable having so much private property when her husband's family was poor, so she contributed all to a common pool. Most women guarded their dowries with vigilance, kept their marriage chests under lock and key in their bedchambers, and never lost sight of their property or the larger family's. In the Song era the husband had to have his wife's consent to use her dowry, at least in theory.

The position of daughter-in-law was not easy. Leaving her parents' home, she took up residence with her new husband in a room or wing of his parents' house. In theory, families and husbands should treat the bride with dignity. In practice, family patriarchs imposed male authority. The daughter-in-law was often seen as a disloyal outsider and the crux of moral threat housed in the home's inner quarters. This view projected blame onto daughters-in-law, although the real threat to family solidarity often was rivalry between brothers and fathers and sons.

A bride in her new family also faced her initiation into sexual relations with her new husband. The attitude of the Chinese elites toward sex changed from curiosity to prudishness from the Tang to the Song eras. Many sex manuals had appeared during the Tang era; they were a popular and entertaining form of didactic literature that many men read. Some popular beliefs showed women as sexually aggressive and dangerous. One Tang folktale told of a fox spirit who transformed itself into a beautiful young woman and seduced men, draining them of vitality. Erotic literature of the eighth century shows heroes falling in love with teenage girls, 11 to 16 years old; such pubescent innocence wakened men's desires. Daoist writings on longevity techniques encouraged men to have sexual alliances with as many young women as possible and bring their partners to orgasm without expending semen. Men were to redirect semen to the brain and strengthen their intellectual pursuits. Sexual intercourse on some level was envisioned as a battle between men and women, each trying to take without giving. On the other hand, the writings of Buddhists, a large and growing group in Tang China, extolled celibacy. Buddhists saw sex as vile and dirty, and carnal desire as an impediment to spiritual progress.

In the Song era, sex manuals came to be classified as medical texts. The Neo-Confucian elite saw sex as beneficial to one's health, given appropriate emotional and physical restraint. However, excessive sexual appetites endangered family harmony, and erotic energy was believed to undermine fecundity. Adultery happened because women were lewd and promiscuous, and they thus needed to be secluded and separated from men in the inner quarters of a Confucian household. Foot binding was thought to improve women's sexual performance along with man's sexual pleasure. Women's medicine of the thirteenth century and later focused on fertility and healthy children. For example, one text argued that not until 20 years of age were a woman's yin forces strong enough for bearing children.

In the house, each Song married couple had their own sleeping quarters, space permitting. For a wife, sleeping quarters consisted of a single room she shared with children, or in a wealthy house, a wing or several rooms. A husband spent no daylight hours in his wife's room, nor did he spend every night. He might spend nights with his concubines, or if the couple was still young, the husband's mother might control access to his wife's chamber. The marital bed was part of the bride's dowry and was highly valued for its role in maintaining the patriline. It was a sumptuous piece of furniture for the wealthy, and much ritual care went into its production and installation, with a study made of its most favorable orientation. The bride used this space to sleep, read, or recline. Sons and wives rose early, washed and dressed, and went in to ask if the parents spent a good night. The "morning inquiry" and "evening wishes" were part of daily ritual. The daughters-in-law prepared breakfast for senior couples. Sons dispensed medicines.

In the larger picture, despite all the constraints, the institution of marriage in Song society set daughters-in-law on the path toward fulfillment and power. Marriage gave them a long-term stake in the family system. The process for daughters-in-law to gain power was demanding. A new bride knew that at some time she would be a grandmother if she lived long enough. Before that day, a desperate daughter-in-law would herself become a mother-in-law in charge of conveying and modeling traditional family values. The path to success as a new bride was fitting into the household order and obeying disciplinary guidelines. For example, in a typical family, no one ate on his or her own, and males and females never sat together. A daughter-in-law complied with the family rules and sought favor with the real power brokers in the family: the elders.

All wives faced many duties in the inner quarters: childbearing and child-rearing obligations, mourning duties, ancestor worship, serving and caring for in-laws, participating in filial acts, and generally managing the household. Filial actions toward in-laws were foremost (from cutting one's own flesh to preparing healing medicines for parents-in-law or offering them special delicacies). A daughter-in-law lived under the eye of her mother-in-law, who was manager of the inner quarters:

> The mother-in-law has to admonish any who are jealous or gossipy; reprimand them if they carry on; divorce them if they refuse to stop. If wives chat endlessly about shameless things, or if they muddle in the affairs outside the inner quarters, they should be asked to perform punitive bowing to shame them.[12]

One husband's testimony provides evidence of how absolutely respectful wives must be to their mothers-in-law: "My mother was yelling at my wife, and my wife was talking back. I couldn't take it. In my anger, I beat her. By accident I killed her." He did not receive the death penalty. "Beating an unfilial daughter-in-law is not the same as beating a wife," wrote the judge in his memoirs.[13]

Most important for Chinese wives was the fact that the Song husband-wife bond was considered the foundation of human reproduction and socialization of children. This could be a source of power and status. In theory the husband was expected to treat his wife with respect and consideration. In reality, patriarchal authority was often exercised as tyranny, and wives were often regarded as slaves, not partners. However, some men wrote of loving marriages, and conjugal love as a beautiful thing. A Song poet compared a close married couple to mandarin ducks staying paired, floating side by side around a pond. Husbands also wrote of bright-minded wives appreciating, listening from behind the screen when husbands carried out business, sometimes warning them against untrustworthy people, as good inner helpers reaching to help husbands deal with the outside world. In his *Precepts for Social Life,* Yuan Cai (1140–1190 CE) reported that some wives played a very independent role, actually acting as managers and saviors of families. "Some women whose husbands are stupid and unworldly can manage the family on their own, keeping account of monies paid out, and people cannot take advantage of them."[14]

What did Song women think about their marriages? One elite Song-era woman celebrated marital love in poetry. Li Qingzhao (1084–1151 CE) was very well known as a poet. Fortunate in enjoying close companionship with her husband, an official, she wrote an account of her marriage, their life and work together, and the disarray of the Jurchen invasion of 1127. Li Qingzhao's very popular poem, "Written by Chance," expressed poignantly her lasting grief at the death of her husband:

> Fifteen years ago, beneath moonlight and flowers,
> I walked with you
> We composed flower-viewing poems together.
> Tonight the moonlight and flowers are just the same
> But how can I ever hold in my arms the same love.[15]

MOTHER

According to a Song saying, "There are three unfilial acts and the lack of descendants is the most serious."[16] In Confucian theory, a barren woman or a woman who bore only daughters could be equally blamed for family extinction; she could also be divorced. By the Song era, however, that rarely happened, because "descendants" of a Song patriarch could be born from any womb, although giving birth to a son made a wife an official member of the family lineage. However, many barren wives of elite families procured concubines for their husbands (or pushed a maid his way), since a son bred from any of the women of a man's household was an heir. Indeed, high-status families appropriated the fertility of families lower on the social scale. Thus, unlike other societies, in which a mother's fertility defined her and bearing sons trumped all other feats, in Song China, rearing sons and daughters successfully could replace fertility as the core task of motherhood.

Childbearing was demanding for women. From ages 25 to 30, a typical fertile wife would be pregnant repeatedly; those who lived to be 45 averaged about six surviving children from 10 or more pregnancies. Childbirth was considered dangerous and polluting. It threatened to disrupt family life. Certain infants were thought to be evil spirits and cause a family and the world harm. Texts from the Tang era and before show that laboring mothers were moved outside the main house to give birth and remained outside for a month until the pollution had dispersed. By the Song era and later, women no longer gave birth outside because families believed that the pollution was contained within the mother's room. Dying in childbirth was quite common, even among the elite educated class.

Rearing children was arguably the most important role for a Song wife, especially preparing her daughters for marriage. Elite mothers not only instructed daughters on how to be good wives, but gradually more mothers regularly arranged the binding of their daughters' feet. Foot binding signified a family's social status by showing that its women need not engage in physical labor. This practice slowly spread through Song and post-Song China, as other social groups sought social mobility for their daughters. Foot binding also reinforced patriarchal authority and the authority of older women over a household's younger women.

CONCUBINE

Concubinage, or female slavery, became increasingly important in Chinese family life during the Song era. Concubinage flourished among the well-to-do, because with the increased money economy and the growth of commercial cities, men could bring courtesans home as concubines. Men could have only one wife, but they could keep as many concubines as they could afford. By the mid-Song period it was extremely rare for a man—even a peasant in some regions—not to have a concubine. Wives often bought concubines for their households and husbands.

Song society recognized different grades of concubines, serving families in a wide range of roles, from housekeepers and companions-when-there-was-no-wife to women who functioned as sex partners to produce sons. Concubines were trained as young girls in much the same way that other female bondservants were, but their attractiveness, mastery of entertainment arts, or refinement may have distinguished them from young women who became maids or other sorts of domestic servants.

Concubines ranked in the female family hierarchy between the wife and other female servants. They had separate sleeping quarters and kept their young children with them. If a concubine bore children and died, the master and her children would mourn her for three months, whereas she would mourn a dead master for three years. A concubine had few legal rights. Men could not legally make a concubine a wife, but this law had not been uniformly enforced until the Song era, when it became a serious breach of social ethics to promote a concubine to wife. As producers of offspring, concubines had no rights to their children. A childless wife could take the children of her husband's concubines to raise as her own. Concubines' sons inherited their fathers' status and had the same rights as wives' sons. After her master's death a concubine could inherit property from him, or at least the use of it until her death or marriage. A concubine could equally be driven away by stepsons or be pensioned off. Oddly, a concubine could not be sent to a close male relative of her deceased master. Most often, concubines would be kept on as charity, although some concubines retreated to convents for security in their old age.

Concubines could be the objects of wives' jealousy. Because Neo-Confucians saw a man's doting on concubines as self-indulgent, wives had some leverage in their relations with their husbands. Jealousy could impair wives' ability to manage. Wives often beat concubines, or worse. The wife's potential to harm a husband's favored concubine or preferred maid was one aspect of the power dynamics in marital relations.

DIVORCEE AND WIDOW

Tang law allowed both voluntary and compulsory divorces. Among the many grounds for compulsory divorce was mutual killing between two families, or a husband killing or beating the wife's natal family members, or his adultery with his wife's mother. Song men had more liberal grounds for divorce, which ranged from a wife scolding a dog in front of her mother-in-law or serving an unripe pear; to talkativeness or disruption of family harmony; to jealousy or lack of filiality or appropriate submissiveness; to outright adultery. Legally Song women could not initiate divorce. Being divorced was far rarer for wives than widowhood.

Traditionally in Han China widowed women could expect the support of sons and daughters in their old age. Many writers testify to the respect and honor they felt for the senior women in their families and how attached they felt to them. Legal and ritual safeguards existed: No male could claim them as mate, no one could stop them from using family property to support their children, no one could stop them from adopting an heir for the husband.

From the Tang dynasty to the Song dynasty, a tension developed among the elite between filiality (the obligation of a son to serve and respect his mother) and the Third Obedience (a widow obeys her son) in mother-son relations. In the Tang era and before, widows had the status of their dead husbands. According to the legal code, the widow was the household head, and sons could not divide property without her consent. By the Song period, a son could show his widowed mother respect for Confucian harmony and yet control her behavior—particularly forbidding or forcing her remarriage.

Thus widows faced changing conditions of widowhood, gradually lost control of their lives, and had fewer options. During the Tang and early Song eras, a widow retained rights to the original dowry, or her natal family did. Widows still retained control of their dowries during the twelfth century, although by the late Song era, that claim was questioned. By that time, strictures against widow remarriage developed based on arguments that the dead husband's family line would suffer. The natal family no longer retained negotiation rights in the remarriage of its widowed daughter. Widows, if they chose remarriage, could expect to be disadvantaged in the marriage market. In later eras, some accounts report that many widows chose suicide or were assisted toward suicide by male relations eager to enjoy the enhanced status of families whose women were so virtuous. Male Song writers celebrated widows loyal to their in-laws and determined to remain chaste. Men also could demonstrate loyalty to the family by not remarrying as widowers. Stepmothers could be bad for the family's sons. "In current custom it is rare for a second wife not to ruin the family."[17]

In a Song commoner family, widows faced different issues: The death of the primary economic provider imperiled the family's very survival. The tax burden alone was weighty. Widows commonly brought in "a continuing husband"; in this event, a widow continued to be the head of the household, and no new household was established. Lopsided sex ratios (in which there were not enough women) encouraged this practice. Song-era Neo-Confucians such as Cheng Yi criticized this practice: "It is a small matter to starve to death, but it is a grave matter to lose one's integrity."[18]

WOMEN'S WORK AND PRODUCTIVE ROLES

As in the Mediterranean world and Gupta India, the productive work of Song Chinese women showed diverse participation in the economy. The work of female slaves or purchased women whether as textile workers, courtesans, or entertainers, was increasingly central to household and local economies in Song China. Indeed, productive roles of women, whether elite or commoner, were the only arena in which women played a public role at all in Song China.

In Confucian thought, work brought harmony and prosperity to the family and the state. "Men till, women weave." Women's work had many meanings beyond the material value of what was produced. For common women, work itself seems to have been one of the only appropriate expressions of filial piety, the supreme virtue. Although Neo-Confucian theory placed women's productivity "inside" and men's "outside," with men and women strictly separated, in practice, commoners lived and worked under different circumstances than the elite. Given the lack of household space, more commingling of males and females was unavoidable. Furthermore, commoner women worked outside the inner quarters when they participated in productive labor with men. Whether in rural or urban settings, women participated in many work activities. The increasing prevalence of bound feet did not really restrict the mobility of common women, nor prevent them from doing every kind of fieldwork, such as picking cotton, plucking tea, and harvesting grain. In coastal villages women also fished and navigated. Women engaged in commerce across rural and urban China, and some owned restaurants, wine shops, or tea houses. However, the majority of women's productive work was done within the context of family households.

TEXTILE PRODUCTION

All women, Tang and Song, elite and peasant, rural and urban, produced cloth. Sericulture (silk making) was sacred. Court rituals had long been held in honor of the goddess of sericulture. The empress and her ladies tended silkworms in a special shrine; the emperor performed the parallel "first furrow" ritual in which he worked a plow. Both rituals ensured good harvests of cocoons and of grain throughout the empire. During the Song era this ritual was no longer practiced regularly and soon disappeared altogether.

Textile production was not only politically and religiously important, but also economically essential. Cloth making fed the family. By the twelfth century, the women in a family of 10 raising 10 frames of silkworms produced 31 bolts of silk worth 3,000 kilograms of rice, more than enough to feed the family for a year.

Cloth making had special social meaning as well. Female networks of kinship were marked and sustained by women's exchange of embroidered items. Women could be heroines through creativity in textile work. Huang Daopo, a woman who helped replace hand processing of cotton with better spinning and weaving equipment, so transformed the local economy that the village established shrines to her memory.

Women were originally responsible for every stage of silk processing, from hatching silkworm eggs, to processing the cocoon into spun thread to weaving cloth and sewing clothes. Women tended mulberry trees and picked the leaves to feed the worms, which would spin extremely fine, strong fibers hundreds of yards long. Then they undertook the tedious process of untangling the cocoon's fibers and twisting them into a stronger spun thread. Silk cloth production became women's work because these stages of making silk thread had to be carried out in spring and early summer, when farming activities were also very demanding. Weaving, dyeing, and embroidering cloth could be accomplished at any time of the year. Poor young teenage girls spun and wove huge amounts of many kinds of textiles—some cloth to be sold in order to earn their own dowries for marriage, and some to be kept. Such hope chests remained their own property in marriage and gave some status in their new households. In the Tang and early Song eras the technical and management skills that it took to make cloth, from simple weaves to highly valued patterned fabrics, were still seen as quintessentially valuable women's knowledge.

This female productive sector during the Tang dynasty made obvious women's contribution to the household economy and to the state. Textile production was essential not only for individual girls' futures and for the family, but for the survival of the government. Imperial taxation had always relied equally on peasant families' tax payments in cloth (produced by women) and in grain (produced by men). The state needed huge amounts of basic cotton textiles to clothe the army. Silks were especially important to clothe the court elite and imperial family, to pay bureaucrats and soldiers, to purchase horses from Tibet, to buy off current nomadic enemies in the north, or to impress rulers in Southeast Asia. Hundreds of millions of bolts of cloth and skeins of silk were levied each year from Tang Chinese households.

Before the mid–Song dynasty, all but a tiny proportion of textiles were produced by rural women in peasant or manorial households. After the tenth century, the Song lost silk-producing regions to invaders and had to replace lost taxes (cloth levies) by forcing sericulture's development in the southern Yangtze provinces. As the Southern Song gradually built a new national economy, transitions occurred in textile production. Commercialization and specialization in textiles brought new divisions of labor, which gradually marginalized women's real and perceived contribution. Taxes were no longer assessed in cloth, but in cash. Families came to specialize in certain cloth or in particular stages in the production process, and specialists, full-time weavers, were more likely to be men. By the late Song period, women were no longer solely responsible for textile production, nor were they valued for their productive work. They came to be valued primarily as good Confucian wives and mothers.

How and why did this happen? Urban workshops to dye and weave fancy silk cloth proliferated as demand for silk fabrics rose. Fashion sensibilities of the Neo-Confucian educated elite rejected the older tastes. Fine silk gauze became fashionable. This could not be produced by the looms of peasant weavers. Mostly state factories and new private urban workshops, organized by men, used the complex, expensive gauze looms. Women were absent or only auxiliary workers in these factories. A putting-out system developed where rural women had the inglorious, but indispensable work of supplying male weavers in urban workshops or their own households with thread for the thriving textile production industry: Women still bred silkworms, reeled raw silk, and spun silk yarn, but they had lost their central position of weaving silk fabric. Many other societies in transition to a commercialized economy undergo a similar process of women's economic marginalization with new divisions of labor. As a consequence, seclusion became more oppressive when women no longer were taxpayers and textile producers. Dowries became more burdensome. Women sought other opportunities to earn income, but the alternatives they faced often offered them less autonomy than they had enjoyed before. Changes in women's cloth making from the Tang to the Song Dynasties clearly show women's deteriorating position in China. Tang women's textile production made important contributions of taxes and goods to the economy, but by the end of the Song dynasty, that was no longer the case. A harsher form of patriarchy developed concurrently. Increasing numbers of women were sold by their families, or sold themselves, to meet a growing demand for purchased women and for patrilineal heirs.

ENTERTAINERS, PROSTITUTES, AND SLAVES

Increasing commercialization of cloth and rice production expanded the demand for purchased women. Women had been entertainers, courtesans, and servants for centuries. During the Song dynasty, however, such work became both more common, and debased, as ways for women to make a living without marriage. This resulted partly from the increasing popularization of Neo-Confucian values among the elite.

Because of its cosmopolitan culture and its prolific cultural interactions with other parts of Asia, Tang dynasty writers and painters had celebrated female entertainers from other regions working in the capital, such as a "Dancing Girl of Kuchai" and a Japanese equestrienne. Tang elite households sought Southeast Asians and Koreans as personal maids and concubines. Dancers, entertainers, and official prostitutes were sent from other lands for the pleasure of the court and emperor. For example, in 733 CE a Turkestani king sent female musicians. Foreign dancers dancing Tashkent's Dance of Chach to rapid drumbeats were all the rage, especially those in Western costumes that could be tweaked to reveal bare shoulders. Twirling girls were the most loved of all young dancers from beyond the frontier. Tang courts lionized such entertainers, but Neo-Confucian morality of later eras would criticize these pastimes as frivolous and corrupting.

Many common Chinese women also worked in Tang cities as professional entertainers, "government hostesses," prostitutes, singers, and courtesans, serving the aristocratic and servitor elites. Tang writers and poets often wrote of their exceptional musical artistry and appreciated their poetry. Li Ye was a Tang courtesan and poet who mastered the qin-zither music. She also wrote poetry vividly describing the music's sounds with literary images of towering cliffs and swift-flowing rivers. Wang Funiang, a singing girl who worked in a brothel in the capital, inspired male Tang poet Sun Qi to write in new ways about an ancient honored Daoist goddess. The poet invited Wang Funiang to imagine the Queen Mother as a madame, disciplining and protecting her girls.

The highly celebrated work of a few female Tang writers reveals a great deal about Tang attitudes toward courtesans. Zhao Luanluan was a courtesan who wrote erotic verses. Yu Xuanji (844–868 CE) was a woman poet and Daoist nun who wrote homoerotic love poems dedicated to three orphaned sisters, courtesans, of refined literary and musical accomplishment, who were her neighbors at a guest house. Comparing the three girls to luxurious pet birds—startlingly lovely and possessing supernatural talent—the poet exclaimed that they must have been immortal attendants of the Queen Mother of the West. Xue Tao (768–831 CE) was a government hostess and a famous poet. She corresponded with many of the great male poets and writers of her day and was nominated to the title of Collator of the Imperial Court in recognition of her outstanding literary abilities. However, a great change in elite attitudes toward entertainers and prostitutes occurred between the Tang and the Song dynasties: From being independent women worthy of respect (as well as objects of male fantasy) during the Tang era, they had become unchaste and lowly, without honor, or in other words, outside the Song family system.

During the Song era, lower-class families gave daughters special training to make them more marketable. Young girls learned household activities, as well as the vocational skills they would need to be the wife of a common man or to be sold as a concubine, maid, or servant in an elite household, or to work as an entertainer in the capital. Maids and concubines came from the same social strata, and their personal attractiveness or mastery of entertainment arts determined their futures.

Most Song families preferred that women eventually be married, but those young girls unable to secure a marriage could be sold or contracted out for a set period of time by their parents. The prosperous Song elite demanded specialized domestic servants and personal maids for running the household and producing offspring. When elite males had more wealth, they acquired more concubines, women slaves, and bond servants. New specialized markets for buying and selling women developed during the later Song dynasty (1127–1279 CE). Female brokers offered all manner of purchased women, concubines, as well as singers, dancing girls, cooks, seamstresses, and maids.

When the Chinese economy expanded and diversified in the late Song era, the organization of women's work began to change and its evaluation also changed. For laboring classes, women's reproduction of sons became more important than women's production of textiles and other goods. A more restrictive form of patriarchy had been established in women's work and productive roles.

WOMAN AS ARTIST-CALLIGRAPHER

In the late Song era, the problem of managing Neo-Confucian constraints and achieving some measure of self-expression through work was particularly poignant for female artists, though it must be said that patriarchal societies rarely considered art as appropriate work or a productive role for women. Guan Daosheng (1262–1319 CE) was the first recognized woman artist. Born into a prominent elite family and raised in the last years of the Song dynasty, she enjoyed the unusual encouragement of both her male kin and a new dynasty's emperor. In 1311 CE, Yuan Emperor Ayurbarwada commissioned her to write *The Thousand Character Classic* (in which no character is repeated) for the imperial library. The Mongol emperor wanted future generations to "know that our Dynasty [the Yuan] had a woman who excelled in calligraphy." She recognized that she broke Song-era taboos as she worried, "To play with brush and ink is a masculine sort of thing to do, yet I make this painting. Wouldn't someone say that I have transgressed propriety? How despicable, how despicable . . ."[19] But she continued to paint and write.

WOMEN AND RELIGION

In the era of disunity and continuing through the Tang and Song dynasties, Chinese women experienced a special link to the ancient goddess Queen Mother of the West, around whom ancient Chinese had created a cult. After the Han era, the Queen Mother cult merged with beliefs about the balance and harmony of yin and yang, light and darkness, and male and female. By the time of the Tang dynasty, the Queen Mother of the West had become the most powerful Chinese divine being, representing creativity, femaleness, transcendence, and communion with the divine. The Queen Mother of the West had a special relationship with all women. She was the teacher, registrar, and guardian of female believers. She was above the family circle that circumscribed their lives and above the domestic economy that bound women's work. The Queen Mother protected and encouraged women and helped them in their work and personal life to find the way to happiness and immortality. She taught and empowered men and women alike, but women addressed her as *"amah,"* or wet nurse, with a touching intimacy and a closer familiarity than men could address her.

In this same era of disunity, both Daoism and the arrival of Buddhism began to offer women deeply satisfying religious experiences. By the Tang era, Daoism became very popular: The Tang royal family traced its virtuous ancestry back to Laozi (Daoism's founder, sixth century BCE), and by 700 CE several members of the Tang royal family became Daoist nuns, such as Tang Princess Jade Verity. Daoism emphasized spontaneity and noninterference. Water, women, and infants were seen to share qualities of softness or weakness, but were able paradoxically to overcome "the hard and strong because of [their] immutability." "The female always conquers the male through her stillness. Because she is still, it is fitting for her to lie low."[20] Daoist practice for women could include fasting, abstaining from sex, meditating, and imbibing elixirs.

Buddhist practice at this time also came to provide many Chinese women with a fulfilling religious experience, and some could even enjoy freedom and autonomy from family constraints as nuns in Buddhist monasteries. By 600 CE, China had become predominantly Buddhist, and Buddhist institutions enjoyed the support of ruling aristocratic families. Buddhist missionaries had originally come from India and Central Asia on the Silk Road. Tang Buddhism assimilated existing religions and used Daoist vocabulary. Thousands of Tang Buddhist monasteries across China played important social roles; conducting services for the dead; celebrating festivals; and overseeing hostels, baths, hospitals, and pharmacies. Many women were drawn to Buddhist practice, even given the fact that Chinese Buddhism contained some misogynist descriptions of women. (Some Buddhist texts blended with folk beliefs to see women as polluted, and "the lack of rationality and specter of danger was . . . explicitly linked . . . to female sexuality."[21]) But the appeal of popular Buddhist practice for women outweighed male Buddhist masters' misogynistic beliefs.

The extreme forms both Daoism and Buddhism removed the practitioner from society and family. Since marriage and motherhood were basic to Chinese female identity and place, a woman's decision to leave a family and pursue a religious vocation, whether Daoist or Buddhist, went against the grain. Daoist holy woman Xu Xiangu compared leaving home to facing wild beasts. "I am a woman who has left the household life. . . . I do not fear serpents and dragons or tigers and wolves."[22] During the Tang era, Buddhist women who sought to join a monastery faced the same familial opposition as their Daoist sisters. One girl named An Ling-shou wanted to become a nun. Her father reportedly said, "You ought to marry. How can you be like this?" She replied: "My mind is concentrated on the work of religion, and my thought dwells exclusively on spiritual matters. . . . Why must I submit thrice to father, husband, and son, before I am considered a woman of propriety?" When her father accused her of selfishness, her response was: "I am setting myself to cultivate the Way exactly because I want to free all living beings from suffering. How much more, then, do I want to free my two parents!"[23] She could transfer the merit she earned by following Buddhist practice to her family, and the family could accrue merit by supporting the convent and clergy. An Lingshou herself went on to found five or six monasteries and is said to have converted 200 nuns. Nomadic women, as well as women in the settlements in the western regions, encouraged the growth of Buddhism and were attracted to the spiritual refuge it offered.

Such spiritual paths allowed women considerable scope for literacy, cultural contributions, and leadership during the Tang era. Female masters of Daoism cultivated mental attitudes of faith and inner resolve and dedicated their lives to good works (caring for the sick or hungry, burying the dead, restoring shrines, and defending the faith). They spoke in public, wielded power, and lived independent lives. Discipline and belief in their immortality made them revered by both men and women and gave them male and female disciples. For some, the religious life functioned as a refuge or retreat at the death of a husband, a way to purify themselves, or as an intermission between marriages. It was a survival tactic for members of the imperial harem who were dismissed during the anti-luxury campaign of certain eras, an escape from palace intrigue and danger. It was also a means of avoiding marriage and living an individual life outside the family. The long lives of some nuns suggest that celibacy may have been easier on women than married life. Becoming a nun was also a way to attain an education, as it was in medieval Europe a bit later. Some parents sent their daughters to convents to cure their sicknesses or to ensure their survival during famines, when daughters were in greatest danger of starvation. Professional religious women practiced asceticism, which gave them enormous power in Chinese society at the price of physical comfort, as it had for Buddhist women of Gupta India and Christian women of late Imperial Rome.

Tang women developed popular cults within Chinese Buddhism. Worshippers, rich and poor, Daoist and Buddhist devotees, revered many faces of the Queen Mother: For Daoists, she was "the Ninefold, Numinous, Grand and Realized Primal Ruler of the Purple Tenuity from the White Jade and Tortoise Terrace";[24] for others, she was both Weaver Creator and Tiger Destroyer. Tang-era poets, professing to seek a divine teacher, believed that love affairs between Daoist priestesses and laymen were under the jurisdiction of the Queen Mother of the West, the embodiment of ultimate yin. As in ancient Mesopotamia, the divine sexual union between a priestess and a male worshipper preserved cosmic harmony. Such yearly meetings (remembered or imagined by Tang-era poets) had taken place long before for the mutual completion of yin and yang and for the periodic re-creation of the universe.

As in family life and productive roles, Neo-Confucian culture dominated Song women's religious life. The Song era's dominant religious tradition was ancestor worship and Neo-Confucian rites. Before the Tang and early Song eras, only families of high rank had ancestral tablets in homes. Commoners were forbidden the rituals of ancestor worship that marked the status of the aristocracy. During the Song dynasty, however, a broadly inclusive Neo-Confucian cult developed. Powerful Neo-Confucian elite writers advocated ancestral tablets for servitors (that is, members of the imperial bureaucracy) as well as all others. One important impetus for revised Song Neo-Confucian rites was to wean people away from the popular "foreign" cult of Buddhism. Neo-Confucian organizations were initiated to compete with Buddhist community and charitable organizations. All patriarchal homes were to have altars, spirit tablets, lineage temples, and access to genealogical records. Song families lived "under the ancestors' shadow."[25]

The center of each house was a family shrine, the ritual area that held ancestral tablets and sheltered the sacred male family line, dead and living. Spirits of generations of immortal forebears dwelled at this center, their names and titles inscribed on the tiles. It was believed to be a magical shelter from wind or evil influences, a site to channel cosmic energies for the family's benefit. The ritual space held four generations of tablets, sacrificial vessels, and a spirit pantry to hold the dishes used to offer food to ancestors. The ancestors required constant attention from the living descendants. Ritual responsibilities shaped life in the inner quarters. The whole purpose of the Neo-Confucian world was to ensure an unbroken line of worshippers for the forebears of the patriarch. Women of the family attended major ancestral rites, lined up on one side of the hall by age and gender twice a month, at the new and full moons, on New Year's Day and solstices. The wife of the family patriarch handled the tablets for female ancestors and put out offerings of food and drink. Everyone elaborately bowed to their superiors in recognition of the Confucian family hierarchy. The presiding woman was a partner in elaborate ceremonies. She was presented to ancestors as a family member when she entered the house as a bride. Only a legal wife could address an ancestor. Indeed, she was obligated to announce her comings and goings to the ancestors. Concubines and all other women were barred from participation in the family cult.

Nevertheless, Neo-Confucian religious culture gave wives a clear central role in the worship of their husband's ancestors, and women were able to achieve a measure of power as wives in family rites even as options for autonomous life within alternative religious traditions narrowed.

As it did in family and work life, Neo-Confucian patriarchy restricted women's ability to follow alternate religious practices that would empower them. Those activities were seen as improper and unfilial, although the presence of a holy woman in the family was touted as an auspicious omen showing the continuing mandate of heaven. Given the authority of Neo-Confucian family values, by the era of the Song dynasty, Daoist masters seldom advocated imitating the Queen Mother and her jade maidens to the extent of refusing marriage and retreating from society. However, each stage of a woman's life, even in a family, offered a special path for practicing Daoism. In youth and childbearing years, a woman could do good works and practice devotion; in old age, she could practice more extreme and ascetic forms of Daoist worship.

By the Song era, conflict between competing religious traditions sometimes challenged female Daoist devotees to exert their special powers. According to a Daoist record of holy women from 920 CE, one holy woman, Xu Xiangnu, lived for hundreds of years from the Sui to the Tang dynasty, always as a 24-year-old.

> Once she was set upon by several . . . Buddhist monks using insulting expressions and insinuating words. The maiden abruptly and unceremoniously cursed them. Roused to anger, the flock of monks was about to stab her with their knives. . . . The maiden said "I am a woman who can reject the household life. Ants, clouds and water I do not shun, serpents and dragons or tigers and wolves. Why should I be afraid of you rats?" Then she undressed and lay down swiftly, snuffing out her candles. The . . . monks [were] happy thinking they would get their way. . . . But the maiden had devised a plan to emerge safely from the mountains the next day. . . . [All of a sudden] they became stiff, standing like corpses. Their mouths were stopped so they could not speak. After the maiden departed, the monks returned to their former selves.[26]

Her Daoist power enabled her to reverse the aging process and conquer powerful aggressors who outnumbered her. In another Daoist holy story, Buddhist monks attacked a mountain shrine and hermitage of the holy woman Gou Xiangu, whose only companion was a bluebird, which happened to be the messenger of the Queen Mother of the West. The monks were eaten by tigers (the alter ego of the Queen Mother).

Here we see that women of the Tang era, whatever their professed belief, experienced richly blended religious traditions. Confucian loyalty and filial piety continued to be important to Buddhist nuns, just as family background continued to play a role in their careers. Nuns' monastic careers affected the fortunes of secular families. The life of Qiwei (720–781) a Buddhist nun, shows that Buddhist women held diverse Daoist and Confucian values. Qiwei was born into a Daoist–dominated noble family but became a Buddhist nun as a teenager because of her own piety, against the wishes of her family, much like An Lingshou. Her family had taken Daoism as their hereditary religion (even naming sons after Daoist classics). Qiwei became an extraordinary and prestigious Buddhist preacher who upheld Confucian values even as a Buddhist nun. She maintained close relations with her family, and many of them became Buddhist believers. Qiwei and other nuns maintained strong ties to their families, although as nuns they had supposedly left the family life. They were commemorated by their families upon their deaths, and their kinswomen followed them as disciples. Ultimately their careers as nuns were influenced by their family ties.

The transmutation of the male Indian deity Guanyin into a powerful female divine figure in Chinese Buddhism shows how Song Chinese women blended religious traditions. Stories about a *bodhisattva* Guanyin became linked to a real Chinese woman named Princess Miaoshan, and the mythical Indian deity was feminized, humanized, and sinicized (made Chinese). The princess refused to marry because she wanted to practice Buddhism. She was persecuted and executed by her angry father. The gods restored her to life, and she achieved enlightenment. She then saved her father from death.

> "My one desire is that the remedy may match the ailment and drive out the king's disease. The king must direct his mind toward enlightenment. . . . " With these words she gouged out both her eyes with a knife and then told the envoy to sever her arms. At that moment the whole mountain shook and from the sky came a voice commending her "Rare! how rare! She is able to save all living things, to do things impossible in this world."[27]

Finally she converted her father to Buddhism. Her unfilial behavior (the greatest Confucian offense) was overshadowed by her sacrifice of parts of her body to save her father, in the true embodiment of compassion. Her story illustrates the great conflict for women between an individual quest for spiritual autonomy and pressures from family to fulfill social expectations. Miaoshan's triumph offered women hope and inspiration as the basis of her cult. Miaoshan and Guanyin merged. *Bodhisattva* Guanyin became the goddess of mercy, a fertility goddess (despite her virginity), and the goddess of safe childbirth—almost a female Chinese Buddha! Guanyin gave rise to a major cult. Holy women of many different regions were believed to embody Guanyin and had magical powers deriving from their discipline, sacrifice, and energy, leading to their transcendence.

Especially in the last 150 years of Song China, the worship of popular deities and temples increased, possibly because the Buddhist monastic path was no longer open to women. Most women could not easily follow textual religious traditions that required the ability to read and write. Popular religions, which had no recognized clergy and no established texts, were far more accessible to the majority of women. During the Song dynasty, village and elite women increasingly followed popular cults like that of Guanyin. An older village woman of Huzhan, Wu Jie, suffered an aching arm. One night in 1161 CE, a white-clothed woman appeared in her dreams and said, "I am also like this. If you cure my arm, I'll cure yours." "Where do you live?" "In the west corridor of the Revering Peace Monastery." Wu Jie woke, went to town, and told the monk of the western hall about her dream. He replied that the white-robed image must be Guanyin. He led Wu Jie to the western hall, where they saw that because of a gap in the roof, Guanyin's arm had broken off. Wu Jie ordered workmen to repair the figure. When the figure was complete, Wu Jie's disease was cured.[28]

The Song goddess Mazu's cult was also widely practiced on the coast of Fujian. Mazu Lin was a rural woman born in a fishing village and grew up on the seashore. Skilled in spiritual healing, she cared for villagers, and she could also read signs of the weather and the nature of the sea. As a boat navigator, she saved distressed sailors. After Lin died, villagers built a shrine on an island, and the cult spread from island to coast. She was worshipped as "the Protector at sea." In 1135 CE Emperor Gaozong canonized her, naming her "Bright Efficacy" and "Excited Fortune." She was neither an ancient goddess nor a mythical figure, but a commoner woman of Song, demonstrating that rural women could achieve fame through their spirituality.

Elite Song women were also drawn to popular cults, blending what they had learned from nuns and female family members in the inner quarters about textual religions (such as Buddhism, Daoism, and Confucianism) with popular beliefs. In some cities, women's clubs met every month to study Buddhist sutras. Women's religious practice was a blend: Reciting and counting the names of Buddha on a rosary coexisted alongside chanting secret incantations to dispel hungry ghosts. For example, the Purple Maiden was the object of a late Song popular cult, which began with a fifth-century CE concubine who had been hounded to death by her master's first wife. On the fifteenth day of the first month of every year, women placed an image of the Purple Maiden by the toilet. Later in the Song era this cult inspired spirit writing, with men and women asking earnest questions, setting a cloth doll who held a chopstick onto paper or in sand, and observing crude writing appear. Sometimes elite women's spirit writing sessions devolved into game-playing, with attendees asking spirits to compose poetry on ouija board–like surfaces.

As in other societies, men of institutionalized religions held the important offices, performed the rituals, and wrote the texts. Within Neo-Confucian, Buddhist, and Daoist religious hierarchies, men wielded enormous power. The widespread appeal of ancient goddess cults of Hera, Kali, or the Queen Mother of the West did not translate into elevated status for women of Athens, Rome, Gupta India, or Song China. But women had special and honored places in China's diverse religious cultures. Neither Chinese Buddhists nor Daoists directly challenged Confucian family ethics. By the Song era, women were rarely recognized by the Neo-Confucian elite as spiritually powerful and independent as they had been in the Tang era. Holy women, Daoist and Buddhist, were no longer celebrated and revered in written records in the same way, and the government no longer supported convents. However, most Chinese women continued to blend Confucian, Buddhist, and Daoist practices and even began to turn to new popular cults in their private spirituality during the more restrictive patriarchal era.

WOMEN IN PUBLIC LIFE

Women do not have public affairs, [for if they did,] they would stop their weaving.

—LADY ZHENG, CA. 730 CE

As with other regions we have examined, such as the Mediterranean world and Gupta India, with only rare exceptions, women were absent from political power in the Tang and Song dynasties. However, at the creation of the Chinese nation, according to Tang Daoist legend, it was the Queen Mother of the West who initially gave power to a ruler to make China great. During the Tang and Song eras, women certainly made many contributions to China's political life, but only one woman, Empress Wu Zhao, actually took the supreme public role and ruled in her own name.

Power in ancient China had been given to the first ruler by the Queen Mother, who continued to advise emperors, even Han Wudi (141–87 BCE). She created order and could break it. She was associated closely with the Mandate of Heaven, which was given temporarily by the heavens to a favored dynasty to rule. When a dynasty lost the Dao, or the proper Way of the cosmos, the Great Gods reacted negatively in their own way: "The Old Lady of the West breaks her *sheng* [headdress]; the Yellow Thearch whistles and intones."[29] When the Queen Mother (who is also the Weaver Mother), smashed her sheng headdress (which is also her loom), the structure of the cosmos (created and sustained by weaving) fell to pieces. The Queen Mother had diverse political implications: Just as her approval and gifts could support the rule of an ancient, sage king, her worship by rebellious subjects could threaten a ruling dynasty's hold on the Mandate of Heaven. Cults suppressed by the government and ignored by the dominant Daoist leaders could easily turn to revolt; popular "Mother" cults were one source of social instability in the Tang and other eras.

During the Tang dynasty, females who were wives and mothers of emperors sometimes could exercise extraordinary political power deriving from their family. Empress Wu Zhao (625–706 CE?) became the most notorious woman in public life. She began as a concubine of Tang emperor Taizong in the mid-seventh century CE. She used her court connections and relations with the imperial successor to rule from behind the thrones of husband and sons and later founded her own dynasty, the Zhou, which reigned from 690 to 705 CE. Wu Zhao carried out many government reforms: Official bureaucracy became a more effective meritocracy, one in which talent could outweigh aristocratic heritage. The dynasty achieved its widest geographical expansion in her reign, and cultural religious and commercial exchange with South Asia along the Silk Road proliferated. Given Chinese aversion to women in power, the lack of precedent of female rule, and the unconventional nature of her rise to power, Wu Zhao was hard-pressed to legitimize her rule. To do so, Wu Zhao made special use of Buddhism and magical rituals of Daoism. One sutra prophesized that a female world-ruler would appear 700 years after Buddha. Wu Zhao claimed to be this world-ruler, the incarnation of the Buddha Maitreya. The empress was an avid patron of Buddhist monasteries. She promoted expansion of Buddhism intellectually and artistically. However, Confucian court historians of later dynasties chose to remember her reign as disastrous and prudishly wrote of her stables of young male concubines, her evil and destructive nature, and how she, with other females meddling in public affairs, had so abruptly ended China's golden age.

Another royal woman, Yang Guifei, known as the Precious Consort of Xuanzong (713–756 CE), was held responsible for the collapse of Tang power. According to later Neo-Confucian accounts, her emperor had ruled with impressive Confucian virtue until he succumbed to the corrupting seductress and made her his Precious Consort. Led by raging erotic passions according to the poem "Song of Unending Sorrow" by Bo Juyi (772–840 CE), "He forsook his early learning and lavished all his time with her with feasts and revelry."[30]

During the Song dynasty, women were excluded from overt political power in imperial China. By spinning the stories of Yang Guifei and Wu Zhao, Neo-Confucian political writers warned later generations against the diabolical nature of women's active role in imperial affairs. Some authoritative Neo-Confucians in the Song era argued that relations with courtesans and concubines were often a dangerous political weakness for prominent officials in imperial service. Sima Guang, of the eleventh century, wrote of several incidents of men experiencing political vulnerability when linked to women who were bought: One official was accused of hiring expensive government courtesans for a party and paying for them with government funds; another official's favorite concubine beat a female slave to death, so he lost his post for "failure to manage his household properly."[31] The message was clear: Contact with lower-class women—concubines—was dangerous. They were seen to be prone to violence and malice, and men, having selected them because of sexual attraction, could not properly govern them. So women could wreak havoc in public affairs in several ways.

However, women played other highly significant political roles in the empire. Women of imperial families were irreplaceable as pawns in the Eurasian alliance game. Alliance through marriage functioned as an essential instrument of diplomacy and of foreign relations with nomadic pastoralist neighbors who loomed large, especially as the empire expanded its borders westward. Earlier emperors had attempted to cement friendly relations with the Xiongnu empire on the frontier by sending imperial princesses as brides. A Song dynasty writer commemorated this sole appropriate political role for imperial women in a well-known play, *Autumn in the Palace of the Han.* The Chinese bride, Wang Chaoshun, though married off to a nomadic chief a thousand years before, became for the Song audiences a much-beloved, tragic heroine through suffering "barbarian" meals of "tasteless salted flesh" and only "clabbered milk and gruel" to drink. Her story not only shows princesses as pawns helping imperial dynasties cement friendly relations, but also was used as propaganda by Song writers to encourage Chinese ethnic identity in opposition to the northern dynasties such as the Liao and the Jin.[32]

Thus, whereas Tang Chinese women often played a behind-the-scenes political role advising their husbands or sons, much like Roman and Indian women, Song women faced backlashes against women overstepping their bounds, as Cleopatra had in Imperial Rome. Song Chinese women, like Imperial Roman and Gupta Indian women, were legitimizers of men's political authority by dint of marriage and kinship relations. Wu Zhao notwithstanding, Buddhist ideology combined with Neo-Confucianism to exclude women from public roles. By the Song era, a more restrictive patriarchy had been established in women's public life. A woman in a public role contravened the natural order of things and, to Song dynasty men, was "like a hen crowing."

CONCLUSION

In Tang and Song China, women's experiences shifted as the political, socioeconomic, and cultural contexts of their lives changed. Chinese patriarchy evolved with China's changing Eurasian frontier, its economic growth, and its sociopolitical change, as the center of development shifted southward and Neo-Confucian elites came to the fore. With the reestablishment of the hegemony of Confucianism during the Song era, ideals of feminine virtues shifted so that family roles superseded any other productive or religious role that women had played in earlier eras. Chinese wives and mothers were seen by Neo-Confucian writers as foundations of the imperial family and state, even as women became more constrained and secluded, and their options for autonomous life within religious traditions narrowed. Even as they developed popular cults within Chinese Buddhism, women of diverse social groups upheld the newly emerging Neo-Confucian patriarchy in households across late imperial China. Women's virtuous behavior and personal comportment increasingly became the main measures of a woman's status. It was the efforts and accomplishments of individual women that redounded to their credit. This new Song development precluded public roles for women, even as it empowered them through their private and individual personal sacrifices, such as bound feet, which became a source of pride.

CHAPTER FIVE

MESO-AMERICAN CIVILIZATIONS (CA. 200–1500 CE)

Other chapters focus on women's experiences on the continent of Eurasia, an area of the world with a relative abundance of documentation. They observe how the development of agriculture and creation of states fostered the domination of elites and tended to erode women's influence, although not uniformly. A woman's social standing, her age and place in a family, the value of her work, and expectations about her spiritual life were also factors that shaped her role in society. The rich evidence from the area of Central America known as Meso-America—running roughly from modern Mexico to the Pacific coast of Costa Rica—presents another arena of women's history. We see the same factors here shaping women's lives, but with distinct results stemming from the historical background of Meso-America.

As early as 2000 BCE, farming villages formed here, providing the origins of a world that retained a cohesive culture despite the centuries of turmoil that witnessed the rise and fall of many civilizations. Some typical characteristics of these societies include enormous buildings in the form of temples and pyramids, a sacred calendar, ritual ball games, plaster floors, marketplaces, the use of obsidian (a glassy black volcanic rock) for tools, overlap in certain deities, and human sacrifice. Two of these civilizations, those of the Classic Maya (about 200–900 CE) and the Aztecs (roughly 1200–1519 CE), developed a rich body of sources, both written texts and archaeological remains, allowing historians to draw conclusions about women's history that would have not been possible otherwise. The evidence from Meso-America is, as with other early societies, biased in favor of an elite male perspective, but here a further difficulty in interpreting the past is the fact that much of the material was either destroyed by the Spanish invaders of the sixteenth century or has been infused with a Christian, post-conquest worldview. An analysis of the Classic Maya and Aztec societies demonstrates the fact that Meso-American cultures produced great differences among their peoples, despite the enormous degree of commonality that prevailed throughout the centuries. Whereas the political structure of decentralized states provided many opportunities for elite Maya women in both political and religious realms, the aggressive colonial policies of the Aztec Empire often eroded women's influence in these areas.

QUESTIONS FOR STUDENT ANALYSIS

1. What economic activities did Maya women engage in?
2. What were characteristics of the feminine ideal and female deities of Meso-America?
3. How did Meso-American women's involvement in politics change from the Maya period to the Aztec period?
4. Was the rigidity of gender roles in Aztec society more of a boon or an impediment for women, and why?

CLASSIC MAYA CIVILIZATION (200–900 CE)

HISTORICAL BACKGROUND

The Maya were builders of great cities filled with temples and palaces. They rose to power in Meso-America between 200 and 900 CE, and then declined. The Maya realm formed on the Yucatan peninsula, but it never coalesced into a single centralized state. Instead, city-states grew, analogous to those in the Classical Greek society. These Maya city-states were governed by elite families who sometimes ruled for generations, and they fought among themselves incessantly. These families made up the Maya aristocracy, from whose ranks priests were also drawn. Commoners included artisans, peasants, merchants, and slaves.

Most Classic Maya cities were fairly uniform. A city's "downtown" had elegant structures carved and painted, pyramids, platforms, and residences. Large numbers of people could meet together in the open plazas surrounded by terraced pyramids and temples. Pyramids were built to imitate mountains and were lofty platforms for political and religious rituals.[1] Maya city-dwellers even enjoyed the sports arenas of the time: ball courts, shaped like an I, with a flat playing surface surrounded by walls. Both pyramids and ball courts placed Maya squarely in long-standing Meso-American traditions. Maya buildings were covered in hundreds of stone sculptures depicting god masks, human figures, undulating serpents, and astronomic symbols. The sculptures probably communicated messages to Maya people almost like political posters communicate to us today. Other sculptures on buildings show how the Maya lived: that they worshipped beside shrines, ate near the small vegetable gardens next to the thatched homes of commoners, and cleaned themselves in sweat baths.

Classic Maya civilization existed from the third through the ninth centuries CE, but most of the sources about women are drawn from the later years of this period, a time scholars refer to as Late Classic Maya (700–900 CE).

THE FEMALE IDEAL OF THE MAYA

The ideal female of Maya civilization can be explored through the creation myth recorded in the Maya text *Popul Vuh*. In it, twin brothers magically created a garden with the help of their grandmother, Xmucane. To make people, "the substance of human flesh," Xmucane ground her corn (maize) and mixed the resulting flour with water.[2] Thus, this myth illustrates that food processing was central to the ideal female and to female identity and sacred in the Maya worldview: It was through food production by a woman that humanity originated. Classic Maya civilization placed women in an usually high position in religious spheres, in some cases even equal to men. In fact, one of the most important Maya gods was the ancestor god Totilmeiletic, "Father-Mother," which suggests that the Maya may have seen the cosmic order in terms of an androgynous figure. This may imply a belief in mutual dependence among men and women.

IDEALS OF ELITE FEMALE BEAUTY   Evidence suggests that Maya aristocracy went through elaborate physical changes in order to achieve an ideal look. Unlike the foot-binding women of Song China, however, their mutations did not hamper movement, and many of their alterations were also undertaken by males. For instance, the elite considered sloping foreheads and crossed eyes beautiful, and thus the heads of newborns were bound to wooden boards to flatten their foreheads, and a small bead was tied to children's bangs, encouraging crossed eyes. Female aristocrats tattooed themselves, painted their bodies in red paint, and carefully styled their hair around their flattened foreheads. They decorated themselves with hair ornaments that resembled sprouting plants and with ear and neck jewelry of jade, shell, or precious jewels. Some aristocratic women filed their teeth to points and inlaid them with iron, fool's gold, obsidian, jade, or shell.[3] The fact that the most drastic of physical changes were made by both genders again suggests a kind of parity unusual for premodern, settled societies.

WOMEN'S LIFE CYCLES IN CLASSIC MAYA SOCIETY

From birth to adulthood, Maya social customs shaped the experience of women, and here archaeology allows us to analyze the lives of common-ers as well as aristocrats. Burial sites suggest that Maya girls were fed less nutritiously than boys were, because the bodies of adult women were much shorter than men's. Despite this disparity, Maya children of both genders were seen to have worthy roles, as rituals celebrating the place of girls and women demonstrate. For instance, the Maya ritual *hetzmek* occurred when a girl was three months old. During the ritual, her fam-ily displayed a miniature loom and corn-grinding stones for the baby's future work.[4] If daughters survived, at 12 years old they participated in an elaborate rite marking the beginning of adolescence. Older women were assigned as godmothers to help expel evil spirits from girl children as they became women.

Marriage was essential for both men and women, allowing each to fulfill their potential for mutual dependence in Maya society. The promi-nent position played by a bride's natal family as well as the ease with which a woman could divorce were both customs used to Maya wives' advantage. As with many premodern civilizations, aristocratic men could have many wives and slave concubines, but monogamy was practiced by commoners. Girls were usually married at 14 or 15 years of age, and boys at 18. Marriage was arranged by the parents: The father of the groom found a matchmaker and, once marriage arrangements were complete, the father of the bride gave a marriage banquet. Notably, matrilocal mar-riage was practiced among commoner families in many regions, whereby the new husband moved to his wife's family, assisting his father-in-law and proving his abilities. As with many Southeast Asian cultures, adult common women benefited by living with their birth families because they avoided domination by the groom's family. Furthermore, Maya common marriages could be dissolved rather simply by a declaration by husband or wife, and a woman continued to control her possessions after divorce.[5]

Classic Maya society defined motherhood as biological reproduction, and her pregnancy and labor amounted to a sacred blood sacrifice. In fact, birth was seen as a battle in which an infant could kill its mother; during labor an image of Ix Chel, the goddess of childbirth, was placed under a laboring woman's bed. Ix Chel was a wizened midwife who supported the mother as she fought between life and death. The association of labor with a battlefield is borne out by archaeological records, as many excava-tions show that women's life expectancy was shorter (35 years old) than men's (45 years old), possibly because of the young marriage age and early childbirth.[6] The birth of a child had great significance as well, for several reasons. Children represented personal wealth and good fortune for mother and family. An elite Maya woman's social persona was determined by her role as a mother perpetuating the lineage of her kin group (in contrast to Song China, where motherhood also included adoption and child rearing).

WOMEN'S WORK AMONG THE MAYAS

A Maya woman's economic position seems to have been much stronger than that of her peers in other cultures. Daughters could inherit property from their families, though sons were favored as inheritors, and the textile work of a Maya woman gave her an important place in her society and her city-state. Home was a common Maya woman's domain and the typical setting for her work—though she would occasionally work in the fields, and her husband might occasionally work in the home. Common women carried out three main activities in the home besides child bearing and rearing: producing cloth, tending small gardens, and processing food.

The work of elite women held an unusual degree of importance in Maya society. As in the civilizations of the ancient Mediterranean and Tang and Song China, they were recognized for their textile work. Among the Maya, however, some aristocratic women became matchmakers, artists, craftspeople, or scribes (keepers of the books); two examples are Noble Lady Scribe Sky of Yaxchilan and Lady Jaguar. Such women were often highly trained and educated. Indeed, elite female matchmakers had to painstakingly consult historical and tribute rolls, so they had to be proficient in reading.[7] Few other civilizations we have examined offered even elite women the rich education evidenced by the Maya female scribes and matchmakers.

TEXTILE PRODUCTION   Weaving was women's central occupation and even featured prominently in the sacred Maya cosmology, in a manner analogous to Tang and Song China. The Maya weaving goddess carried spindles in her hair ornaments in much the same way that the Chinese weaving goddess wore a loom headdress. When women wove, they were following the lead of the Moon Goddess, the inventor of weaving and the special patron of women.

Commoner women most often wove their cloth from a fibrous plant called maguey, which involved extremely time-consuming work. In fact, the creation of maguey cloth was so demanding that community-wide workshops developed to process it. First the women's teams softened the plants' leaves with heat, and then they scraped and beat the leaves to separate fibers and flesh. Some cloth was famous for being made of maguey with spines intact, but other cloth was made from single maguey spines. Women met in a processing and weaving building, or outdoors, weather permitting. They worked in public spaces that were also associated with community festivals and celebrations.

Cotton cloth was made and worn only by aristocrats and was important for Maya social, religious, and political life. Use of cotton in ritual activity ranged from its employment in ceremonial costumes, to providing offerings to gods, to wrapping sacred objects. Cotton textiles were also important as gifts of tribute to other city-states or for exporting in trade, thus forming an essential component of the government's economic well-being. Evidence for this comes from Maya vases, which regularly show stacked heaps of cloth for use in political transactions.

Wealthier Maya women worked with elevated materials, such as feathers, pearls or beads, and expensive dyes—cochineal from tiny red insects living in the prickly pear, purple dyes from snails, or blue from indigo. High-ranking females may have supervised and controlled high-quality textile production similarly to elite Tang Chinese women's oversight of silk works.

OTHER WORK: FOOD PROCESSING AND PREPARATION, FARMING, AND CERAMICS The centrality of common women's role in food provision for Maya communities was probably a major reason for their strong position in their civilization. They were associated with the production of flour, the tending of small gardens, and the raising of deer for venison. Processing dried corn into maize flour required persistence and patience on the part of Maya commoner women, who had gnarled knees, calcified toe bones, and powerful arms from years of kneeling to grind maize. Indeed, one of a Maya common girl's first possessions as a child was probably her stone-pounding kit of *mano* (tubular hand stone) and *metate* (flat grinding stone). Every day, women first soaked and boiled maize kernels in lime to remove the hulls and release the nutrition in the plant; then, after straining the maize, they knelt in front of a grinding stone on the ground and ground the kernels with their manos on metates.

Maya women also tended small gardens, where they grew a variety of vegetables and fruits: beans, squash, cotton, sweet potatoes, tomatoes, chili peppers, avocados, papayas, cacao, and other medicinal plants. For meat, women raised many animals, but perhaps the most significant were deer. Women tamed wild fawns and brought them into the household compounds to be raised, and venison in some cities accounted for 90 percent of all animal meat consumed. According to the Maya text *Popul Vuh*, deer were the first creations of the Divine Mother, before jaguars and humans. In Maya communities, half the women were buried with deer bones, showing the important association of deer farming with women.

Maya women's participation in farming changed after 700 CE when agricultural intensification occurred in some regions. In the earlier Maya communities, making tools and preparing food was done in the same outside space. Women cooked in large open bowls preparing soups and gruels, which were not very time-consuming meals. Men, women, and children participated collaboratively in many aspects of farming.[8] After 700 CE, terracing began and agricultural productivity intensified, and eventually women invented new kinds of food processing, including making tortillas, which demanded more time than corn gruels of earlier centuries.[9] Other occupations of Late Classical Maya common women included helping men to produce pottery and clay products, sculpting stucco, and creating latticework on rooftops.

MAYA WOMEN AND CITY-STATE POLITICS

Aristocratic women were important to Classic Maya city-state politics through marriage alliances, rule as regents, and court rituals. Only rarely did Maya women rule directly. Women's political position in this era, however, was extraordinarily strong, as shown by enormous numbers of sculptures of female leaders. This prominent public role for royal females arose from a combination of incessant city-state struggles and the Classic Maya view of female spiritual power.[10] Elite women played a central role in marriage alliances among city-states. These alliances were essential for survival and prosperity in the divisive political world of the Classic Maya. Such marriages brought political support from the natal city of a princess-bride, as well as trade and military connections. Especially notable for women's position is the fact that social and political rank came from mothers as well as fathers, since the Maya word "noble" (*almehen*) combines words denoting "women" and "men."

Women were also important as royal widows, ruling as regents for their minor sons. One example comes from Dos Pilas, one of the most powerful city-states. In 682 CE, the rulers sent a princess-bride named Lady Six Sky to marry into the ruling family of the neighboring lesser city-state of Naranjo, which was undergoing political crisis. Representing the power of Dos Pilas royalty and their bloodline, she initiated a new dynasty and reinvigorated Naranjo with rituals involving her own bloodletting. Indeed her husband's name is notable in its absence from ritual inscriptions. Upon the death of this unnamed husband, her son Smoking Squirrel came to the throne at five years old, and Lady Six Sky governed as regent. Later, as an adult ruler, Smoking Squirrel continued

FIGURE 5-1   LADY XOC'S BLOODLETTING RITE
As her husband holds a torch aloft, Lady Xoc pulls a thorny rope
through her tongue—a Maya ritual thought to give access to
powerful visions.

to honor his mother, and she continued to perform sacrificial rites until
her death in 720 CE.

Women of the ruling families played important roles in court rituals of the Maya city-states, especially in blood rituals, which served to
unify their state and maintain their royal power. Blood rituals of kings
and their female consorts (perhaps commemorating women's blood
sacrifice at childbirth) were seen as essential. Some of these ceremonies
meant death for the one performing the sacrifice: One 20-year-old woman
decapitated herself with a flint knife to accompany the Lady of Altar in
death.[11] However, most bloodletting did not have such drastic results
and instead capitalized on the power held by these royal women. For

instance, in an exquisite temple built for the Lady Xoc by her husband, Shield Jaguar (681–742 CE), a series of carvings depicts how the lady's blood sacrifice gave her access to supernatural forces. The carvings show her carrying out a sacrificial bloodletting by drawing a thorny rope through her tongue and catching her blood in a bowl and on special paper. Shield Jaguar appears, holding a burning spear or torch over her head to illuminate the nighttime ritual. The carvings depict the results of the sacrifice: a vision of a monstrous beast coming from the bowl holding her bloodied rope and paper, with an armed warrior coming from its mouth. Armed with this vision, Shield Jaguar is then depicted receiving the weapons of battle from Lady Xoc.

Finally, though political power was generally held by men, on rare occasions, women not only ruled as regent for young sons, but also held power directly. In Palenque, several women ruled outright. This state of affairs was possibly legitimate because the royal line was purportedly descended from a mythical female ancestor, "Lady Beastie." Two female Palenque rulers were Kanal-ikal (r. 583–604 CE) and her granddaughter, Zac K'uk (r. 612–615 CE). Descendants of Zac K'uk likened her to Lady Beastie, that first creator goddess, and justified coming to power through ties to her. When women did come to the throne, a special story had to be developed to make female rule acceptable in Maya political culture. For instance, Zac K'uk's grandson retroactively built up his grandmother's reputation by having a special myth recorded about a divine mother who gave birth to three male gods. He wanted this story to parallel his own ascension to power.

Elite women held an unusually high profile in Maya warfare, although they were not soldiers and could not use their military leadership as a route to power. Yet they were depicted as central characters supporting battles and were considered serious threats by their political enemies. At the coronation ceremony of the Lord Pakal (615–683 CE), the ruler's mother, Zac K'uk, handed him the royal headdress, the mark of his ability to lead in combat. In a rare instance, one ruling queen of a city-state created carvings crediting herself as a victorious war commander, standing on top of prisoners, though she very likely did not actually lead the forces on the battlefield. The treatment of aristocratic or royal women in wartime was often far harsher than the treatment of royal elite men, suggesting that the Classic Maya civilization respected and feared them. For instance, in the Yaxuna city-state inter-family war, many royal women—including the daughter and heir-presumptive, as well as a pregnant young wife of the deposed ruler—were tortured and buried ritually by their enemies in the course of takeover, whereas the male ruler was simply decapitated.[12]

MAYA WOMEN AND RELIGION

Rituals performed only by women, the essential role of goddesses, and the sacred power of women's fertility gave female spirituality a high place in the Classic Maya world. Furthermore, in elite Maya households, as in Chinese households, ancestor worship—which included deified men and women—was also a significant component of religious life.

In the Classic Maya civilization, many goddesses existed, and they were referred to as either "mother" or "grandmother," which shows the sacred reverence Maya had for the power of female fertility and the wisdom of aged women. Two in particular stand out: the moon weaver goddesses, O (Ix Chel or sometimes Chak Chel) and the young goddess I (Ix Tab). The Maya revered the moon and credited it with governing women's menstrual cycles and the planting of maize, and thus these two deities held considerable powers. Although the elder O was affiliated with the waning moon, and the younger the waxing moon, the goddesses were sometimes blended in Maya thinking and practice. In fact, the physical trinity of earth, moon, and maize was known as "Our Mother." The Maya, in this way, associated conception with sowing. Maya goddesses not only embodied a loving life force that could offer guidance when needed, but also personified chaos and dangerous heralds of death.

CROSS-DRESSING ROYALTY AND FEMALE RITUALS   In their rituals, Maya kings and queens impersonated gods and goddesses in a way that combined male and female powers of the cosmos. The way in which kings impersonated the most important god, the Maize God, in special rituals to commemorate his birth, sacrifice, death, burial, and resurrection show how important was female power in Maya civilization. The Maize God was androgynous: He was the first father, but he also wore a net skirt, albeit not in the style typical for Maya women. On his cheek the hieroglyph "Il" was written, a variant of "Ix" (which meant "goddess"). He also wore a fertility seashell in the center of a Xoc monster belt. (This monster refers to the Maize God's rebirth underwater.[13]) The Maya perhaps understood the anatomy of maize itself—that the plant possesses both male tassels and female ears and silk and is thus able to fertilize and give birth in the same body. In Copan, King Eighteen Rabbit wore skirts for his bloodletting rituals to combine male and female power. Shedding blood from the penis imitated the menstrual cycle, and he appropriated such female fertility symbols to strengthen his power. Female rulers also impersonated male deities. In Palenque, Queen Zac K'uk sometimes wore a male haircut and a loincloth when impersonating the Moon Goddess. Mixing gender meant that the rulers, especially female, could break from the normal domains of common Maya and become deities to wield extraordinary power.[14]

Many city-state occasions required rituals and ceremonies in which women participated. We have already discussed the bloodletting of the Maya political scene. On some occasions women were charged with special religious duties. For instance, some women were thought to be able to bring rain in a time of drought. Carvings and vases suggest that Maya women participated in other rituals in many ways. Festivities included paying respect to the gods, praying, and burning copal. Women assisted men engaged in consuming mind-altering substances, such as peyote, or consumed such substances themselves. Women gave intoxicating enemas to men. Ceremonies often required sexual abstinence and purification techniques before rituals. Following rituals, women danced, feasted, and drank *balche* (an alcoholic beverage). In these ways women played a prominent public spiritual role in the Classic Maya city-states.

WOMEN OF A DISAPPEARING WORLD:
THE LATE CLASSICAL MAYA

The Maya world view placed women in a high position for their reproductive powers. Women were respected for their blood sacrifice and resulting children and thus had a strong position in their families, although common women were nutritionally deprived. Maya women contributed to the economies of their families and city-states in many ways, such as weaving cloth and preserving and processing food. Royal consorts played critical roles in the political scene, whether through religious bloodletting rituals, forming political alliances, or as outright leaders. Female goddesses with multifaceted power were important to Maya society for their fertility and wisdom.[15] Not only did the Maya cosmology require mutual dependency between men and women in marriage and society, but kings also needed access to female spirituality in various ways to wield power. Although Maya women had many more paths open to them compared with women in other civilizations, some evidence suggests that even their status was gradually declining compared with earlier Meso-American civilizations. For example, Maya women had been prominent players in the ancient Meso-American ball game, but they ceased playing by the eighth century. The farming techniques of common women had become more time-consuming by this time too. Regardless of this trajectory, by the end of the tenth century, the Maya civilization faded rapidly and somewhat mysteriously, although the increasingly destructive inter city-state warfare probably played a role.

AZTEC CIVILIZATION: FROM THE YUCATAN PENINSULA TO THE CENTRAL VALLEY (750–1519 CE)

The collapse of the Classic Maya civilization did not herald an end to Meso-American cultures. Indeed, in the centuries that followed, several highly developed urban societies emerged, continuing the cultural homogeneity of this area in Central America and all the while developing new characteristics. The last great state to thrive before the coming of the Europeans was that of the Aztecs, who embraced wholeheartedly the civilizations that had preceded them, especially those based on the city of Teotihuacán (150–750 CE) and the Toltec peoples (950–1150 CE). Such was the desire of the Aztecs to conflate their own history with these ancient cultures that Aztecs pointedly imitated them. The great capital city of the Aztecs, called Tenochtitlán, was built on a grid pattern similar to that of Teotihuacán, and the rulers intermarried with the descendents of Toltec people. In their recorded histories, Aztecs attempted to promote the connections between their society and those who had come before.

The Aztecs were particularly interested in highlighting these connections because they were relatively recent immigrants to the central valley of Mexico. In fact, they came from the north at the beginning of the thirteenth century. As recent arrivals, they realized that they lacked the legacy and political traditions of other Meso-American kingdoms. Sources that describe these migrations cultivate an image of these early Aztecs as uncouth, yet determined and impressive warriors who managed to secure swampy land in the central valley of Mexico, defend themselves against preexisting peoples, and intermarry among indigenous people they believed were related to the ancient Toltec civilization.

One account of an early alliance between the Aztec and their neighbors demonstrates how the Aztec ruling class perceived themselves in relationship to the communities around them. According to legend, the Aztecs had made a political arrangement with a more powerful kingdom that allowed the newcomers to stay on a meager allotment of land in exchange for the Aztecs' military services. Eventually, the neighboring king granted them his favorite daughter and princess in reward for their assistance in battle. The Aztecs gave the king a horrifying surprise, for when he visited them, he saw that his daughter had been killed and her skin flayed off of her body, with an Aztec priest wearing the princess as part of a religious sacrifice. Needless to say, the alliance broke down. This tale demonstrates that the Aztecs viewed themselves as interested in interweaving their fortunes with those of the great civilizations they encountered, but also wanted to show that they would never stand for secondary status. Instead, they would gain their power in society through bloodshed—whether in battle or human sacrifice.

Through incessant warfare, the Aztecs began their ascent to power in Central America, founding their great city of Tenochtitlán in 1325 CE. Eventually, their overlordship extended throughout most of the central valley of Mexico, encompassing numerous peoples from a wide range of linguistic groups and environments. Until the fifteenth century, the Aztecs ruled in conjunction with two other powerful city-states, finally becoming the singular power in the central valley only in the late 1400s. Although their economy thrived on the cultivation of corn and the development of extensive trade networks, the real basis for Aztec power was the tribute extracted from the conquered cities and tribes. In this regard the Aztec state resembled that of Classical Sparta, which was completely dependent on its colonial policies for maintaining power. The Aztecs established an empire, allowing conquered territories some degree of independence in terms of setting up their own laws and maintaining their own infrastructure. Yet these rulers demanded periodic tribute in the form of goods and services. Thus, various Aztec subjects paid cloth, exotic feathers, and gold, as well as soldiers to their masters. In return, the Aztecs made only a minimal attempt to have an equitable relationship with their colonies. When they invited the tributary states' officials to the capital city of Tenochtitlán for feasting and religious occasions, the Aztec rulers made a conspicuous show of public human sacrifice as an intimidation technique. The message sent by the Aztecs was clear: They demanded subservience and staged blatant reminders of their authority.

The colonial policies so dependent on warfare worsened the livelihoods of many people in the Aztec lands. This stress was augmented by demands for constant tribute and an increasing desire on the part of Aztec leaders for captives to provide human sacrifices. Additionally, a growing overpopulation problem was emerging in Central America that strained ordinary people's food resources. The Aztec leaders could make subservient communities, but they were not actually making loyal allies. Their policies left opportunities for those who wished to turn the tables against the Aztec overlords. In 1519, the European explorer and warrior Hernando Cortés used the ruthless relationships the Aztecs had cultivated among their subjects and neighbors to ally his men against the once-mighty empire, which collapsed within three years.

THE IDEAL AZTEC WOMAN

In many ways, the expected behavior of Aztec women was comparable to that of other early societies. According to the Spanish friar Bernardino de Sahagún, who interviewed a variety of Aztec nobles about how their society functioned, females were expected to be obedient, patient, chaste, and modest:

> The good maiden is yet a virgin, mature, clean, unblemished, pious, pure of heart, benign, chaste. . . . The good noblewoman [is] patient, gentle, kind, benign, hard-working, resolute, firm of heart. . . . The good mature woman [is] . . . long-suffering; she accepts reprimands calmly. . . . The bad maiden [is] corrupt, incorrigible, rebellious—a proud woman, shameless, brazen, treacherous, stupid. . . . [16]

When women married, they received this advice from their elders: "be most considerate of one; regard one with respect, speak well, greet one well. . . . Arise in the deep of night [to begin domestic tasks]."[17] From these statements, it seems like an almost universal constant that women were expected to assume a passive and obedient role in ancient societies. Yet, some unusual ideas about appropriate female behavior did exist among the Aztecs. For instance, it was considered proper etiquette for a small girl from a noble family to act energetically and with enterprise. Furthermore, the idea that women ought to be sequestered did not exist, as it had in Classical Athenian and Song Chinese civilizations.

A closer look at the ideal version of Aztec women reveals a contrast between valuing their special place in society and constricting them to inflexible gender roles. From the beginning of children's lives, they were reminded of the difference between male and female. Whereas a boy infant received a tiny shield with arrows at his birth, a girl baby was given a miniature broom as a reminder of her duties. Similar to practices among the Classical Maya, Aztec female infants received spinning tools. A synonym for "woman" in Aztec society was "skirt," so closely connected was gender with apparel. Critical for understanding the expectations of women is the way that Aztecs understood a woman's place in the house. As in other ancient civilizations, women tended to assume the household duties. Unlike practice in many other societies, the assumption of these tasks gave women a great amount of social value. "Thou wilt be in the heart of the home, thou wilt go nowhere, thou wilt nowhere become a wanderer, thou becomest the banked fire, the hearth stones," went the statement that midwives chanted to newborn infant girls.[18] Thus was a woman's identity conflated with that of her domicile. Although she was not sequestered from public view, her real essence belonged in the home. In fact, an infant girl's umbilical cord was buried under the *metate* (grinding stone) of the household, almost chaining her spirit there in a ritual act.

The association of women with the home actually elevated her status in Aztec society, however. The reason for this has to do with the way that Aztec society was molded by warfare. Like pastoralist societies in premodern Eurasia and Classical Sparta, Aztec civilization was more conscious of women's contributions to the economy and management of the family household. In both cases, men spent much of their time away from home fighting or preparing for war. Whereas Aztec men also farmed (work which the Spartans left for their conquered subjects), their dependence on women for maintaining their homes was tangible. In fact, it was reinforced by their conception of the universe. The areas outside the home were thought to be a construction parallel to the areas inside the home. By maintaining order in their domiciles, women played a crucial role in maintaining the overall harmony of society. The Aztec state's constant focus on military conquest had critical ramifications for women. Not only was their expected role in society shaped by the incessant warfare, but so too were other aspects of women's lives, such as their economic contributions, religiosity, and access to public power, as we shall see.

WOMEN'S LIVES ON THE HOME FRONT

BIRTH, CHILDHOOD, AND ADOLESCENCE   The importance the Aztecs placed upon differentiating the two genders—as well as the relatively high social value placed on each—can be seen by the typical life cycles of women and men. As we have already seen, even from birth the destiny and duties of infant girls were carefully pronounced by the midwife. Throughout early childhood, however, little distinction between boys and girls seems to have been made. Both baby girls and baby boys were welcomed into the world with days of feasting and celebrations. These festivities contrasted with the words spoken by the midwife to the newborns:

> You have now come into the world where your parents live amidst cares and toil, where glowing heat, cold and winds prevail, where there is neither real joy nor satisfaction, for it is a place of work, cares and want.[19]

Parents doted on their young children, with mothers not weaning them until the child was perhaps four years old, and it was after this time that boys and girls began to spend time differently. Six-year-old boys followed their fathers around their fields or trained in their crafts, while girls began to learn the basics of cooking and weaving. Parents demanded obedience from their offspring, and sources recount grim punishments when boys and girls disobeyed. According to one source, "they punished the eleven-year-old boy or girl who disregarded verbal correction by making them inhale chile smoke, which was a serious and even cruel punishment."[20] Notable among the Aztec civilization was a lack of taboo or even interest in marking the menstruation of adolescent females, traditions that in other ancient cultures went hand-in-hand with an overall denigration of women.

The children of Aztec nobility led different lifestyles than their poorer counterparts, which became apparent in early adolescence as they were trained in different schools. Young men and women from common society attended local schools, where they learned to perform ritual songs and dances. There, the male youths learned the arts of warfare while the young women were presumably taught their domestic duties (sources for formal female education say little on this subject). The youth of the nobility attended a different type of school, where they studied writing and the sacred duties of priests. The young men learned about governance and leadership in war, while the young women trained in embroidery and sacred rituals.

Elite women did not have to learn the skill of cooking, but it was a major preoccupation for their common sisters. As with the Maya, maize provided the major source of nutrition. Meat was largely absent from the typical Aztec's diet, and peasants depended on treating the maize with lime and eating it alongside beans to consume adequate protein. This necessitated the constant grinding of maize upon the metate, which took up to five or six hours of work per day. Both noble and common women, however, were expected to learn the skills required for weaving. This was an obvious necessity for the average Aztec woman, who, like the women living in the Classical Maya civilization, made cloth out of the maguey plant fiber. The fabric they produced served three functions: It was their family's clothing, it often furnished tributary payments to the nobility, and it was also a source of income, since it could be sold in the public markets. For elite women, their talents as weavers were hallmarks of good upbringing. Nobles wore the more prestigious and expensive cotton cloth, which was forbidden by law to commoners. Also restricted to the elite, who made up perhaps 5 to 10 percent of Aztec society, were two-story houses and fancy jewelry.

FROM MARRIAGE TO WIDOWHOOD   Except in rare circumstances, such as when a noble person desired to take up the priesthood, marriage was an anticipated event for both men and women. Here again is notable the unusual degree of gender parity that had existed in earlier phases of the Aztecs' lives. Men on average married at 20, women at 18: a fairly equitable age difference. When a man desired a certain woman for his bride, he sent delegates to his intended's home, asking both parents for her hand in marriage. Whereas parents made the final decision about their daughter's betrothal, the couple-to-be likely had a large influence in selecting each other. This was because of the older age of the bride and groom and the fact that both would have probably been neighbors. The marriage and formal courting rituals were quite extensive, expressing the importance of rituals and of the advice of elders in the community. For instance, as the potential groom's representatives queried the desired woman's parents about her eligibility, her own relatives ritually critiqued her, decrying her laziness, her stupidity, and her ugliness. The marriage ceremony actually began with the faked kidnapping of the bride by the groom's male relatives. Ritual meals and advice from both male and female elders finally cemented the relationship, and then the couple usually established their own households.

Male and female sexual drive was recognized as a legitimate desire, although women lacked the sexual freedom that men possessed. Aztecs regarded sexual intercourse as a notable pleasure, referring to a vagina as a "place of joy."[21] As with early Southeast Asian societies, women considered sexual gratification their right. One Aztec father advised his son to always maintain a good sexual relationship with his wife, or else "thou starvest her. . . . she longeth for the carnal relations which thou owest."[22] Despite the Aztec belief in the legitimacy of sexual desire, different observations about sexual practices existed for the two genders, as they did in other ancient civilizations. Penalties for adultery were meted out for both men and women, yet an Aztec man committed adultery only when he had intercourse with a married woman other than his wife, whereas any sexual relationship outside of marriage was considered adulterous for women. Thus did an Aztec father remonstrate his daughter about the perils of extramarital sex: "If you are seen, if this is known, you will be put in the streets, you will be dragged through them, they will break your head with stones, they will turn it into pulp."[23] As with the Maya, monogamy was typically practiced by commoners, but Aztec noblemen routinely took up multiple wives and concubines.

As with other ancient civilizations, the bearing of children was one of the most important motives for Aztec marriages, and in the age of premodern medicine, childbirth was a time of danger for women. As a sixteenth-century source recounts, "it is the woman's portion to be miserable when she is pregnant; when she bears a child she is much afflicted; she suffers."[24] As with Maya civilization, the Aztecs compared childbirth to entering a battlefield. One Aztec poem reads: "Is this not a fatal time for us poor women? This is our kind of war. . . ."[25] Yet Aztec mothers had distinct advantages over many of their counterparts from other cultures, for Aztec medicine was very advanced, and Aztec women usually bore children after their bodies had reached adulthood. The Spanish conquerors of the Aztecs noted the vast knowledge of medicines possessed by the Aztecs, which included plants that induced abortion and those that would bring on a woman's labor. The medical lore known to the midwives about delivering children was such that they could safely deliver breech babies and maintained a much higher standard of hygiene than did their European medieval counterparts.

As Aztec women aged, they gained respect as elders of their communities. They were sought out for advice, and society acknowledged their powers in judgment. Widows in Aztec society had no problem remarrying, and they usually exercised even more choice in their later marriages than they had in their first. Both men and women had the ability to divorce with relative ease. Thus, in many ways the life cycles of Aztec women maintained a high degree of equity with those of men, whether through the opportunities to receive education (albeit girls received a different curriculum than men), through comparable choice of marital partner, the enjoyment of sexuality, or through an increased social standing for the elderly.

WOMEN'S WORK AND WEALTH IN AZTEC SOCIETY

Aztec women enjoyed a great deal of economic influence in society, sometimes even approaching parity with men. They were able to control wealth in ways similar to women of the Classic Maya civilization, and perhaps their influence came about because of continuities among Meso-American civilizations. It can also be understood in light of the great value that Aztecs placed on women's contributions to the domestic sphere. Since women's daily tasks were thought to provide a critical source of social well-being, their communities may have taken for granted that they should also be able to exercise economic power. Thus, daughters could inherit property as well as sons. When a woman did marry, the wealth she carried into her new relationship remained hers, even if she divorced, as was the case with Classical Maya women. One source documenting the control that women had over their own finances praises a resourceful wife, stating "much would she gather, collect and save, and justly distribute among her children."[26]

Even within a marriage, women were sometimes able to develop an economic standing distinct from their spouses. Thus, a common woman who excelled at trade in the local marketplaces built up a clientele who would invite her to their feasts, and she would invite them to hers. Rather than serving a merely social function, these feasts marked a subtle bond of the clients' dependency upon their economic superior. Noblewomen often played an even more important economic role, since they were often given the duties of managing their family's considerable estates. Like elite women in Classical Sparta and in Tang China, the female duty to manage estates was publicly acknowledged. As one Aztec source records, "the good noblewoman [is] careful of her estate. She governs, leads, provides for one, arranges well, administers peacefully."[27]

The enormous amount of work for which common women were responsible within the domestic sphere has already been discussed: cooking, cleaning, making fabric, and child care. Another critical component of women's labor was their role in the marketplaces. Unlike Classical Athens, whose commercial centers were dominated by men, women exhibited a high profile in Aztec markets. In fact, married women took it as a matter of course that they would sell goods such as their homespun cloth or food there, and husbands actually gave their wives fabric to start them off on this task upon marriage. Women also shopped for their own family's needs, often bartering for desirable prices using their cloth as currency. Some women hailed from wealthier merchant families and took a prominent role in managing specialized long-distance trade in crafts or large-scale transactions. Aztec society recognized a type of merchant, usually a wealthy long-distance trader, called a *pochteca*. A woman married to a *pochteca* did not accompany her husband on any trading ventures, since she was not supposed to roam far from home, but she did locally sell the goods obtained by her spouse. Women also played an important, although secondary, role in the manufacture of specialized crafts. Thus, some Aztec artisans excelled in working with the beautiful and costly feathers of tropical birds. Such an artisan would design the patterns to be woven and apply the feathers; his wife would sort out and dye the feathers beforehand. This type of labor, like that of long-distance trading, was engaged in only by women acting in consort with their families, and men dominated the overall process.

Midwifery was one area in which women gained economic and social prestige outside of their families. Midwives held a high position in Aztec societies, and their training was both extensive and specialized, as discussed above (see pp. 141–142).

The lowest-ranked women in Aztec society were prostitutes and slaves. Many prostitutes came from outside the local area in which they worked, and, as elsewhere, there were different rankings within this profession. For instance, some prostitutes displayed their wares in the marketplaces and were notable for their disheveled hair and garish clothing. Although their lives were difficult and undesirable, they roamed the streets freely, without a male protector. It was considered unseemly for men to use their services. The other sort of prostitute dwelled in the "Houses of Joy" that young Aztec peasant warriors-in-training were encouraged to frequent. The women in these places were likely to have been slaves captured in raids. Indeed, slavery was the common fate of foreign women on the losing side of battles with the Aztec armies. Female slaves who did not end up as sexual servants often worked under the employ of noble families, weaving cloth or performing other domestic tasks. Their children were not considered slaves, however, and could rise in social standing.

The degree to which Aztec women could control their wealth certainly speaks well for their position in society. There was an underside to this situation, however. If the militarization of the Aztecs gave women a high, if rigid, social value, and if it did allow women to develop significant independence in their financial affairs, it also created a great deal of additional labor for them. All commoners owed some sort of tribute to their local lord, but the expansion of the Aztec state placed additional heavy burdens upon them. Furthermore, as the empire grew, more and more tribute was demanded from the population. For men, this usually meant military service. For women, the payment was rendered either in cloth or, in urban areas, food. In fact, the demands upon commoners for these goods were such that some even began to practice polygamy, something that before the late fifteenth century only nobles had done. Households with more than one wife could combine the labor and provide payments more easily. Even noblewomen experienced some negative repercussions as the Aztec ruling class put ever-more emphasis on their aloofness and distinction from ordinary society. Their economic duties became narrower. Although there was a continuing expectation that they work with embroidery, they were not encouraged to embark on merchant activities. One source gives the advice that elite women should "not walk and know of plants or sell wood or sell *aji* or salt or saltpeter."[28] These negative trends, combined with the sheer amount of labor demanded of most women, should warn against painting too bright an image of Aztec women's financial power. The bellicose expansion of the Aztec Empire also had a negative impact on the role of female spirituality, as we shall see.

SACRED DUTIES AND FILTHY GODDESSES:
AZTEC WOMEN AND RELIGION

Much of Aztec religion derived from earlier Central American civilizations, including many deities, such as the Great Goddess from the civilization of Teotihuacán. In the Aztec culture, she became known as Xochiquetzalli ("Flowery Plumage") and was associated with sexual love and handicrafts. Nevertheless, Aztecs also made their own contributions to the religious culture. With intricate artwork and sophisticated rituals, the Aztecs wove together a belief system that put an extreme focus on human sacrifice and horrific imagery. Aztecs believed that their gods and goddesses had slain themselves in order to maintain the universe: The sun and the moon, for instance, were both deities who killed themselves in order to become these celestial bodies. In reciprocation for their own deaths, the Aztec divine beings demanded human bloodshed. Thus, Aztecs believed that the tears of sacrificial children could bring about rain, that the sun could be kept in its orbit with a freshly removed heart of a victim, or that a priest wearing the flesh of a woman representing a goddess could help to prepare Aztec communities for the war season.

The Aztec ruling class promoted these violent beliefs for their own political agendas. They depended on conquest through warfare for their livelihoods, and they used fear to keep their tributary states in check. The very public sacrifices, the sometimes gruesome rituals of the priests, and the gore-covered deities served as a highly visible reminder of the divinely given power of the Aztec Empire.

FIGURE 5-2   STATUE OF COATLICUE, THE AZTEC SERPENT-SKIRTED GODDESS
This statue, built ca. 1500 at the height of the Aztec state's power, wears gruesome apparel and a terrifying expression, which were intended to inspire fear and respect.

As with other aspects of women's lives in this society, female spirituality was infused by the militarism of the Aztec Empire. This can be seen in two areas: first, in the way Aztecs worshipped female deities, and second, in the religious observances expected of women. The Aztec state promoted the worship of many goddesses, whose appearance and function often reflected a militaristic agenda. Thus, some goddesses were depicted holding both brooms and shields, mixing the household duties of women with those of the male warriors. One stone monument depicts the goddess Coyolxauhqui equipped and dressed for a losing battle, her limbs torn asunder. Many goddesses reflect the militarization in a more abstract way, by hearkening to fearsome powers and gory visages. Thus, a 10-foot-high statue, usually identified as Coatlicue, the mother of Huitzilopochtli, bears little resemblance to a woman. Her face is made up of two serpents abutting each other, and her skirt is a twining mass of undulating snakes. Her arms are in an attacking position, and adorning her neck is a string of human hearts and hands depicted with great attention to realistic detail. Such imagery was not born out of a fear of the power of female sexuality (as was the case for the terrifying Hindu goddess Kali), but rather out of a more generalized idea that Aztec deities' authority rested in the fear they could inspire in their subjects and enemies.

The militarized goddesses and the prominence given to terrifying aspects of these divine beings were most important for the ruling classes of Aztec society. Evidence suggests that, at least among peasants, a different religious sensibility existed. Archaeologists who have examined the homes of Aztec peasants have recovered hundreds of small statues of deities, and their appearance and function differed greatly from the gods and goddesses promoted by the Aztec state. To begin with, most of the recovered peasant statues were of women, and most of these wore benign expressions.

The two most common have been called "goddess with temple headdress" and "goddess with tasseled headdress." Without corresponding written evidence, it is difficult to surmise the roles or origin of these deities, but it is possible that the former represented agricultural fertility (she holds ears of corn) and the latter represented waters close to home. In either case, these statues demonstrate an important connection between female divinity and agricultural fertility lacking among the state deities. These statues also reveal expectations about female roles in society. The goddess with temple headdress literally wears her domicile on her head and thus remains and reigns inside her temple in the manner that women both governed and were bound to their homes. The goddess with tasseled headdress is most often depicted kneeling with her hands in her lap, the most proper and demure position for Aztec women to assume.

FIGURE 5-3   SCULPTURE OF AN AZTEC CORN GODDESS
This small statue of an Aztec corn goddess
(note ears of corn in her left hand) was
likely used for private devotion.

Domestic religion, so often observed by women in ancient civilizations, took on a heightened role in the Aztec world. As with other layers
of society, the private rituals performed by women in their homes were
shaped by the militarization of the Aztecs. Women's religious duties were
recognized by society as being critical for maintaining the welfare of the
Aztec population, especially for protecting the men in their communities
who were constantly called out to war for the Aztec state. For instance,

one of the domestic duties of women was to sweep their houses. Aztec sources state that women were advised to "take charge of the sweeping."[29] This was not merely for the sake of cleanliness, but to maintain a kind of cosmic harmony in the household. The facts that priests performed ritual sweeping and that deities swept in several myths show that sweeping was actually an important and sacred act. More obvious religious rituals performed in women's homes included lighting incense, ritually eating earth, and letting blood from their ears—all in service to gods and goddesses. Through these services, women's prayers for protection for their warriors could perhaps be more effective. In fact, when wives' husbands were at war, women would hang the leg bones (femurs) of men their husbands had killed in battle from their house beams, which was thought to bring protection to their men.

Although Aztecs did think that women's domestic religious duties were critical for the maintenance of social well-being, the public religious role of women in the empire was limited. On the one hand, noblewomen frequently attended priestly schools, learning embroidery and weaving. There, older women strictly chaperoned the students, preventing them from engaging in degrading behavior. Some women did become priestesses, serving in deities' temples, but most left the schools for marriage. Even the women who became priestesses had a limited role. In public ceremonies when these women danced or sang, they were always led by men.

A final aspect of women's spirituality to consider is the role they played in the afterlife. The souls of deceased Aztecs were thought to have different fates, depending on the manner of a person's demise. One of the most important ways an Aztec could expire was in battle, and both women and men were thought to be able to meet a "warrior's death." In this aspect, Aztec belief corresponded to the Classical Spartan view of women, for dying in childbirth in such warlike societies was overtly compared to death in battle. In the Aztec belief system, however, the afterlife of these warriors differed greatly according to gender. For men, death in battlefield would lead to a period of four years in the underworld, followed by a reincarnation in the form of hummingbirds or butterflies. Women who died as "warriors" in giving birth experienced a different sort of fate. First, their bodies were removed from their homes by way of a hole drilled expressly for this purpose, avoiding the doors for the living. Second, their remains were thought to be potent magic: Some body parts were thought to be able to cause paralysis. Thus, they had to be carefully guarded by midwives and husbands. The souls of these women initially endured to become spirits who escorted the sun along its path, but eventually became demonic-like spirits who caused great harm to the living. They turned either into *Cihuapipltin*, "female nobles," or *Cihuateteo*, "female deities," powerful beings of ill-will. In either case, they appeared in artwork as skull-faced, open mouthed, and often fanged. They caused convulsions and deformities in children and haunted certain areas.

THE LIMITATIONS OF POWER: THE SUBORDINATE ROLE OF AZTEC WOMEN IN POLITICS

Like most of the urban civilizations examined in this book, the Aztecs effectively shut out women from positions of state power. Women were technically forbidden to speak on formal public occasions. Nevertheless, women did make important contributions to the political direction of the empire and even exercised leadership roles in informal ways, such as through the management of large estates, as discussed above. Perhaps their most important influence took place at the local neighborhood levels, where older women were approached for advice and played significant roles as marital matchmakers, thus allowing them to shape the dynamics of Aztec society. Also, although women were prohibited from giving formal political speeches, sources indicate that it could be perfectly acceptable for them to argue their minds when the occasion called. For example, one account of the Spanish conquest tells of a group of noble warriors who fled Tenochtitlán during the takeover. Apparently, a group of women gathered around them, chastising and humiliating them, yelling: "Have you no shame? No woman will ever paint her face for you again!"[30] Evidence suggests, however, that women's opportunities in the political realm diminished as the Aztec state grew, with its bellicose expansion contributing to the silencing of female political voices.

As with the ruling classes of the Roman Republic, Tang and Song China, and the Classical Maya, one of the most critical political roles of Aztec women was in forging alliances through marriage, even if their betrothals were typically arranged by others. The marriage of an Aztec royal daughter to a nobleman of another kingdom was one of the few ways that the empire maintained relationships outside of the imperial policies of warfare and fear tactics. It was common among Aztec leaders to "marry down" their female children to nobles of tributary states. This practice was not a generous way of including these subordinate kingdoms in the empire; in fact it was a prominent reminder of the subordinates' dependency upon the Aztec ruling class. These sorts of marriages also appeased colonized areas that may have resented the military overlordship and incessant demands for tribute made by the Aztec leaders.[31] The progeny of these marriages emphasized their relationships to their mothers rather than their fathers, since they achieved greater status by being related to the ruling class of Tenochtitlán.

Less typical among the Aztecs was the occasional public role played by a female member of the royal family who managed to secure power in exceptional instances. For example, the daughter of the leader Moctezuma I, Atotoztli, succeeded him upon his death. Scholars dispute the extent to which she ruled in her own right, but she was powerful enough to have legitimized imperial descent through the progeny of herself and her non-royal husband. The Aztec Queen Tecuichpo, child of Moctezuma II, did not govern the empire but did show amazing political savvy during the time of the Spanish conquest. She used her diplomatic skills and knowledge of law to secure large amounts of property for herself and her children, an impressive feat that most indigenous peoples in Central America were unable to achieve. The way in which one source discusses the proper behavior of Aztec women rulers also indicates that more may have existed than the traditional accounts suggest:

> The good woman ruler [is] a provider of good conditions, a corrector, a punisher, a chastiser, a reprimander. She is needed, obeyed; she creates order; she establishes rules.[32]

In fact, it is likely that Aztec women exercised more political authority than the extant sources show, particularly in the first century and a half after their arrival in Central America. For instance, local neighborhoods in the Aztec world were called *calpulli*, and in the earliest years of Aztec settlement they had governed themselves by means of a council of elders who elected one leader in warfare and another leader in civic and religious affairs. Some scholars have suggested that early calpulli leaders might have included women. Evidence for this can be seen in the title given to a male calpulli leader—"*Cihuacoatl.*" This term had originally meant "female snake," perhaps indicating a reverence for female gendered leadership in the distant past. At any rate, the calpulli laws regarding divorce and the inheritance of property generally promoted the interests of both genders. The emergence of a centralized Aztec state, whose power was based on the prominent use of warfare, seems to have eroded the public role of women in a couple of ways. First, women could not be soldiers. Even though they might have played complementary roles with men in their domestic duties, with both male and female roles recognized as critical for the maintenance of social well-being, women were denied access to what eventually became the most critical avenue to public honor. Aztec leadership emphasized the characteristics of warriors, and good leaders were expected to be good generals. Furthermore, as the Aztec Empire developed, the power of the state was emphasized at the expense of the authority of the calpulli, limiting the local public voices that might have been more conducive to allowing women a political role.

CONCLUSION

Women in Aztec Mexico enjoyed many privileges denied to their sisters in other ancient civilizations. The ideal Aztec women, although expected to be obedient and solely concerned with affairs related to their domestic spheres, also were expected to be energetic in youth, maintainers of social harmony in marriage, and providers of advice when aged. Whereas the work of most women was a grueling challenge, demanding hours of grinding corn, weaving, and attending to child care, there were important financial opportunities available to them. Noblewomen were expected to be able to manage their large estates, careers as midwives were well respected, and most women played an active role in the bartering and exchanging of goods in the public marketplaces. In their social lives, they also had some degree of parity with men, in terms of their ability to divorce, the degree to which they (or the common women, at least) participated in marriage arrangements, and their inheritance rights.

Nonetheless, in important ways Aztec women's roles in society were limited compared with those of men, particularly in the realms of politics and religion. Thus, they could not hold political offices and they were not supposed to speak publicly on formal occasions. As priestesses their duties were far more limited than their male counterparts, and the most significant Aztec deities were masculine.

For both positive and ill, the growth of the Aztec state by means of constant warfare, fear tactics, and economic colonization influenced the treatment of women and the way women shaped their communities. Militarization fostered the ossification of gender roles in society, even as it upheld the importance of women's contributions to social harmony through their attention to their domestic duties. It may have supported the important economic standing possessed by Aztec women. Nevertheless, it also militarized their goddesses and gradually limited their role in state political affairs. Many Aztec women survived the Spanish conquest to continue their richest traditions, allowing the Meso-American culture that began so many hundreds of years ago to continue to develop.

Aztec and Classical Maya women shared many similarities, particularly in their social and work experience. This can be seen in the types of work they performed, especially grinding corn, producing textiles, and caring for children. Some women's experiences, such as the identification of a girl infant with spinning tools, the economic rights of divorcees, or the comparison of childbirth to warfare, were so alike that they probably were passed on through the transfer of Meso-American traditions. Nonetheless, in two important ways the lives of Maya and Aztec women differed. In the Classical Maya era, women's public role in politics and their prominence in important religious rituals far surpassed those of their Aztec counterparts. Images of women in positions of power adorned the large stone sculptures, visible for every traveler in the Maya world to see. The Maya tradition of placing women in such high positions of public spiritual authority was not repeated among the Aztecs, whose political structure depended on the upholding of constant warfare as state policy, which led to the erosion of women's roles in the realms of religion and politics.

CHAPTER SIX

WOMEN IN THE ISLAMIC WORLD: PRE-ISLAMIC ARABIA TO ABBASID CALIPHATE (CA. 500–1258 CE)

Men have authority over women because Allah has made the one superior to the other, and because they spend their wealth to maintain them. Good women are obedient. They guard their unseen parts because Allah has guarded them. As for those from whom you fear disobedience, admonish them and send them to beds apart and beat them. Then if they obey you, take no further action against them. Allah is high and supreme. (4:34, p. 370)

Those who surrender themselves to Allah and accept the true faith; who are devout, sincere, patient, humble, charitable, and chaste; who fast and are ever mindful of Allah—on these, both men and women, Allah will bestow forgiveness and rich reward.[1] (33:35, p. 293)

Muslim theologians use the above suras—Quranic verses—as examples to argue their opposing positions in the ongoing debate on the status of women in Islam. Traditionalists commonly cite the first sura to justify the religion's patriarchal control over women. Modernists use the second sura as a basis to assert that Islam accords spiritual equality to both men and women and reiterate that the notion of gender inequality is not limited to Islam but is prevalent in all the great world religions. Therefore, analyzing the status of women in Islam is a complex task, as it has been open to interpretation. This chapter will show that, because the boundaries of Islam extended beyond the Arabian Peninsula to encompass a vast territory, the condition of Muslim women did not remain static. Instead, the broader political and socioeconomic factors molded and shaped their position in society.

As happened elsewhere, the rise of centralized, economically and culturally vibrant empires sometimes went hand-in-hand with women's roles becoming more constricted. During the Abbasid caliphate (ca. 750–1258 CE), the compilation of the *Sharia* (Islamic law) reintroduced, altered, and added injunctions affecting women's status adversely. Many pre-Islamic or regional practices, such as veiling and harsh punishments for women's sexual impropriety, were transcribed in the Sharia, thus reinforcing patriarchal control. This gave rise to a popular image of Muslim women as helpless victims leading secluded lives. However, as we will see, these customs were not universally practiced. Overall, when comparing the lives of Muslim women in the early years of Islam with those living under the Abbasid caliphate, one cannot but help notice a gradual decline in their status. First let us focus on the condition of women in pre-Islamic Arabia, as this will help us evaluate the reforms that Islam instituted for women.

QUESTIONS FOR STUDENT ANALYSIS

1. What was the impact of Islam on women's lives in Arabia during Muhammad's lifetime?

2. To what extent did women in the Abbasid caliphate retain their privileges established by Muhammad and to what extent did they lose freedoms?

3. To what extent was the declining status of women in the Abbasid caliphate, Tang and Song China, and Gupta India related to the centralization of the respective empires?

4. Foot binding, physical and spatial segregation *(purdah),* and *sati* are all different examples of patriarchal control. Why is this so? Discuss the factors that prompted the rise of these practices in Song China and Gupta India and during the Abbasid caliphate.

WOMEN IN PRE-ISLAMIC ARABIA

Pre-Islamic Arabia was shaped like a triangle and comprised roughly two unequal regions: the vast inland desert area and the peripheral areas bordering the Red Sea (the *hijaj*). This geographical divide led to the birth of two groups practicing very different lifestyles: the Bedouins, who were pastoral nomads interspersed throughout much of the desert areas, and the sedentary communities who lived along the hijaj.

BEDOUIN WOMEN

Approximately 75 percent of the Arabian peninsula was and is made up of arid land suited to the development of nomadic pastoralism. Bedouins were pastoral nomads, who were organized into tight-knit kinship groups and pursued a seasonal migratory lifestyle. The entire clan migrated together, shared common pastureland and spoils of war, and in times of emergency presented a united front. Most of the year they lived in the desert in tents. During the winter months, when pasture for their domesticated animals became sparse, they raided settled areas in hopes of acquiring sustenance. This lifestyle left little room for the accumulation of private property and wealth. Besides exhibiting fierce group solidarity, the Bedouin valued qualities such as upholding honor; protecting the weak; and practicing generosity, patience, and persistence in revenge.

Bedouins did not live in matrifocal families. Instead, the basic family unit was the extended patrifocal family, where two to three generations resided together. These types of family units had several characteristics that promoted relatively positive social arrangements for women. For example, different forms of marital arrangements were prevalent. Some Bedouin women practiced polyandry (a wife with multiple husbands) and could have as many as 10 sexual partners. Another common practice known as "temporary marriages" allowed women to simultaneously reside with two brothers. The most common form of marriage was the polygamous arrangement where a man married multiple wives. He had the liberty of either bringing them to his own residence or permitting them to continue living in their own clans, visiting them on a rotating basis. Generally the oldest patriarch of the family arranged the marriages. Both customs of giving dowry and bride-price (gifts from the groom's family) were common in Bedouin society. In cases of abusive relationships, a wife could return to her natal group, and both men and women could terminate a marriage arrangement if they so desired.

In Bedouin society women were highly valued for their procreative roles. Therefore, once married, a Bedouin woman's primary responsibility was to bear children. Infant mortality rates were relatively high, and any pregnancy was welcome news. As in other urban societies, there was a distinct preference for boys over girls. Some Bedouin groups practiced female infanticide, and baby girls were often buried alive hours after their birth. Frequently in times of emergency when the survival of the entire group was at stake, little girls between the ages of one to four were left behind to die or hastily buried alive.

If they survived infancy, Bedouin girls learned the techniques of surviving the harsh desert conditions and living under a constant threat of inter-group rivalry. They learned the skills to defend themselves, their immediate family, and the group. It was common for older Bedouin women to assume leadership roles when their men went off on plundering raids, especially during the harsh winter months. Sometimes, young Bedouin women accompanied the men to serve as nurses behind battle lines, although we have no specific evidence suggesting that they participated in warfare. One can only speculate that, given their training from childhood, they might have fought battles if the need arose.

Bedouin women contributed economically to the group's survival by raising livestock; making pastoral products from milk such as butter, cheese and curd; and weaving and spinning. In addition, they fulfilled a wide range of household chores from food preparation to pitching and cleaning tents to tending infants, the sick, and the elderly.

Another area to which Bedouin women contributed substantially was in the evolution of Arabic lyrical poetry, which was orally transmitted from one generation to another. Generally Bedouin poetry concerned the universal themes of unrequited love, survival, betrayal, revenge, and bravery. This genre also popularized the image of the ideal beauty in Bedouin society: a voluptuous woman with large black eyes, shiny long black hair, and a smooth complexion of the color of honey and milk. This image was very far removed from the reality of the weather-beaten bodies of most Bedouin women, who were merely trying to survive day-by-day under harsh conditions.

Al-Khansa (600–670 CE) was one of the greatest Bedouin poets in the pre-Islamic Arabia. She belonged to the Madar nomads, who were renowned throughout the Arabian Peninsula for their lyrical poetry. From an early age, she exhibited great talent and independence and fiercely resisted getting married until she had found the man of her choice. Subsequently, she married three times and had four sons. She often challenged her male peers in public recitation contests. During one of these competitions, when she had finished reciting one of her poems, a disgruntled, envious male competitor taunted her by saying that he had not seen a better "woman" poet. She is believed to have retorted, "Don't you want to say that I am the best poet, male or female?"[2]

Al-Khansa eventually converted to Islam and lost her four sons in the Battle of Qadasiyah (637 CE). After she heard the news, instead of regretting the idea of having sent all her four sons to die for Islam, she regarded it as an honor. Because of her personal losses, Al-Khansa's poetry took on a melancholic tone but was nonetheless magnificent. Muhammad, who found much of the poetry of his time very distasteful because of its erotic content, admired Al-Khansa's because it extolled the Islamic way of life. She died at the age of 70 in the desert, where she spent her final years as a recluse.

Other Bedouin women poets were regarded as dangerous to the newly emerging monotheistic religion of Islam, because they ridiculed Muhammad through their verses. For example, Asma' bint Marwan emerged as Muhammad's strongest critic, lampooning him through her lyrical poetry. Perceived as an enemy of Islam, she was assassinated by an ardent follower of Muhammad. Subsequently, several Bedouin women poets converted to Islam, thereby becoming the religion's earliest supporters.

WOMEN FROM THE HIJAJ

In contrast to the desert areas, the hijaj was interspersed with oases and included the southernmost tip of the Arabian Peninsula, which experienced some summer rainfall. As a consequence, this region saw the emergence of pockets of urban centers mostly populated by farming and mercantile communities. Although the women in the hijaj still continued to enjoy some of the social freedoms of their Bedouin sisters, their lives underwent crucial changes as a direct consequence of the growing economy in the century prior to Muhammad's lifetime (ca. 470–570 CE).

The influx of long-distance trade led to the gradual erosion of communal sharing of land and other resources and was replaced by acquiring private property and wealth. This change in turn dictated the urgency of establishing patrilineal descent, since this was one crucial way of maintaining a family's inheritance over time. An example to corroborate the shift toward patrilineal descent was the issue of the control of the *Ka'ba*, a repository of pagan idols in Mecca, the seat of pre-Islamic worship. Before Muhammad's lifetime, the guardianship of the Ka'ba passed through the female line; in later years this was not the case.

Further, polyandry and temporary marriages were no longer allowed: Women lost their ability to marry more than one partner. However, polygamy remained the dominant form of marriage arrangement, and the number of wives a man had became a reflection of his economic status in society. Divorce became the sole prerogative of the husband, and was achieved with relative ease. There were no guidelines protecting wives, so divorces would often have disastrous financial and emotional consequences on women.

With the growing economy was a corresponding rise of nuclear patrifocal families. This prompted another important change in the lives of women belonging to the wealthy farming and mercantile families. They were now increasingly discouraged from participating in the public arena and instead pressured to focus their attention on fulfilling their traditional roles of being a wife and mother. Keeping women within the confines of the house became an honorable practice, as it reflected the socioeconomic status of the family.

Despite these slow changes, women continued to contribute visibly to the economy and to the pre-Islamic pagan religion. Some women were involved in the traditional long-distance caravan trade, as is evidenced by the example of Khadija bint Khuwaylid, the first wife of Muhammad. In addition, women openly assumed leadership positions in the pagan religion. For example, there were several priestesses, especially in the southern part of Arabia—where Muhammad would eventually face his strongest opposition when he began his teachings. These priestesses were overjoyed at the news of Muhammad's death, believing that the new religion of Islam would die with him. Instead, as the popularity of Islam grew, they became increasingly marginalized from society, prompting some to voluntarily convert to Islam.

From this discussion, now let us focus on the reforms Islam instituted and how they affected the status of women from the time of Muhammad to the end of the Abbasid caliphate in 1258 CE.

WOMEN'S POSITIONS FROM MUHAMMAD'S LIFETIME TO 750 CE

BACKGROUND: MUHAMMAD, THE FOUNDER AND HIS TEACHINGS

Unlike other regions—where differences in ecology dictated the existence of great linguistic, ethnic, religious, and cultural diversity—the peninsular geography of ancient Arabia, surprisingly, helped forge a homogeneous Arab society. The tribes, both Bedouin and merchant, who populated the region spoke one language: Arabic. They all practiced a polytheistic religion in which once a year, the different Arab groups would congregate for a pilgrimage at Mecca, where the Ka'ba, the repository of pagan idols, was situated. It is from this geographical setting that "Islam"—meaning submission to the will of Allah—first burst upon the tribal, polytheistic world of the Arabs.

Muhammad-ibn-Abdullah ("highly praised"), the founder of Islam, was born around 570 CE in Mecca. His family belonged to the powerful Quraysh tribe. Orphaned at an early age, he was brought up by his grandfather, Abd al-Muttalib, and uncle, Abu Talib. He married a rich 40-year-old widow, Khadija, who entrusted him with her family caravan business. It was not until the age of 40 that Muhammad started receiving Allah's revelations through Archangel Gabriel. He would continue receiving these for the next 23 years. At first he communicated these revelations only to family and close friends. After he won the confidence and support of his wife, Khadija, and his close allies—Ali, Abu Bakr, Zaid, and Omar—he turned to a larger audience. The next 10 years of Muhammad's life proved to be difficult. He became the target of verbal abuse and derision from Meccan society. Such treatment was common for religious founders who professed a message different from the one the people were accustomed to hearing.

The essence of the new religion that Muhammad taught was the obligatory adherence to the Five Pillars: The first was the *sahada*, or declaration of faith, that reinforced the monotheistic principle that there is only one God, Allah, and that Muhammad was the seal of prophethood. The other pillars were *salat*, praying five times a day facing Mecca; *zakat*, giving alms to the poor; *sawm*, fasting during the month of *Ramadan*; and *hajj*, pilgrimage to Mecca. Muhammad preached a monotheistic religion that was a direct departure from the polytheism and paganism prevalent in ancient Arabia. Furthermore, he voiced his dismay at idolatry and the exploitation of the poor by the rich mercantile community. In doing this, he directly challenged the powerful Quraysh oligarchs who were the keepers of the Ka'ba, the main seat of pre-Islamic worship, and also further angered those who were content with the pagan religion.

Encountering considerable resistance in Mecca, Muhammad fled in 622 CE to Yathrib (later renamed Medina), where he found a more receptive audience and formed a strong community of both men and women followers known as the *umma*. In 630 CE, Muhammad finally decided to return to Mecca to cleanse the Ka'ba of its idols and proclaim it to be the seat of Islam. This mission was accomplished with some resistance from the Meccans. By the time he died in 632 CE, Islam had been successful in marginalizing the pre-Islamic pagan religion. It was Muhammad's message of a simple ethical order based on a monotheistic belief and sense of interpersonal justice that accelerated the momentum of Islam's success.

THE WOMEN OF MUHAMMAD'S HOUSEHOLD: THE IDEAL ROLE MODELS FOR ALL MUSLIM WOMEN

As the family formed the basic unit of the *umma*, the newly formed Islamic community, women played an important role in its perpetuation through their procreative roles. The Quran laid out numerous injunctions on women's familial and societal behavior that were primarily aimed at the preservation of the newly emerging Islamic umma. In particular, the Quran accorded an elite status to Muhammad's wives and daughters. They were given the honorific title of "Mothers of the Believers" and deemed to be ideals for all Muslim women. As a consequence, they had the enormous responsibility of adhering to the ideals stipulated in the Quran. For example,

> Wives of the Prophet, you are not like other women. If you fear Allah, do not be too complaisant in your speech, lest the lecherous-hearted should lust after you. Show discretion in what you say. Stay in your homes and do not display your finery as women used to do in the days of ignorance. Attend to your prayers, give alms to the poor and obey Allah and His apostle (33:33, p. 293)

As the above sura attests, these women were expected to be devout Muslims by practicing the Five Pillars, exhibiting humility in speech and modesty in dress and behavior, and being obedient and loyal to Muhammad. The Quran stipulated that they lead a life of quiet domesticity and practice frugality but be charitable when the need arose.

Certain additional stipulations were laid down in the Quran to protect the honor of Muhammad's wives. For example, as the following sura suggests, ordinary men were prevented from entering Muhammad's household unannounced and conversing with any of his wives directly:

> Believers, do not enter the houses of the Prophet for a meal without waiting for proper time, unless you are given leave. But if you are invited, enter; . . . If you ask his wives for anything, speak to them from behind a curtain. This is more chaste for your hearts and their hearts. (33:51, p. 295)

The first time veiling appears in the Quran is in the form of a revelation aimed specifically at the women of Muhammad's household:

> Prophet, enjoin your wives, your daughters, and the wives of true believers to draw their veils close around them. That is more proper, so that they may be recognized and not molested. (33:59, p. 295)

Historians differ on how exactly this sura was revealed to Muhammad. Some suggest that his enemies harassed him by spreading malicious gossip about his wives. Others point out that it was after a particular incident when Muhammad caught some guests overstaying their welcome and hovering around the area where his wives were believed to be living. Some have suggested that Muhammad was not happy when one of his wives accidentally touched the hand of an unrelated male. Other scholars argue that, even if the above reasons seem preposterous, what actually prompted Muhammad to start secluding and requiring the women of his household to wear the veil when they went out in public was his concern for their safety. It slowly became a mark of distinction. Being Muhammad's wives, they enjoyed a privileged status in society, and wearing the veil was a way to distinguish them from the rest of the populace.

However, although the Quran dictated that the women of Muhammad's household appear before unrelated males veiled, it also specified that they could interact unveiled with the male members of their immediate and extended family.

> It shall be no offense for the Prophet's wives to be seen unveiled by their fathers, their sons, their brothers, their brothers' sons, their sisters' sons, their women, and their slave-girls. (33:55, p. 295)

The Quran gave Muhammad the right to marry several times but, given their special status as "Mothers of Believers," his wives were barred from remarrying after his death.

> You must not speak ill of Allah's apostle, nor shall you ever wed his wives after him; this would be a grave offense in the sight of Allah. Whether you hide or reveal them, Allah has knowledge of all things. (33:54, p. 295)

Over the ensuing decades, these rules, originally meant to safeguard the prestige of the Prophet's wives, came to be applied to other women.

MUHAMMAD'S WIVES

The nature of Muhammad's polygamous household has been a source of great controversy. Not only do historians differ on the exact number of wives Muhammad had but also on his motives for these marital alliances. Some refer to 14 wives, others cite the *hadiths* (sayings of Muhammad) and argue that he had only 12 wives—of whom only 9 survived him. Most agree that he married two Jewish women, two slaves, a Coptic Christian, and a concubine, and that the rest were either widows or orphans. The only virgin Muhammad married was Aisha, who was the daughter of his close friend Abu Bakr and who became his last and youngest wife.

Some historians have defended Muhammad's polygamous arrangements by citing the following sura, which clearly stipulates the nature and number of women Muhammad could marry, given that he was Allah's last prophet and no ordinary commoner:

> Prophet, We have made lawful to you the wives to whom you have granted dowries and the slave girls whom Allah has given you as booty; the daughters of your paternal and maternal uncles and of your paternal and maternal aunts who fled to you; and the other women who gave themselves to you and whom you wished to take in marriage. This privilege is yours alone, being granted to no other believer. (33:50, p. 294)

Further, given his special status, Muhammad was granted the right to deal with his wives as he saw appropriate, as is evidenced from the following sura:

> You may put off any of your wives you please and take to your bed any of them you please. Nor is it unlawful for you to receive any of those whom you have temporarily set aside. That is more proper, so that they may be contented and not vexed, and may all be pleased with what you give them. (33:51, p. 294)

Scholars argue that all of Muhammad's marriages were contracted before he received the revelation legally restricting men to marry only four wives (provided they could treat all of them equally). Still others have argued that Muhammad married for humanitarian and political reasons: Islam as a religion emphasized the need to help the weak and needy. They point out that most of Muhammad's wives were either widows or orphans or slaves. By marrying them, he wanted to set examples for other men to follow. He entered into some marital alliances for political reasons in order to consolidate the position of Islam. For example, the first five *caliphs* (successors to Muhammad) were all linked to him through marriage. Abu Bakr, the first caliph, was his father-in-law; Ali, the fourth caliph, was married to Fatima, Muhammad's youngest daughter.

Muhammad's first wife, who has been considered an ideal role model for all Muslim women, was Khadija bint Khuwaylid, whom Muhammad married when he was around 20 or 25 years old. Khadija had been married and widowed twice and was very affluent. It was she who proposed marriage to Muhammad, and he accepted the offer immediately. This marital alliance provided Muhammad with some unique opportunities. Muhammad earned the respect of the mercantile community because of his fair business dealings. Consequently he was nicknamed "al-Amin," trusted one, and was able to make his financial mark on the Arabian caravan circuit. This alliance gave him access to the much-needed social status and recognition that would eventually prove crucial for the initial propagation of the rising religion of Islam.

Together, they had four daughters—Zaynab, Ruqayya, Umm Kulthum, and Fatima—and several sons. None of the boys survived their infancy. For 24 years, Muhammad remained completely devoted to Khadija until her death at the age of 65 (619 CE), after which he started remarrying. Therefore, Khadija's historical significance in early Islamic history can be summarized as follows: (1) She was the first to believe in Muhammad's revelations and provide him with unconditional support during those crucial years when he was trying to create the umma; (2) she was the only wife to bear him children; and (3) she never wore the veil or practiced physical seclusion, because Muhammad received this revelation a few years after her death.

Even though the women of Muhammad's household were regarded as the ideal role models for all Muslim women, they often encountered difficulties living up to the Quran's high expectations. Like any typical polygamous household, jealousies and scandals were common among Muhammad's wives. Perhaps the best example to highlight was the contentious relationship between Aisha, Muhammad's youngest wife, and

Fatima, his youngest daughter. The animosity between the two exploded with disastrous consequences after Muhammad's death.

Aisha bint Abu Bakr (613–678 CE), the youngest surviving wife of Muhammad, is historically best known of all his wives apart from Khadija. Over the years, two distinct images of Aisha have emerged. The Shiites portray her as a jealous schemer ruining the peace of Muhammad's household, a rival of Fatima and supporting the creation of the rift between Muslims over the succession of Ali, the fourth caliph. The Sunnis, on the other hand, revere her as a loyal wife and widow of Muhammad who played a very important public role in promoting Islam after his death by transcribing as many as 1,200 hadiths (sayings of Muhammad).

Aisha (literally translated, "life" in Arabic), the daughter of Muhammad's close friend Abu Bakr, was only six (seven, according to some) years old when Muhammad married her. Aisha continued to live with her parents for another two years until she reached puberty (as was the norm). When she moved in with Muhammad, she still played with her dolls. It was at the age of nine that her marriage to Muhammad was finally consummated. As she matured physically and emotionally, her intelligence and beauty intrigued Muhammad. However, the hadiths refer to several incidents when Muhammad became impatient with Aisha's childlike jealous outbursts against the deceased Khadija, to whom she often referred to as a "toothless old woman." This jealousy is said to have stemmed from the fact that Aisha was never able to bear any children of her own. She resented Khadija's lasting importance as being the only wife of Muhammad to bear four surviving daughters who reached adulthood. Muhammad is believed to have been very understanding and to have reasoned with Aisha to remember that she should not be envious of Khadija, but rather be respectful toward her, because she was the first to believe in his revelations:

> "She had faith in me and she shared her worldly goods with me when everyone else scorned me, and Allah has granted me her offspring and no other woman's."[3]

However, over a period of time Aisha clearly emerged as Muhammad's favorite wife and was called *habiba* (the favorite one), even though the traditional sources emphasize that Muhammad treated all his wives with respect and care. His preference for Aisha in turn generated much jealousy among some of the other wives, especially the beautiful Umm Salamah. Known far and wide for her beauty, Umm Salamah actually turned Muhammad down three times before accepting his proposal of marriage. She greatly resented Aisha and often complained to Fatima (Muhammad's youngest daughter) about Muhammad's preference for

Aisha. Gradually Aisha won most of them over to her side with her quick wit and charm. Soon all the wives consulted Aisha on everything—from mundane things such as how to apply cosmetics, to what clothes they should wear, to who should be with Muhammad on certain weeks.

Historians agree that Muhammad's death was an important turning point in Aisha's life. Widowed at 19 and faced with a lonely future—being both childless and without the prospect of remarriage—Aisha transformed herself from leading a life of quiet domesticity to becoming a major political player in the events that unfolded concerning the successor to Muhammad. She soon became embroiled in a conflict that very publicly exposed the existing long-term tensions between Fatima's family and herself.

Aisha is best remembered for her role in the famous Battle of Camel (656 CE), which took place after the assassination of Uthman, the third caliph. Unable to reconcile with the fact that Ali, Fatima's husband, would be the next caliph, Aisha joined with those opposed to Ali's accession to power. She rode to battle and commanded her camel troops and was disastrously defeated. Taken captive, she was later freed and allowed to return to Medina to lead a reclusive life. She dedicated the last years of her life to charitable endeavors and transmitting some of the *hadiths*. Although her political and military leadership reveals Aisha's great ability to transcend typical women's roles, her actions had a long-term negative impact on the status of Muslim women. For example, from her death onward, Muslim women were dissuaded from fighting battles and even excluded from formal participation in government. Also her action made succession via women impossible for the Sunnis. However, despite her failure in the Battle of Camel, Sunnis extol Aisha as being one of the primary transmitters of some 1,200 hadiths.

Fatima, the youngest daughter of Muhammad, was Aisha's main adversary. Shiites revere her as the mother of Muhammad's grandsons Husyan and Hasan. Being the Prophet's youngest daughter, Fatima was naturally very close to him but, along with her other stepmothers, she deeply resented her father's overt favoritism toward Aisha. Historians speculate that the tensions between Aisha and Fatima originated from childhood squabbles. Fatima was at least two years older than Aisha, and it must have been very difficult for Fatima to get accustomed to her. Soon after Aisha moved into Muhammad's household, Fatima was married off to Ali, the first cousin of Muhammad. Fatima often intervened on behalf of her other stepmothers when she felt that Muhammad was not being fair to his other wives. The animosity between the two became more pronounced after the death of Muhammad.

Fatima had wanted her husband, Ali, to be elected the successor after her father's death. The normally shy and quiet Fatima briefly came out of her seclusion and forcefully proclaimed that Ali was a legitimate choice. She argued that the leadership of the Muslim world should rest in the hands of individuals directly related to Muhammad and not outsiders. However, when the umma chose Abu Bakr (Aisha's father) as the first caliph, Fatima refused to acknowledge him as Muhammad's legitimate heir. She died six months after her father's death, convinced that the umma had not done justice to Muhammad's legacy. Subsequently, Ali lost three more battles and finally compromised and accepted the verdict of the umma. Anarchy prevailed after the assassination of Uthman (the third caliph), and some members of the umma elected Ali to restore political order. Far from securing peace, Ali's choice as the fourth caliph engulfed the Muslim world in more turmoil, eventually resulting in the creation of two distinct sects: the Shiites and Sunnis.

The Shiites believe that Ali and his descendants were heirs of Muhammad, because they were related to the Prophet. They recognize Ali as their first *Imam* (spiritual leader), thereby rejecting the legitimacy of the first three caliphs.

The Sunnis on the other hand argued that any devout Muslim could be a leader of the umma and accepted the first three caliphs as rightful successors of Muhammad.

The tension between Aisha and Fatima's family was not resolved after the latter's death. When Aisha publicly denounced the choice of Ali as the fourth caliph and allied with those willing to overthrow him, Zaynab (Ali and Fatima's daughter) decided to take up the mantle on behalf of her deceased mother. In the process, Zaynab lost her two sons in the Battle of Kufa (680 CE). Instead of being consumed with sorrow, Zaynab decided to participate in the battle. During a crucial moment when her brother Husayn was surrounded by troops loyal to Yazid (the next caliph), she threw herself on top of her brother to shield him from the wrath of Yazid, who came very close to killing him. When captured and brought to the royal court before Yazid, she displayed exemplary courage. Zaynab was later released and, just like her grandmother, led a reclusive life practicing Islam.

Briefly, then—after the death of Muhammad, some women belonging to his household displayed exemplary leadership qualities unusual for women's history and did not even hesitate to take up arms for the new faith.

REFORMS AIMED AT IMPROVING MUSLIM WOMEN'S STATUS

We know that some of the first women converts belonged to Muhammad's immediate family. Others came from different backgrounds and decided to convert after diverse experiences. Sources indicate that Muhammad had as many as a thousand female companions or early believers. It was the teaching of spiritual equality among all believers that drew many of these women into the expanding fold of Islam. Muhammad personally accepted devout male and female converts as spiritual partners as long as they adhered to the Five Pillars. His ideas are clearly reflected in the following Quranic verse:

> Those who surrender themselves to Allah and accept the true faith; who are devout, sincere, patient, humble, charitable, and chaste; who fast and are ever mindful of Allah—on these, both men and women, Allah will bestow forgiveness and rich reward. (33:35, p. 293)

Another sura from the Quran points out that

> The true believers, both men and women, are friends to each other. They enjoin what is just and forbid what is evil; they attend to their prayers and pay the alms tax and obey Allah and His apostle. On these Allah will have mercy. He is mighty and wise. (9:71, p. 328)

Perhaps the most famous of these non-familial early women converts was Hind, who married Abu Sayaf, a prominent member of the powerful Quraysh family. Initially, Hind was angry at Muhammad after her father, uncle, and brother were killed in the Battle of Badr (623 CE). She decided to avenge their deaths by participating in the Battle of Uhud (625 CE). It was only after her husband's conversion to Islam that Hind decided to follow him and fight for the religion rather than against it. Being a member of the leading family in Mecca, her conversion gave Islam additional social approval.

Some privileges that Islam guaranteed to women may seem ambiguous and over the ages have been subjected to reinterpretations and manipulated to strengthen or weaken the position of women. Nevertheless, one thing remains certain: The Quranic verses reforming marriage, inheritance, and divorce were aimed primarily at preserving the institution of the family, which formed the basic unit of the umma.

For example, the Quran stated that marriage was a legal contract between two believers and within this institution, men and women were expected to play a complementary role. However, there is considerable debate among historians about whether the Quran actually dictated complete obedience and loyalty from wives or whether the clause was added later. During this period, women did have a say in the choice of their partners. Even though Quranic injunctions limited a woman's ability to have several sexual partners, it specifically allowed women the right to equal sexual fulfillment within the legitimate institution of marriage. The Quran allowed the practice of *coitus interruptus* as a legitimate means of contraception. Concubinage was tolerated, though discouraged. Women could negotiate a separation based on the lack of sexual satisfaction in the marriage or if the husband had not had sexual relations with the wife for over a period of four months. The rationale behind this was that a sexually frustrated wife was more likely to commit adultery.

Polygamy became the norm in the Arabian Peninsula among males of all classes, but the number of wives a man could legally marry was restricted to four. Again there was a stipulation that all four should be treated financially and emotionally equally:

> You may marry other women who seem good to you: two, three, or four of them. But if you fear you cannot maintain equality among them, marry one only or any slave-girls you may own. This will make it easier to avoid injustice. (4:3, p. 366)

The Quran also specifically encouraged men to marry orphans, widows, or slaves, but categorically banned them from marrying non-Muslims. In addition, the Quran reformed the institution of marriage by outlawing adultery and instituting strict punishments for both adulterous men and women.

One of the popular stereotypes associated with Islam is that the laws regulating divorce were very lax. Some of the Quranic verses on divorce read as follows:

> Prophet and believers, if you divorce your wives, divorce them at the end of their waiting period. Compute their waiting period and have fear of Allah; your Lord. Do not expel them from their homes or let them go away unless they commit a proven crime . . . (65:1, p. 385)
>
> If you are in doubt concerning those of your wives who have ceased menstruating, know that their waiting period is three months. And let the same be the waiting period of those who have not yet menstruated. As for pregnant women, their term shall end with their confinement. (65:5, p. 385)
>
> Do not harass them so as to make life intolerable for them. If they are with child, maintain them until the end of their confinement, and if after that, they give suck to their children, give them their pay and consult together in all reasonableness. (65:6, p. 385)

A careful analysis of these suras reveals certain provisions laid out for the protection of women. For example, there was a three-month waiting period to determine whether the wife being divorced was pregnant. If she was, then the husband had to promise to financially support her until the child was born. This trend seems to be related to the broader changes taking place in society. The gradual consolidation of power in the hands of men resulting from the increased economic prosperity gave them the motive to divorce to consolidate their familial assets, and this was legitimized in the Quran.

Perhaps the greatest change that Islam brought to women's legal position was granting them the right of inheritance and possession of wealth. In pre-Islamic Arabia, as we have seen, patrilineal descent was the most common practice, and even though there were rich women (like Khadija) who controlled their wealth, they were the exception to the rule. Patrilineal descent largely left women economically dependent on men. The Quran reformed and implemented new rules of inheritance in favor of women:

> Women shall have a share in what their parents and kinsmen leave:
> whether it be little or much, they are legally entitled to their share.
> (4:7, p. 367)

Even though the Quran stipulated that a male child would inherit twice that of a daughter, women still were guaranteed inheritance from their fathers and, when widowed, from their husband's estate. Eventually, over a period of time, as the status of Muslim women fluctuated and many social restrictions were placed on them, the right of inheritance would become an asset for Muslim women. Women were also allowed to stipulate their alimony. In case of a divorce, the bride was entitled to her alimony and to all bridal gifts: "Give women their dowry as a free gift" (4:2, p. 366).

The Quran categorically denounced the pre-Islamic practice of female infanticide, as some of these verses suggest, and warned that if anybody violated this law, they would be punished later by Allah on the Day of Judgment.

> When the birth of a girl is announced to one of them, his face grows dark
> and he is filled with inward gloom. Because of the bad news he hides
> himself from men: should he keep her with disgrace or bury her under
> dust? How ill they judge! Evil are the ways of those who deny the life to
> come. But most sublime are the ways of Allah. He is the Mighty, the Wise
> one. (16:57, p. 308)
> When the infant girl buried alive is asked for what crimes she was
> slain; when the records of men's deeds are laid open and heaven is
> stripped bare; when Hell burns fiercely and Paradise is brought near:
> then each soul shall know what it has done. (81:8, p.17)

However, the Quran was ambiguous on the issue of whether women could publicly participate in religious ceremonies and pray in mosques. Muhammad did not exclude the women of his family from praying in the mosques, but he did ask them not to participate in religious activities during their menstrual cycle.

After the reign of the first four caliphs, the Umayyads came to power in 661 CE. They were successful in extending the boundaries of Islam into Africa, Spain, and frontiers of Asia, thereby creating the *dar-ul-Islam* (lands under Islamic rule). Even though the Umayyads gave preference to Arabs over other subjects, cross-cultural exchanges allowed for certain non-Islamic practices, such as veiling, to become an acceptable practice for upper-class Muslim women. The Umayyad caliph Walid (705–715 CE) required all women in his royal harem be veiled. Walid was attracted to beautiful non-Arab women, but to conceal this secret addiction from his Arab queens, he kept them secluded so that the two groups would not interact with one another. Emulating his example, several court officials and wealthy mercantile families adopted this practice. Historians argue that gradually the practice of veiling became more of a reflection of the family's social status rather than just display of modesty. Plagued with internal problem from the beginning, the Umayyads were a short-lived dynasty and ultimately fell to the Abbasids in 750 CE.

WOMEN IN THE ABBASID CALIPHATE (CA. 750–1258 CE)

The Abbasid caliphate ruled from a new capital at Baghdad, which became the center of an Islamic cultural efflorescence. The early Abbasids succeeded in balancing the political and religious tensions existing among the Shiites and Sunnis and other ethnic groups, thereby leading to the creation of an economically vibrant and culturally diverse empire. The Quran and the hadiths provided the guidelines to individual caliphs and theologians on how to administer the empire. As the Abbasid caliphate became too far-flung, one of the caliphs' priorities was to ensure a stable government. They did this by establishing a uniform legal system, among other things. Though the Umayyad caliphs had experimented with the idea of establishing a uniform legal code, it was under the Abbasids that the four orthodox schools of Islamic law were formulated. Collectively known as the Sharia, it was a product of not only Arab culture but also assimilation of customs from the adjacent regions and the conquered peoples. Over a period of time, certain sections of the Sharia came to be regarded as immutable. However, there is consensus that sources such as legal commentaries and *fatwa* collections (legal opinions) did interpret and re-interpret the Sharia. Nevertheless, this wide-ranging corpus of legal principles regulated the personal, commercial, property-based, and sexual relations of all Muslims. Therefore, these laws became indispensable as a guide for creation of subsequent Islamic societies.

Similar to the *Laws of Manu* in Gupta India, the Sharia dictated the lives of women by reintroducing and mandating practices limiting women's participation in society. In addition, respected Muslim theologians through their writings reinforced the notion that uncontrolled female sexuality was dangerous for society. Therefore, they argued for ways in which they could control female sexuality and, in the process, provided the rationale for adopting laws constricting women's behavior. Veiling and physical seclusion were made mandatory, and the Sharia instituted ghastly penalties for any form of sexual transgression. Purity of women's bodies now reflected family honor. Therefore, beginning with the Abbasid caliphate, the burden of upholding family honor shifted primarily to women, and the ideals spelled out in the Sharia greatly affected the eventual development of Muslim tradition.

FAMILIAL ROLES

The ideals laid out in the Sharia dictated the lives of elite Muslim women during the Abbasid caliphate. Although the caliphs and theologians wanted these laws to be applied universally, in reality it would have had the strongest impact upon the lives of elite Muslim women. In the absence of sources from lower-class women, we can speculate that these laws must have had a limited impact on them. Overall, the imposition of the Sharia led to the loss of some freedoms Muslim women had enjoyed previously. Many of the changes are similar to those we have seen in other parts of the world.

DAUGHTERS: CHILDHOOD, ADOLESCENCE, AND MARRIAGE. A common pattern that is reflective of all patriarchal societies is that the birth of a girl was not a joyous occasion, irrespective of the economic status of her family. Arabic poems often express the pessimism that parents felt at the birth of a daughter, as does this example from an anonymous source:

> How can I help it that she is a girl?
> She washes my hair and is a credit to me
> She brings me the veil that has fallen down,
> And when she is bigger and is eight,
> She will look splendid in a Yemenite gown,
> I will marry you to a Marwan or Muawiya,
> Noble men, for a high dowry certainly.[4]

Right from her birth, the parents were worried about her marriage and began saving for her dowry. Usually on the seventh day after her birth, the girl's hair was ritually cut off and she was formally initiated into Islam.

In the absence of formal sources, one can only speculate that girls belonging to affluent families must have been taught Arabic by the male family members. A common pattern was that little girls were socialized into familial roles from an early age. They were also familiarized with the Quranic injunctions on sexual propriety and modesty. In some areas under Abbasid control, pubescent girls underwent an important rite of passage in preparation for the next stage in their life cycle as wives: the veiling and physical seclusion of girls from their male peers.

Veiling as a custom was widespread among the upper classes throughout ancient Mesopotamia and the Byzantine Empire. The first time it appears in the Quran was as a revelation to protect the honor of women belonging only to Muhammad's household. Though the Umayyad caliph Walid was the first Muslim ruler after Muhammad to require the women of his royal harem to be veiled, it did not became an official policy until the time of Abbasid Caliph Mansour (754–775 CE). He went to the extreme of ordering the construction of a separate bridge for women to cross the Euphrates River. This became a mandatory practice rather than a voluntary one once it was ordained in the Sharia.

During the Abbasid period, the growing popularity of veiling was most likely associated with economic prosperity. More and more men could now afford to keep their wives in seclusion, as it came to reflect a man's socioeconomic status in society. Another argument used to justify the increasing popularity of veiling was the concept that the image of women's bodies was a threat to the stability of society. In other words, women were viewed as *fitnas*—femmes fatales. This concept was totally new to Islam, as the Quran was ambiguous about the nature of women. Historians speculate that it was probably the result of cross-cultural connections. Thereafter, women's sexuality was seen as a dangerous force that needed to be controlled, and one way this could be achieved was by secluding them.

The writings of Imam Abu Hamid al-Ghazali (d. 1111), the noted Muslim theologian, were representative of this genre of thinking. In his famous manual *Nasihat al-Muluk* ("Advice to Kings"), Al-Ghazali argued:

> A woman's piety and seclusion are favors from God. . . . It is not permissible for a stranger (male) to hear the sound of a pestle being pounded by a woman he does not know. If he knocks at the door, it is not proper for the woman to answer him softly and easily because men's hearts can be drawn to women for most trifling reason and the greatest number of them. However, if the woman has to answer the knock, she should stick her finger in her mouth so that her voice sounds like the voice of an old woman.[5]

Another noted Muslim theologian, Nasir-al-Din Tusi (d. 1274), concurred with al-Ghazali and warned husbands to keep their wives preoccupied with housework or else they might be tempted to have an extramarital affair. This theme occurred repeatedly in popular Arabic fictional works, for example, *The Arabian Nights.* In the many of the short stories, women were depicted as using their beauty to seduce men.

Historians are still debating the impact of veiling and physical seclusion on lower-class women and those who lived in the regions to which Islam spread subsequently. In the Islamic heartland (the Arabian peninsula), veiling and physical seclusion were practiced mostly among the upper-class women. However, by the beginning of the Abbasid caliphate, Islam had arrived in sub-Saharan Africa via trade in a manner similar to the spread of Hinduism and Buddhism to Southeast Asia. Initially only elites and affluent mercantile families adopted the religion to consolidate their political and economic positions. It was only over time that Islam percolated down to other classes. As a consequence, many traditional sub-Saharan practices were diffused within the fold of Islam, leading to the rise of a highly syncretic form, very different from the that in the Islamic heartland.

This pattern is clearly evidenced from the travel accounts of Muhammad ibn-Abdullah ibn Battuta (1304–1369). A Muslim scholar from Morocco, he was commissioned by the local ruler to travel across the *dar-ul-Islam* (territories under Islamic rule: Spain to China) and record his observations. The result was a voluminous travelogue that recorded his observations on social customs and behavior of kings. In addition, Battuta vividly talks about physical seclusion and veiling in the Islamic states of Mali and Ghana. Being a devout Muslim, he was stupefied to observe ceremonial nudity in Mali. He wrote:

> One of their disapproved acts is that their female servants and slave girls and little girls appear before men naked, with their privy parts uncovered. During Ramadan, I saw many of them in this state, for it is the custom of the *farariyya* [princes] to break their fast in the house of the sultan, and each one brings his food carried by twenty or more of his slave girls, they all being naked.[6]

He also pointed out that the royal women did not conform to the Islamic practice of veiling and that they appeared before strangers without covering their breasts.

> Another is that their women go into the sultan's presence naked and uncovered, and that his daughters go naked. On the night of 25 Ramadan, I saw about 200 slave girls bringing out food from his place naked, having with them two of his daughters with rounded breasts having no covering.[7]

Another anomaly from the Islamic heartland that Battuta discusses is the relative freedom with which the two genders interacted in Islamic sub-Saharan Africa. Referring to the small town in Walata, he recounted how Muslim men were not jealous of their women befriending foreigners of the opposite sex.

Most of the inhabitants there belong to the Masufa [a Berber people] whose women . . . have a higher status than the men. . . . These are Muslims who observe the prayer and study *fiqh* [religious laws] and memorize the Koran. As for their women they have no modesty in the presence of men and do not veil themselves in spite of their assiduity in prayer. . . . The women there have friends and companions among foreign men. . . . One of them may enter his house and find his wife with her man friend without making any objection.[8]

Due to limited evidence, we can only speculate about how the practices affected lower-class women in the Islamic heartland. They likely wore more apparel than their sub-Saharan sisters, but were unlikely to have practiced veiling and physical seclusion. As we have seen elsewhere, lower-class women had to work outside the house in order to support their families. It is likely that practices such as veiling and physical seclusion (like foot binding in China) would have interfered with their day-to-day activities.

WIVES. Another common pattern was that marriages were made compulsory for girls during the Abbasid caliphate. Pre-pubescent marriages were very widespread. In those cases girls lived in their parents' houses until they reached puberty, after which they were allowed to join their husbands. This lower age at marriage directly reflected the broader changes occurring in society. First, as has already been discussed, family honor became irrevocably entwined with preserving a girl's virginity before marriage. Second, young brides were believed to be more malleable and more easily trained to be obedient and loyal to the mother-in-law, other older wives, and especially the husband.

During the Abbasid caliphate, marriages were usually arranged between Muslim families of equal economic status. The groom's mother played a crucial role in the selection of the bride. After the marriage was arranged, the bride was allowed to state her own alimony in the case of a divorce. Weddings were generally elaborate affairs full of festivities. Many of the customs surrounding a Muslim wedding were intended to bring the couple together in the presence of other relatives for the first time. For example, the wedding night was an important event of the ceremony. Female relatives waited anxiously outside the locked door of the newly wedded couple's room just to hear the young bride scream in pain. This cry symbolized that the marriage had been consummated, and after that there was much rejoicing and relief for both the bride and groom's families. By Western standards this seems very intrusive but given the situation in which the marriages were arranged, the girl never really had an opportunity to get to know her future husband. Often she saw his face only on the day of the wedding.

The Sharia reiterated the Quranic injunction that both husband and wife had equal right to be sexually fulfilled in the relationship. The theologian Al-Ghazali wrote extensively in *The Revivification of Religious Sciences* on the subject of female sexuality and pointed out that denying females their right to sexual fulfillment could result in social turmoil.

Though men could legally marry four wives, polygamous households were not universal and were certainly reflective of a man's economic position in society. Lower-class men often could not afford to keep multiple wives. Divorce was viewed negatively and only a last resort for couples unable to solve their marital problems. The Sharia generally advised couples to seek counsel from a judge before the decision to terminate the marriage. When it came to who had the right to initiate a divorce, the balance was heavily tilted to the side of men. But the Sharia also specified that if a woman was not fulfilled in the marriage or if her husband was impotent, then she had the right to legally terminate the marriage. Besides, if a couple divorced, the wife retained the right to her bridal gifts and alimony. To maintain the institution of the family, the Sharia imposed ghastly punishments on both adulterous men and women. For example, if a woman was found guilty, she could be stoned to death in a public place.

As transpired elsewhere, society's privileged men dictated what constituted femininity during the Abbasid caliphate. For example, an eleventh-century handbook entitled *The Book of Marriage* gave women explicit guidelines on how to enhance their sexual attractiveness for their husbands. One of the ideal beauty traits in today's world is slenderness, but the opposite was true for women during the Abbasid caliphate. This handbook pointed out that

> Since a man likes a woman to be fat and plump, for then he experiences, when he sleeps with her, a pleasure which he does not have with a thin woman, I mean, a slight woman, we list here foods which make a delicate woman fat, make her flesh firm, give her skin a clear color and enable her to win the favor of her husband when she always eats them.[9]

The anonymous author listed foods high in calorie content that slender women could consume to increase their weight. For example, honey and different kinds of nuts were prescribed, along with red meat and dairy products.

There were also many beauty manuals targeting the elite women in society. These handbooks suggested different homemade concoctions: compounds for whitening teeth, facials for a flawless skin, potions to cleanse the body, and depilatory agents to rid it of excessive facial or body hair. Deodorants and perfumes of different kinds were also recommended. Henna was an important and popular cosmetic item recommended as a conditioner for black lustrous hair. Jet-black hair was preferred to either blonde or brown hair. Henna paste was applied to the hands during festive seasons and gradually it evolved into a distinct body art form, similar to body piercing or tattooing in Southeast Asia.

The practice of veiling allowed only the woman's eyes to be seen by outsiders, and therefore enhancing them with black kohl was another common way to beautify oneself. During the Abbasid caliphate there was a distinct preference for women with black eyes, since blue or brown eyes were regarded as ominous and the Quran specified that women with black eyes were the ones to go to heaven. Other assets that made up the feminine ideal were a small mouth, straight nose, heavy hips, and ample thighs. A beautiful woman was one who was soft spoken and had a pleasant laugh. During the Abbasid period, poets compared a beautiful woman to "a full-moon" or "a swaying cypress tree" or "flowers from the gardens of Paradise," and her disposition was "sweeter than cool spring water."[10]

According to Al-Ghazali, an ideal wife was one who "was beautiful, non-temperamental, with black pupils, and long hair, big eyes, white skin, and in love with her husband, looking at no one but him."[11] Al-Ghazali also reiterated that an obedient and faithful wife was a rare gift from Allah. His view was corroborated by another theologian who suggested that an ideal wife should diligently observe the following: She should submit to her "husband humbly," "listen and obey him," pay attention to "his wishes to eat and sleep," "watch over his property," "take care of his family," and finally she should not "oppose him, nor betray any secrets."[12]

Elite wives of a polygamous marriage generally resided in the harem— the woman's section of the household (known as the *harim* in Arabic or *zenana* in Persian). The development of this institution coincided with the formal introduction of the practice of veiling and physical seclusion during the Abbasid period. As a consequence, structural changes were made to houses belonging to the upper classes. Often the courtyard surrounding the harem would be enclosed by high walls to give the women privacy.

A common Western stereotype of the harem, perpetuated by Hollywood movies, is that it was where scantily dressed women entertained men and indulged in lascivious behavior. This image was far removed from the reality. Recent research has shown that it was where women performed their day-to-day activities that ranged from cooking, entertaining, relaxing, and taking care of children.

Since most upper-class Muslim households were polygamous, there was a hierarchy among the different wives. The oldest wife would be looked upon as a matriarch of the women's quarters, and she was the one responsible for dividing up the household chores on a rotating basis. The younger wives generally deferred to her suggestions, given that in most cases there were substantial age differences between the senior and junior wives. Another important responsibility of the oldest wife was to set up a schedule for the husband to visit his different wives on a rotating basis. As the oldest wife aged and the sons or stepsons started marrying, she helped socialize the younger daughters-in-law.

It was natural that the wives were jealous of one another and this often led to family problems. On the whole however, these households proved to be mutually satisfying for the wives. Not only did they form long-lasting bonds but during times of tragedy they could depend on each other for emotional support. Further, spatial segregation and veiling did not mean that women never stepped outside the harem. If they needed to go outside the house to watch entertainers or visit relatives, they were usually accompanied by a male relative.

Generally the Abbasid rulers had harems comprising thousands of beautiful women—legal wives, concubines, and slave girls. These imperial harems were under the control of the queen mother—the oldest legal wife of the caliph—and the entire premises were guarded by eunuchs (castrated males), who were imported from Central Asia.

MOTHERHOOD.   The next stage in a woman's life was motherhood. Here as elsewhere, becoming a mother of a son validated a woman's position in society. After the young bride moved into her husband's house, it was expected that she conceive fairly quickly. If she was the oldest daughter-in-law, the failure to produce a male heir could have especially serious consequences. In a polygamous household, this was a legitimate reason for a man to marry other wives or even dissolve the marriage.

Even though the Sharia is ambiguous on the issue of abortion, women had access to different methods, especially when the life of the mother was in danger. Many theologians also agreed that a pregnancy should not be terminated after four months. A woman was generally expected to give birth four or five times but, if she chose not to have more children, she had access to birth control in the form of *coitus interruptus.*

Similar to other cultures, childbirth was a dangerous experience and women midwives played a crucial role in delivering the baby in a secluded room in the harem. It was especially painful for those women who had undergone circumcision, a non-Islamic practice that grew in importance in many Islamic communities as time went on. There were often elaborate rituals performed by the women of the household for the safe delivery of the baby. After the birth, usually the mother and child underwent a period of purification, after which they were allowed to join the rest of the family. As in most cultures, ceremonies involving pregnancy and childbirth were essentially women's.

WIDOWHOOD.   Unlike Gupta India, where the *Laws of Manu* and the prevalence of the custom of sati kept women from remarrying, Islam contained no such rigid rule. During the Abbasid caliphate, the Sharia encouraged widow remarriage and also permitted levirate marriages. Besides, the Sharia allowed widows to inherit a certain share from her husband's estate. If the widow had minor children, then she was the sole executor of her husband's estate until the sons gained maturity. A widow was therefore never financially dependent on her sons. This economic independence gave her the freedom to choose to remarry or remain single if she so wished.

ECONOMIC ACTIVITIES

During the Abbasid caliphate, a woman's legal right to inherit, combined with the widespread popularity of physical seclusion, gave Muslim women unprecedented economic opportunities belied by their physical constraints.

With the influx of trade and economic prosperity, elite women belonging to affluent families no longer performed household chores. Slaves were employed to carry out arduous domestic jobs. Ironically, even though these elite women had help, just as we saw in other world areas, merely supervising the housework took up a significant portion of their time. When they had free time, they concentrated on other ventures. For example, court records and legal documents have revealed that many of these women used their large inheritances to patronize the buildings of community centers, religious schools, mosques, and even public parks. Some even reinvested their wealth in joint ventures and sometimes in import-export businesses. As the practice of veiling barred them from directly negotiating business transactions with men, the deliberations would often be undertaken through an intermediary. The popular fictional work *The Arabian Nights* refers to many women characters who were involved in long-distance trade. It should be emphasized, however, that as more and more women became prosperous, they felt tremendous societal pressure to conform to their familial roles only. For example, the theologian Tusi warned men not to marry women who were involved in any form of business, as this would eventually cause marital problems.

During the Abbasid period as affluent women had plentiful wealth to spend on themselves and their families, one notices an increase in demand for cosmetics, perfumes, jewelry, fashionable clothes, and other exotic items. This phenomenon in turn generated the evolution of small industries that provided employment to lower-class women. Furthermore, the institutions of harem and physical seclusion opened up other opportunities for lower-class women. Not only were they employed in the traditional industries such as agriculture, silk manufacturing, or rug making, they could become hairdressers, matchmakers, seamstresses, embroiderers, professional mourners, or even companions for elite women residing in the harems.

Like Chinese women, those lower-class women employed in the sericulture found their lives difficult and vulnerable to health hazards. They were involved in separating the silk ball from the worm and cleaning, carding, spinning, and finally, weaving the cloth. However, an interesting departure was that Muslim women were not engaged in the textile industry (which manufactures cotton cloth), since textiles were generally produced in large-scale factories where men were employed. Rug making was an industry in which women workers were specifically preferred to men. Some lower-class women were trained by their husbands to contribute to the family business. For example, women became calligraphers or artisans; some learned how to make difficult metal handicrafts.

Abbasid society was hierarchical, and slaves were placed at the bottom of the social ladder. As mentioned earlier, in particular women slaves were employed in large numbers as domestic help for upper-class households. They were also engaged in laborious agricultural tasks. If the slaves were beautiful and knew how to read or write, they were in great demand, as affluent men would buy them at high prices and make them a part of their harem. Since Islam encouraged men to marry their slave women, sometimes women slaves could aspire to gain their legal status through the institution of marriage.

Some slaves who were not so fortunate continued to live as concubines. Concubinage was allowed under Islamic law, and a man could keep as many as he wanted. Muhammad himself had married a concubine named Marya who bore him a son Ibrahim, who unfortunately did not survive his infancy. Prostitution, however, was strictly prohibited by the Sharia. One can only speculate that, given the ubiquity of this profession, there must have been places or areas where this timeless activity took place clandestinely.

POLITICAL ACCESS

Women could indirectly wield power in court circles during the Abbasid caliphate. As previously mentioned, women belonging to Muhammad's household participated prominently in the politics of the early Islamic period. Even though there were no women rulers during the Abbasid caliphate, two women played important roles to ensure that their sons or husbands stayed in power. They were Khaizuran, the mother of the Abbasid ruler Harun al-Rashid, and his wife, Zubaida.

Khaizuran was originally a Yemenite slave and became a part of the royal harem of Caliph al-Mahdi, Harun's father. Gradually, she moved her way up the hierarchy to become his favorite wife and used her special status to help out her other relatives. For example, she acquired for her brother the covetous job of being the governor of Yemen, she married her sister off to a member of the royal family, and she used her position to influence court members to support her son as the next heir. After the death of her husband, in what became a particularly messy struggle for succession, Khaizuran was able to ensure her son's success. She continued to play a behind-the-scenes role until al-Rashid was able to fully consolidate his position. He became one of the greatest Abbasid rulers.

After her death in 789, al-Rashid's wife, Zubaida, emerged as a powerful woman who exercised tremendous influence on her husband. She was also his first cousin and, even though al-Rashid had beautiful women in his imperial harem, he clearly favored Zubaida. It was her wit, charm, as well as intelligence that drew him to her. There was a brief period during his reign when al-Rashid wanted to give up the throne just to spend time with her, but Zubaida persuaded him to continue ruling. She was a very cultured woman, and many historians argue that the cultural vitality that characterized al-Rashid's reign was largely due to Zubaida. She transformed Baghdad and the imperial palace into a centerpiece of Islamic architecture. It is believed that she requisitioned sequined and bejeweled tapestries as well as pure gold plates for the palace. In addition, she set the fashion trend for upper-class women in Baghdad. Later on, she also tried to manipulate the court into accepting her incompetent son, al-Amin, as the next caliph. But she was unsuccessful, as Harun al-Rashid chose another of his sons to succeed him. In many ways then, the wealth and grandeur of the royal court of the Abbasids that has captured the minds of many was largely Zubaida's contribution.

SUFISM AND WOMEN

A commonality that Islam shares with the other world religions is that even though these patriarchal faiths have traditionally excluded women from officiating in public ceremonies, they have played prominent roles in groups emphasizing a mystical connection to the divine. Sufism (from the Arabic word *suf*, which means coarse wool clothing) was a mystical sect within Islam that advocated a direct union of the believer with Allah. Some speculate that it arose around the same time that Muhammad was preaching the new religion of Islam. This movement slowly gained visibility when it began voicing its discontent with the increasing powers of the *ulemas*—the Muslim theologians who became the main interpreters of the Sharia—and the extravagant lifestyles of the Ummayad and Abbasid caliphs. Sufism emphasized leading a simple life, practicing celibacy, and dedicating one's life to Allah. Sufis were itinerant, wore coarse woolen clothes, and spent their entire day in prayer.

Women were attracted to Sufism in large numbers. Due to the absence of any formal monastic order in Islam, Sufism allowed women an alternative outlet similar to that of Buddhist or Christian nuns. Those women who wanted to absolve themselves from familial duties or gain intellectual fulfillment were welcomed into this mystical sect, where their communication with God might be as direct and important as any man's. Another example of the parity of gender relations in Sufism was that women could achieve sainthood.

A woman who played an important role in popularizing Sufism was Rabi'a al'-Adawiyya (ca. 717–801 CE), who was born in Basra, in modern Iraq. Not much is known about her early childhood; some speculate that she was born a slave but eventually freed from bondage. She was known for her beauty and received multiple marriage proposals from an early age. However, she kept rejecting these offers and instead believed that by leading a life of celibacy, she would achieve her goal in life—that was to praise and be with Allah. Rabi'a joined the Sufi order, and by her sheer dedication and hard work, soon emerged as a respected leader. Stories say that, even after renouncing the material life and becoming a Sufi, she continued to receive marriage proposals but declared that her love for Allah was supreme. She professed no romantic feelings for another mortal being.

Sufis today believe Rabi'a performed many miracles during her lifetime, but perhaps she is best known for engaging in theological conversations with her male counterparts, especially the renowned male Sufi, Hasan-al-Basri. He was apparently overwhelmed at Rabi'a's intellectual precocity and eventually admitted to her arguments. Rabi'a also challenged other male Sufis in public debates, often winning these contests. Therefore, she is a rare example of an extraordinary woman who resisted societal pressures and carved out her own destiny.

CONCLUSION

The status of women in the Islamic world changed over a period of time. A comparison of the lives of pre-Islamic Arabian women leading two distinct lifestyles shows that their status was not homogenous, but conditioned by the broader changes taking place in society. Within the patriarchal framework, Bedouin women and women from urban centers both shared certain relative freedoms. For example, women were allowed to participate in economic ventures, could move around freely in society, accompany their men to the battlefield as nurses, and participate openly in the pagan religion. Despite the widespread prevalence of female infanticide, physical seclusion was not yet a universal practice, and women were considered to be valuable contributing members of society. With the initial coming of Islam, reforms benefiting the status of women were introduced. Female infanticide was abolished, veiling and physical seclusion were not widely practiced, and women could emerge as leaders during the early Islamic period. In addition they were granted the important legal right of inheritance and spiritual equality with men. This has led some to argue that Muhammad was a reformer who helped improve women's legal and economic position. However, with the rise of the Abbasid caliphate and the transcribing of the Sharia, women's status overall took a downward turn as their roles became increasingly constricted. Even then, the Islamic world did not create a uniform experience for women during the Abbasid caliphate, as the record of sub-Saharan Muslim women demonstrates. Within this model, certain women were still able to exercise their own independence and challenge the ideals.

CHAPTER SEVEN

WESTERN EUROPE IN THE CENTRAL AND LATE MIDDLE AGES (1050–1500 CE)

An all-pervasive Christian worldview, coupled with the strong influence of an institutional church, distinguished the lives of European women from their counterparts elsewhere in the world during these centuries. The forces of regionalism and social class within Europe certainly existed, varying the daily patterns of life among women, but because of the common culture of Western Christendom, there was also a certain level of homogeneity. This chapter focuses the Central (1050–1300 CE) and Late (1300–1500 CE) Middle Ages, centuries that saw rapid changes in the realms of politics, society, and religion—all of which subsequently made their mark upon women's lives.

During this time, the power of the church hierarchy increased, European cities became more numerous, and political states in some areas grew more centralized. In the broadest terms, these trends eventually corresponded with an increased regulation of women's economic opportunities and narrowed the range of political and religious activities women could undertake with public approbation. Yet the situation for women was certainly not one of unilateral decline: The standard of living for the population generally increased in the Central Middle Ages, and in the Later Middle Ages many women exercised greater control over their marriages. Throughout the period, some women took religious or political paths that risked public disapproval of state and church authorities. It is important to recognize, however, that women who protested their situation or who undertook ventures normally allowed to men acted not out of a belief in women's equality with men but out of medieval concerns: to achieve personal or familial wealth or good standing within their local communities, or to express religious piety. Indeed, the formation of the patrilineal states and the influence of the male-dominated Catholic church would have been impossible without the complicit cooperation of high-status women, as we shall see. In this chapter, we shall examine the ways in which the culture of Western Europe during the Central and Late Middle Ages influenced women's place in society, their access to political power, and their participation in religious affairs.

QUESTIONS FOR STUDENT ANALYSIS

1. As the Middle Ages grew to a close, the variety of women's occupations narrowed, as several important trades became monopolized by male craftsmen. What factors caused these changes?

2. In what ways did the lives of noblewomen parallel the lives of their poorer counterparts? Include in your response the issues of how much control women had over their marriage choices and their business opportunities and take into consideration the differences among women living in different parts of western Europe.

3. How do writings left by medieval churchmen portray women? How do their stereotypes reflect both misogynistic and respectful attitudes toward the female gender? Compare the biases in sources dealing with women written by Christian ecclesiastics from the Middle Ages with those authored by Islamic theologians in the Abbasid caliphate.

4. Why were some medieval women drawn to life in a convent, others to the beguine life, and still others to an existence as an anchoress? Which types of religious lifestyles were most approved by ecclesiastic authorities, and why?

WESTERN EUROPE FROM THE END OF THE ROMAN EMPIRE THROUGH THE EARLY MIDDLE AGES (CA. 460–1050 CE)

The Roman Empire had vanished in western Europe by the end of the fifth century CE, and with it dissolved many of the economic and political connections that had united the Mediterranean world. Whereas northern Africa, Spain, and the eastern Mediterranean came under the control of Islamic emirates, European unity broke apart. In eastern Europe, the

Roman emperors continued to govern a relatively cosmopolitan and affluent region, now called the Byzantine Empire. In the west, however, a wide
variety of political states existed, many of them controlled by Germanic
peoples, whose leaders continued to appropriate the traditions of the vanishing Roman world.

As the political influence of Rome faded, the force of Christianity
gave Europe a new religious cohesion. There, the former western portion of the Roman Empire witnessed an institutional church formed sepa-
rately from state offices. The leader of Western Christendom, known as
the pope, resided in Rome and was regarded as the leading voice in theological matters. In the early centuries of its existence, the papacy exerted
little influence on secular (non-religious) rulers; the pope's primary role
was organizing and influencing the religious officials beneath him. Most
important were the bishops, who governed areas that paralleled the
ancient Roman administrative units called dioceses. Priests served under
the bishops and eventually reached numbers great enough to minister
to the peasants who occupied the European countryside. Since women
were not permitted to fill any of these leadership positions, their influence
in the institutional church came from other avenues. One of these was
through monasticism.

Monks lived amongst themselves, by and large separated from others in society, but they formed a particularly important group during the
Middle Ages because of their education. Most of the extant sources for
European history between the fall of Rome and the Central Middle Ages
were written and preserved by these religious people. Monks were of
course mostly interested in spiritual matters, and therefore most of the
documents from this era are tinged with their special religious perspective. Most monks were men from elite families, and some wealthy women
also took up a monastic vocation, swearing to uphold the tenets of the
church hierarchy and live as sequestered nuns.

Women's status in this early part of the Middle Ages varied widely
across Europe, but the Germanic peoples generally viewed females as
property. For example, when a man raped a woman, his society punished
him for "theft," not for injury to another human. Polygamy, or having
multiple wives, was a common practice, especially among the elite. Even
Christian kings kept numerous wives, despite the fact that this practice
was technically forbidden by the institutional church. Many Germanic
groups prohibited women from inheriting property. Eventually, some of
the harsher treatment of women lessened, and numerous law codes permitted women to inherit and forbade polygamy.

THE CENTRAL AND LATE MIDDLE AGES (CA. 1050–1300 AND 1300–1500 CE)

POLITICS AND SOCIETY IN THE CENTRAL MIDDLE AGES

By 1050 CE, much of the political chaos that had hampered early medieval Europe had come to an end, and the states of Italy, Germany, France, and England were emerging. Various kinds of governments existed in the Central and Later Middle Ages: generally, strong kings ruled in England and France, a (usually) weak emperor tried to rein in the power of princes in Germany. Italy remained a political mish-mash, made up of city-states, oligarchies, papal lands, and individual lordships. During the Central Middle Ages, relative political stability went hand-in-hand with economic prosperity. The most important political conflicts of this time were the Crusades (the First Crusade began in 1096), the holy wars sanctioned by the pope that occurred in the eastern Mediterranean. The object of the Crusades, as professed by the papacy, was to take this area, particularly the land around which Jesus had traveled, out of the hands of Muslim leaders and back under Christian control. In truth, there were many reasons that knights, kings, queens, and peasants of varying ages made the arduous journey from their homelands to fight in the eastern Mediterranean. Piety, greed, and lust for battle were all important motives.

Although the Crusades brought horrific bloodshed to Christians and Muslims alike and ultimately failed to achieve their goal of permanent occupation of the Holy Lands, western Europeans benefited from these wars in several ways. First, the Crusades mitigated the amount of violent bloodshed within Europe, which was helpful in establishing a greater degree of peace, allowing local communities to flourish. Second, they brought Europeans into contact with the trade routes of Eurasia, which was financially beneficial. And third, the new connections with peoples outside of Europe enabled a great transfer of knowledge to take place. The number zero, for example, only came into use in Europe because of the Crusades via contact with Muslim scholarship, and the influence of Islamic learning in the areas of astronomy and medicine also had a long-lasting effect on Western European academics.

Economic prosperity and population growth characterized the Central Middle Ages. Farmers learned to rotate their crops on different fields, utilized more advanced ploughs, and made greater use of windmills, resulting in a greater agricultural surplus than Europeans had seen in centuries. With more food available, the population expanded, and more and more people began to live in the cities, which flourished as they had not done since the heyday of the Roman Empire. Although slavery continued to exist, it was a relatively unimportant part of the economy. In the Central Middle Ages, many of the peasant farmers were serfs—people who were not considered property but who were nevertheless legally bound to the land. This period also witnessed a great era of building, both of fortified stone castles and the ornate churches known as cathedrals, where bishops presided.

POLITICS AND SOCIETY IN THE LATE MIDDLE AGES

Political violence within Europe increased in the Late Middle Ages during the Hundred Years' War (1337–1453), an age of episodic battles between England and France. The Hundred Years' War drove these kingdoms into grave debt, ruined one of the most significant banks in Europe, devastated large parts of the French countryside, and caused countless deaths to both soldiers and civilians caught in the bloodshed. Even greater turmoil was caused by the bubonic plague or the Black Death, which arrived in Italy in 1347 and quickly spread from there. This particular strain of the disease had been ravaging East Asia and the Middle East, but brought particular distress to Western Europeans. By the fourteenth century, the food surplus had ended and peasants were farming on even the poorest land available. Their weakened immune systems succumbed easily to the flea-borne sickness, and the plague's effects were worsened by a lack of medical knowledge and extremely unhygienic conditions. Approximately one-third of the population died from the disease's first wave, and the Black Death continued its breakouts for centuries afterward.

Although the destruction of the plague was immeasurable, the loss of peasant life made labor a scarcer commodity, which pushed wages for peasants higher and enabled farmers to concentrate on the best land rather than scraping by on poor soil. Many peasants who had been legally obligated to farm their lords' lands rose in social status to become free wage earners, and for the first time in history, many ordinary Europeans began to eat meat regularly. Wealthy landlords unsuccessfully tried to resist freeing their peasants and to limit the growth of wages, and in places peasants revolted against their poor treatment. The immensity of the Black Death's influence can be seen in the artwork that developed during the period, as a fascination with death led to carvings that depicted decaying bodies, skeletons leading rich and poor in a dance, and a focus on Christ in death.

RELIGIOUS CHANGES IN THE CENTRAL MIDDLE AGES

Important changes within Christianity also occurred. The papacy's authority began to grow. No longer was the pope a mere theological director with little influence on secular rulers, but his status as a religious leader had become so great that monarchs and prelates began to reckon with him as an equal. On occasion, a pope's threat to excommunicate (exclude from the church) a state official was terrifying enough to alter the political policy of great states. Aside from the pope's importance as a statesman and religious supervisor, the papacy influenced Europe in other ways as well: Papal bureaucracy utilized documents much more than other institutions had done, and this practice became thorough enough to inspire a greater usage of the written word throughout western Europe. A corresponding development in religious affairs was the growth of a revitalized monasticism. Across Europe, monasteries became more uniform in their practices, and monastic leaders (abbots or abbesses) focused on maintaining the vows of poverty, chastity, and obedience that formed their core practices. The culture of Europe continued to be strongly influenced by Christianity, as art, literature, and music mainly bore Christian images and themes. For instance, Latin was the language of the ecclesiastical bureaucracy and thus became the common written language throughout Europe. Ordinary people as well as the wealthy elites partook of this culture: They could read the lessons engraved on the stained glass of the great cathedrals, travel on a spiritual journey (a pilgrimage) to a sacred destination, and pray for miracles at the resting places of the deceased holy men and women, known as saints. To a certain degree this popular Christian culture had also existed before the Central Middle Ages, but now it had become even more infused into the daily lives of most Europeans.

RELIGION IN THE LATE MIDDLE AGES

In terms of religious developments, the Late Middle Ages witnessed the erosion of the papacy's spiritual prestige, even as this institution continued to gain wealth and political power. Popes took a growing interest in their relationships with European rulers and began to amass greater secular authority, gaining lands and even armies to defend their interests. At one point (1309), King Philip of France actually moved Pope Clement V from Rome into France so that the church leader would be more amenable to Philip's wishes. Several decades later, three men each claimed to be the legitimate pope and excommunicated the followers of the others. Europeans became jaded at this and other misuses of the papacy's spiritual powers—practices that eventually contributed to the Protestant Reformation.

During the Late Middle Ages, new expressions of piety developed: An increased fascination with the Virgin Mary as a spiritual intercessor for the sins of humanity occurred. More Europeans turned toward mysticism as a way of obtaining closeness with the divine outside of logic and theological knowledge. Other Europeans broke away from the institutional church to practice their own interpretations of Christianity, a practice that had begun in the Central Middle Ages and that the church hierarchy called heresy. Both secular and religious leaders worked hard to eliminate medieval heresies, but they nevertheless continued.

CHRISTIANITY AND THE IDEAL FEMALE

As with so many ancient civilizations, the sources left to us from the Middle Ages are predominately male-oriented. This is certainly the case when evaluating what expectations medieval people had about female behavior and what qualities constituted "female" versus "male." Similar to writers in other parts of the premodern world, most medieval authors believed women were supposed to be meek and obedient and to preserve a tranquil domestic environment. The prism through which authors in the Middle Ages constructed these ideas had a characteristically Christian perspective, one that reflected the biases of male monastic authors. Monks were not supposed to mingle with women, and upon taking up their religious vocation they swore to adopt lifelong celibacy—to refrain from sexual intercourse. Like the Buddhist monks from the Gupta Empire, these Christian monks' outlook on women was one of distrust and hostility.

As might be expected, then, women's behavior was often described using Christian imagery. Women appear in historical accounts as either "good" or "bad." Good women were described as selfless creatures who knew their place was subordinate to men, accepted social conventions, and quietly suffered whatever misfortunes they encountered in order to ameliorate the lives of the men around them. The very best woman, whom all women were supposed to emulate, was Mary, the mother of Jesus. Mary's chief qualities were obedience and chastity, for she allowed herself to be impregnated by an aspect of God called the Holy Spirit and gave birth—even though she was a virgin.

The opposing female figure in Christian tradition was Eve, whom medieval writers used as a reference point to describe evil women. In the Old Testament of Christian tradition, God created Eve as the first woman to be a companion for the first man, Adam. God gave these first humans every sort of delight in their paradisaical garden, stipulating only that they not eat the fruit from a forbidden tree. God's enemy, Satan (the devil), decided to convince the humans to disobey this one command from their Creator. He appeared to Eve as a snake and told her that she would be as knowledgeable as God if she ate the fruit. Eve gave into temptation,

FIGURE 7-1   PAINTING OF MARY AND THE CHRIST CHILD
Here the Virgin Mary holds the Christ child while angels circle
above. Dating from 1308, this painting testifies to the extraordinary
importance of Mary for medieval Europeans.

ate the fruit, and then caused an even worse catastrophe by tempting her
husband into eating. Because of this, both husband and wife were thrown
out of the Garden of Eden and into the world of hardship. For medieval
Christians, Eve's "original sin" was the reason humans have to work hard
and suffer mortality. Eve's characteristics (and therefore those of all evil
women) were deception and seduction. For the monastic authors who
had forbidden themselves all sexual relations, the powers of women to
lure men to sin using their sexuality were especially dreadful.

Ideas about what was feminine and how women ought to behave had a long-lasting and important influence in the Middle Ages. However, these concepts bore no more resemblance to reality than did the idea of the chaste matron of the Roman Empire or the Confucian wife of Song China. They tell us much more about how men desired to construct their societies than about how real women actually behaved and thought.

LIFE CYCLES OF THE DISTAFF

BIRTH AND YOUTH.   Many of the patterns of women's life cycles in other ancient civilizations also existed for medieval women in Europe: high infant mortality, marriage partners selected for economic versus romantic reasons, enormous danger of childbirth, unequal tolerance for women's sexual relationships outside of marriage, and restricted access to education. An example of how these trends applied to medieval people can be seen in the speed with which the ecclesiastical sacrament of baptism was performed, since so many children died at birth. Baptism was carried out as hastily as possible to ensure that a baby's soul would be able to go to heaven. If it seemed like the infant would not survive a formal church ceremony, the delivering midwife performed the ceremony. Otherwise, the sacrament took place in a church along with a naming ceremony, with girls often receiving the name of their godmothers. Because of widespread poverty, infanticide was practiced, even though the church forbade it—this is in contrast to the legalized infanticide practiced in other cultures, such as ancient Rome. Many parents who could not afford to care for their newborns abandoned them, and they were more likely to abandon baby girls than boys, similar to many premodern societies. In fact, the incidents of abandonment were high enough for church officials to create orphanages. Thus, Pope Innocent III (d. 1216) ordered the hospital of Santo Spirito to be constructed because "so many women were throwing their babies into the River Tiber."[1]

Early childhood for medieval girls was similar to that in other civilizations: Boys and girls mixed together during their first years. Although parents loved their children, they were aware of the often-precarious nature of daily life. Thus, mothers' lullabies tended to recognize the hardships that children would withstand and emphasize the difficult sacrifices that mothers endured in raising their babies. Probably half of the population who survived birth died by age five. If peasant children survived their earliest years, they soon took on work according to their gender. By about seven years of age, peasant boys were following their fathers out into the fields, while girls were performing household tasks.

In elite families, boys and girls received varying styles of education after reaching seven years old. It was important for aristocratic girls to learn the mannerisms of adult hostesses—to obtain what was often referred to as "courtesy." This might include noticeable displays of religious piety, a demure countenance upon receiving guests, and even the ability to sing or play a musical instrument—qualities that were also admired in the young noblewomen of Gupta India. In terms of formal education, wealthy daughters could not attend the new universities of the Central Middle Ages, but often they received private training. More common as time wore on was the likelihood of elite girls learning to read and write in their vernacular tongues rather than the Latin expected of literate men. Because of this, aristocratic women eventually played an important role in the growth of vernacular literature, since they often became patronesses of authors who wrote in their native languages. For example, sources have recorded the existence of several female courtly minstrels called *trobairitz* in southern France. Often of noble birth, these musicians even wrote their own music, and we know that about 40 of these poems were written by women.

Probably the most famous learned woman in the Late Middle Ages was Christine de Pisan (d. between 1429–1434), who married a nobleman of the French royal court but became a young widow. In order to earn a living for herself and her children, she began to write under commission from various aristocrats. She composed poems, tracts on war and history, and works about the nature of women in *The Book of the City of Ladies* and *The Treasure of the City of Ladies or the Book of the Three Virtues*. In these works, Christine argues against the misogyny prevalent in so much of medieval writings and discusses examples of praiseworthy women. She writes about women: "they murder no one, nor wound, nor harm . . . Nor wage war and kill and plunder. . . ."[2] Christine's position as a writer was almost unique in the medieval period, and yet she was not alone in the fact that she was an educated woman. Readers of Christine's works also can see that she, like others from her milieu, accepted the existence of class structures and of the lower position of women in their relationships with men. She believed that the best sort of woman was one who strove toward marriage and supported her husband in all of his decisions. Her special pleas in favor of women, though atypical, argued in favor of collaboration among genders to preserve a Christian hierarchical society. In this Christine was of a piece with her medieval elite peers.

Marriage: Love, Sex, and Money.   The marriage habits of medieval women differed according to region, social group, and time period. Although the bride's family usually selected their daughter's marriage partner, women in the Central and Late Middle Ages did experience more choices in betrothal than did their sisters in other early societies. In fact, medieval peasants probably had more ability to influence their choice of partners than nobles, since commoners' marriages would have occurred in neighboring areas where at least the brides would have known their husbands. As we have seen with women in other civilizations, the older the bride, the more say she tended to have in whom she married. Therefore, because English women married relatively late and often had more economic independence when they came of age, they had more freedom in choosing a partner. After the Black Death in many parts of northern Europe, peasant men and women were marrying in their mid- to late twenties, with prospective brides and grooms working to raise money either for their dowries, in women's cases, or to acquire their means of livelihood, in men's. In Italy, on the other hand, men tended to marry later than women throughout the Central and Late Middle Ages. This was because men were expected to be financially independent, which meant a later marital age, whereas women were supposed to be overtly pure and virginal, which necessitated an early one.

There were many reasons for Europeans to desire marriage. In the eyes of the hierarchical church, this ceremony was critical in order to have legitimate children. As in the religions of Hinduism and Islam, the only way that sexual intercourse was not considered immoral for women was when it occurred in the confines of matrimony. Although many examples of loving relationships between husbands and wives existed, romantic relationships were not a prerequisite for a wedded couple. Indeed, Christine de Pisan did not think that a woman ought to marry for love, but should be devoted to her husband without such expectations. Ironically, considering the medieval church's negative views of corporal pleasure, sexual relations were considered a legitimate function of marriage. Women were thought to be weaker than men in terms of their sexual insatiability, and therefore the institutional church, rather than seeking to eliminate female sexual desire, sought to control it. From the Christian Bible, Saint Paul wrote "Let the husband render to his wife what is due her, and likewise the wife to her husband," which theologians interpreted to mean that either marital partner who demanded sexual intercourse from the other should have it.[3] (The idea that women could legitimately expect sexual gratification from their husbands also existed in Islam.) This requirement would, it was hoped, make people less likely to have intercourse outside of marriage. Another way of controlling the passions of sexual intercourse was to limit the positions in which it could occur: Proper women were expected to remain supine under their husbands. The subject of female sexual desire frequents medieval literature and testifies to the stereotype of the voracious appetites women were thought to have had. The bawdy poem, "A Talk of Ten Wives on Their Husband's Ware," envisions several women discussing the failures of their husbands' penises: "I measured him in the morning," states one disappointed wife, "when he was in his greatest glory, the length of three beans."[4]

Political authorities and both the bride and the groom's family considered finances and inheritance a critical part of marriage. Especially in the Central Middle Ages, aristocrats often had to pay fines to their lords or the king when they wed; peasants who lived before the Black Death often gave payment in food. As we have seen in many early societies, women were expected to bring a dowry into marriage by the thirteenth century in Europe. This wealth was the bride's, although it would often be at the disposal of her husband once she married. In northern Europe, if a husband died first, a widow could take the value of her dowry from his lands as her own. In Italy, a widow was allowed to keep her dowry only if she did not remarry. This geographic distinction indicates the degree to which wives were able to control their finances independently. Thus, it was uncommon for women to inherit in the southern regions of Europe, whereas widows often held land northwest of the Alps. Perhaps as many as 20 percent of landholders were women in parts of northern Europe in the thirteenth century.

The central issue concerning medieval women's inheritance was the financial interest of the maternal and paternal families. This factor, as we have seen, also played a critical role in many ancient societies. In many parts of northwest Europe, tracing one's family through the female family line was acceptable, especially if the maternal line had particularly wealthy or politically powerful ancestors. This meant that female inheritance was possible, since the family's integrity or wealth was not dependent on a male line. That said, however, the practice of primogeniture, in which the eldest son of a family inherits all of his family's lands, was becoming particularly popular across Europe in the twelfth century. Primogeniture emphasized the continuity of a family's line through one male descendant, and its spread testifies to the great power of aristocratic families who wanted to concentrate their assets. Primogeniture and a general attempt to keep a family's lands in the hands of male descendants gradually decreased the number of female landholders across Europe in the fourteenth and fifteenth centuries. In many parts of southern and eastern Europe, the importance of tracing one's lineage through the paternal line was an even more entrenched tradition, and this limited women's inheritance there.

FROM WIVES TO WIDOWS. Once married, medieval women were expected to run a smooth household and bear children. Peasant women benefited more than noblewomen from the nuclear family structure that characterized many parts of Europe in the Central and Late Middle Ages. Unlike their aristocratic counterparts, common women normally did not move into their husband's familial household, but established an independent household after marriage. Thus, most medieval women did not have to try to fit in with or obey their in-laws. Nevertheless, a woman's position was certainly subordinate to her husband. That the husband was considered the most powerful member of a medieval household can also be seen in advice manuals that men wrote for their wives and children in the Late Middle Ages. One such manual from the late fourteenth century, written by an older man to his young bride, discusses matters such as how to worship, why wives shouldn't talk too much, the importance of remaining chaste and honorable, how to manage the chores necessary for the maintenance of a house, and how to get rid of fleas in a bed. Wife beating was acceptable and legal throughout the period.

Women feared great danger in childbirth, as evidenced by the popularity of Saint Margaret, the patroness of women in delivery, and by the fact that so many pregnant women made pilgrimages to ask for a healthy birth and convalescence. Because of the dangers and costs involved with childbirth, both medieval women and men did seek birth control. Though the institutional church prohibited it, evidence survives of a poor medieval Parisian man who practiced *coitus interruptus* because he would not have been able to feed any children.[5] One woman thought that the stomach lining of an unweaned hare might be an effective prophylactic. No doubt women sought many herbs and amulets for such purposes, with some solutions having more effectiveness than others.

One difference between medieval society and other early civilizations is that divorce in medieval Europe was not legally possible: The church hierarchy forbade it. However, the institutional church could annul a marriage—wherein it declared that the sacrament of marriage had never really taken place. Annulments could be granted if one of the marital partners was impotent, if one of them had already married another person, if a wedding had been compulsory, or if the marriage was between people who were related by blood to a certain degree. In effect, this last measure was one that the church was able to use most often to dissolve a failed marriage, since it was fairly easy to find forbidden blood relations—these were defined as almost anyone who shared relatives on any part of a family tree. Nobles were able to have marriages annulled relatively easily, but women did not necessarily benefit. Especially in parts of southern Europe, very little legislation protected their wealth or even access to their children. For most medieval commoners, annulment on the basis of blood relationship was a fairly rare event. Even less frequently, however, did men seek annulments on the grounds of their own impotence. Yet in England, there was a practice in which a group of "wise women" gathered to test male impotence by trying to sexually excite the man, thereby determining whether sexual intercourse in a marriage had indeed been absent or which marriage partner was responsible for not producing children.

Many women outlived their husbands in the Central and Late Middle Ages, for two reasons. First, the good weather and improved farming technology that was developing in the Central Middle Ages meant that more women could eat vegetables, which gave them a greater amount of iron to prevent age-related anemia. Because of this, the average woman lived longer than the average man for the first time in European history. Second, in those parts of southern Europe where a woman married at a much younger age than her spouse, it often resulted in the husband dying first.

The situation of medieval widows was not as challenging as those from some other ancient cultures, where such women were thought to contribute nothing to society. European widows did, however, experience different degrees of independence. Generally, women in northwestern Europe could find that economic and legal independence was most possible in widowhood. In England after the Black Death, for example, numerous widows increased their personal and familial fortunes by remarrying wealthy husbands. Margaret Freville, a fifteenth-century English aristocrat, survived her first husband by almost 50 years and remarried, perhaps causing consternation to her stepsons, who were thereby unable to enjoy their father's wealth. In parts of southern Europe, however, a widow's position was less enviable, because her husband's family put pressure on her not to remarry (and reclaim her dowry). In fact, in late medieval Florence, the children of a widow belonged to their father's lineage, and a woman who remarried gave up her ability to raise them.

HOW WOMEN WORKED

Generalizing about the habits of working women of the Central and Late Middle Ages is nearly impossible: Micro-economies existed all over Europe, as did the variation of women's occupations. Nevertheless, trends do emerge when we examine the types of professions practiced by women throughout the medieval period. First, as in every society discussed here, women's work was of critical importance in sustaining the economy, whether this work took place in the household or in the public sphere. Second, as with each of the sedentary civilizations we have examined, women were the primary caretakers of children and took charge of maintaining their homes. Third, in this period, common women had a relatively important role in the European urban economy compared with women of many other eras. However, business opportunities for European women lessened as the medieval period continued, so that their range of occupations was on the whole more varied in 1050 CE than it was in 1500 CE. In the eleventh through the thirteenth centuries, women had a relatively frequent participation in the urban trade alliances known as guilds, craft-based organizations established to protect the workers of a certain industry. They also played a major role in weaving cloth, brewing ale, and milling grain; they participated—although their appearance was rare—in the medical and legal professions; and their wages were likely on the whole to be higher than in preceding centuries. By 1500, although women's participation in the public workforce continued, men had monopolized the most prestigious occupations that women had practiced during the Central Middle Ages.

Although urbanization was on the rise at the start of the Central Middle Ages, most women were peasant farmers, and thus the bulk of their work occurred in the countryside. On farms, the private work of managing a household was often inextricable from the family's farming chores. Generally, the peasant wife made the most important decisions running her household, deciding what to buy at the market, when to do various chores, or how to clean her home. Some typical women's tasks included fetching water, spinning, milking, doing the laundry, tending to the livestock and poultry, nurturing the small household gardens adjoining the home, and gleaning the remaining grains from the fields after harvest. Records of accidental work-related deaths in late medieval England suggest that, at least in part of Europe, a female peasant's occupations were not as physically dangerous as those of men's. This, however, does not mean that farming women's lives were easier than their male counterparts. The late medieval poem called "The Ballad of a Tyrannical Husband" ridicules the idea that women's work was more desirable than men's when a grouchy husband complains about his wife's lifestyle. "What has thou to do, but sit at home?" he chides.

The peasant wife suggests that she trade jobs with her husband for one day, describing how she has to wake early in the morning after being up at night with her crying children, milk the cows, make butter, tend to the chickens, bake, brew, spin, and perform many other chores besides. Indeed, after spending one day working in his wife's shoes, the husband yields: "'Lady,' said the Goodman, 'I'm going to the plow. Teach me no more house-wifery, for I cannot move.'"[6]

In cities, women were visible in the workforce throughout the Middle Ages, and most medieval crafts were practiced by women as well as men. Women's work, however, was expected to be less prestigious than men's, and their occupations generally did not pay as much. Urban women were more likely than men to change their careers during their lifetimes, which necessarily meant fewer women were able to specialize in a profession. For example, a widow who remarried was expected to give up her craft unless her new husband practiced the same occupation as the former spouse did. Examples of low-status jobs women typically undertook include small-scale retailing, laundering, and spinning.

Prostitution also belonged in the domain of women and—as with the practice in Gupta India—was tolerated by the institutional church and governments, despite the Christian belief that intercourse outside of marriage was a sin. Prostitution was highly regulated by governments, which often limited prostitutes to certain areas of a city or required that they wore distinguishing clothing, such as bells on their heads in Florence. In fact, many authorities viewed prostitution as a necessary evil, something that would prevent unmarried men from having sexual relations with virgins, other men's wives, or other men. In southern Europe, where men typically married later than women, prostitution was considered an especially important sexual outlet for unmarried men.

Several high-status occupations were open to women, especially in the Central Middle Ages. Luxury textile production was one of these, and in the thirteenth century, women in fact often dominated in this field. In Paris, female town guilds included silk spinners, silk ribbon makers, and silk kerchief weavers. These women's guilds were unusual, yet attest to the power that women could have in certain areas of the workforce. Although less prestigious, apprenticeship in textile workshops was a common undertaking for girls in the Central Middle Ages. Women played a critical role for much of the Middle Ages in the important trade of brewing ale. For example, in the Central Middle Ages, the town of Brigstock, England, could claim that about a third of the female population brewed ale for commercial profit.[7] And, although practicing medicine became institutionalized through the newly created—and male-only—universities in the Central Middle Ages, women were still sought after as midwives and, far more rarely, as doctors. In 1265, for instance, records show a certain Stephanie working as a doctor in the French town of Lyons. Stephanie's father was also a doctor, which explains how she was able to receive the complex training needed for this occupation.

Opportunities for women diminished as the Middle Ages ended. Most women's guilds had disappeared by 1500 CE, and women played minor roles in beer production and milling grain. Even brothels were mainly male-run by the 1400s. Several factors account for these changes. One of the most important was the Black Death, which devastated Europe's population in the fourteenth century and afterward. The fact that this plague brought higher wages to the smaller workforce was an ironic turn for many who managed to live through the onslaught of the disease. For women, however, the higher wages and increased job vacancies did not prove to be long-lasting benefits. As the number of deaths rose, the goods and services demanded by the medieval economy waned. Men tended to fill the occupations of the dead, and they did so in a way that often shut out women. Thus, the fact that men came to virtually monopolize guilds in the Late Middle Ages meant that fewer women could practice certain trades. New machinery also contributed to this trend. Animal-powered grain mills took the place of the hand grinding formerly done by women, and large horizontal looms that favored men's upper-body strength began to predominate in the textile industry. Obtaining training became increasingly difficult, as more craftsmen limited the necessary guidance to their sons. Despite the narrowing of paid specialized occupations for women outside their homes, many women continued to practice unpaid variations of textile making, medicine, and brewing within the confines of their households.

IMPASSIONED DEVOTION: MEDIEVAL WOMEN AND RELIGION

Christianity provided a viewpoint that most women and men referenced throughout the Middle Ages, from the popular stories of saints, to the moral code that dictated daily behavior, to common rituals. Thus, it became a cultural expression as well as a set of beliefs. It was also a bureaucratic institution, and from 1050–1500 CE, the centralized church grew in its influence on Europeans. All of this had an enormous impact on women. As we have seen in other cultures, women in medieval Europe had a relatively high profile in religious institutional roles, and there were often important feminine aspects about spiritual beings. Furthermore, the growing authority of the church successfully curtailed the power of women who chose to pursue a life oriented around religion. Although women continued to play a significant role in medieval Christianity around 1500, that role was narrower than that which existed three centuries earlier.

Medieval people's religious beliefs had much more in common with the Muslim world of the Abbasids than with the Romans who had inhabited Europe in earlier centuries. The belief that there was only one God—and this God was masculine—certainly curtailed the possibilities for female divine beings. Christianity's paternal Trinity of the Father, Son, and Holy Spirit reinforced this limitation. It is worth considering what this meant for women in these civilizations. On the one hand, women did not necessarily receive better treatment in societies where goddesses figured prominently: aristocratic women in Classical Athens lived restricted lives despite the importance of Athena. On the other hand, the existence of powerful female figures in a religion does reflect on a society's culture:

The Hindu goddess Kali's unbridled sexuality indicates that women's overt sexuality was considered a powerful force. What female characteristics could be considered so powerful in a civilization that had no goddesses? Female aspects of the divine were present in medieval Europe because of the importance of Mary and the female saints. Although the institutional church clearly pronounced that such beings were not divine, their physical presence prominently figured in the artwork that adorned the parish churches that everyone attended, and both women and men thought them powerful enough to include them in their prayers. Indeed, it is difficult to imagine that Europeans always made a distinction between "spiritual intercessors" and "goddesses" regarding the Virgin Mary and the female saints.

We have already discussed Mary's virtues of obedience, chastity, and humility as a role model for women. The Virgin Mother and the female saints were not merely figures meant to teach women their position in society, but they also represented powerful feminine characteristics to be emulated. Mary's attributes were traits that monastic writers considered feminine: the ability to be nurturing, merciful, and weak. Christian thinkers considered these characteristics important for themselves in their relationship with God. Indeed, they were qualities that God sought out in His worshippers, and theologians believed that acquiescence toward God's will was crucial. God was the dominator who wanted the weak and the powerless. Christ himself was at times portrayed with decidedly female characteristics in Christian artwork and writings from the Central and Late Middle Ages. The female theologian Julian of Norwich made many of these connections in her mystical writings. For example, Jesus' sufferings on the Cross were pointedly compared with the sufferings of women in childbirth. With his own bloodshed he gave spiritual nourishment to all of humanity, in a way analogous to a woman's breastfeeding her child. The caring love that he showed to his people was as unconditional as a mother's love for her children.

Besides the Virgin Mary, many Europeans turned to female saints in their prayers for assistance, as focal points in pilgrimages, and in hopes that the saints' physical remains (relics) would grant some sort of blessing. Female saints were important for women during the perilous time of childbirth. As one fifteenth-century author declared,

> At the time of birth, it is good that the legend of blessed Margaret be read, that she have relics of the saints on her, and that you carry out briefly some familiar ceremonies in order to please your patient. . . .[8]

The French Saint Foy (who perhaps lived in the third century CE) was popular among soldiers and prisoners and provided so many miracles at her shrine that the monks who tended her relics—which included a renowned statue adorned with precious metals and gemstones—grew wealthy and famous. Gertrude of Nivelles (d. 659) was invoked by pilgrims, those who prayed for the recently dead, and believers who wished to ward off pestilence. As the medieval era continued, the number of women whom the hierarchical church officially accepted as saints (in a process called canonization) actually increased.

Many of the characteristics that medieval Europeans found most compelling about their female saints were attributes that most women could never possess. They tended to be stridently virginal, able to control their own destinies, able to defy political authority, and immune to the most violent of physical punishments. In the Central and Late Middle Ages, some of the most popular female saints were from the period of the Roman persecutions of the Christians. The stories surrounding these holy martyrs were often created hundreds of years after their deaths and thus reflect the sensibilities of a much later era. For instance, Saint Christine, a Roman whose life narrative was virtually invented by a late fourteenth-century author, was reputed to have experienced enormous levels of violence for her faith. Christine was a young Roman beauty who refused to worship her father's pagan gods. He trapped Christine in a tower, whereupon the young maid smashed all her father's expensive idols to bits. Her father decided to torture her. He

> . . . commanded that her clear white flesh be scraped from her bones with sharp hooked nails. He ordered all her limbs broken, one by one . . . it was a shame to see what was done to that maiden![9]

Christine was also tortured by being put on a wheel, burned, saturated in burning tar, attacked by poisonous snakes, and by the severing of her breasts and ripping out of her tongue. Even though she was only 12 years old, she endured all these abuses until she was finally killed with arrows.

The lives of female saints did finally end with martyrdom, but only after they had taunted their enemies and often prayed to God to be taken into heaven. These stories were extremely popular in the Middle Ages, probably for several reasons. Perhaps men who knew of these stories found it easier to have female role models whose lives in no way could represent those of the women who surrounded them. (The goddesses Athena and Kali were similarly unrealistic in Classical Greece and the Gupta periods, respectively.) Perhaps the violence endured by these saints represents a kind of misogyny prevalent throughout the era. For many, however, these virgin martyrs could also represent powerful figures—women who were able to control their own destinies and still be held in high esteem by society. Perhaps these were things that medieval women desired for themselves, if only in fantasy.

THE PROFESSIONAL RELIGIOUS.   Another venue for women's spirituality in the Central and Late Middle Ages was as the professional religious, which could take several forms: nun, anchoress, or beguine. Both society at large and the institutional church embraced these various expressions of female religiosity differently, depending on the extent to which they viewed the women involved as threats to the social or religious order. Despite this, women religious did manage to shape medieval Christianity, whether through the wealth of the nuns, the public assistance provided by the beguines, or through the example and advice of anchoresses. In the religious sphere, the Late Middle Ages actually saw a greater range of religious expression for women than existed in the Central Middle Ages, but as time went on, the church's male hierarchy became ever-more critical of women whose religious callings were out of the church's control. (This type of increasing restriction on women's spiritual expression also occurred during the Song period in China.)

Because they were closely supervised by male ecclesiastical authorities, nunneries had generally enjoyed the sanction of church authorities since their appearance in the fourth-century Roman world. Living in their own communities apart from secular society, they placed themselves under the direction of an abbess, but were governed by *Rules*, or church-sanctioned guidelines for both male and female monks. These *Rules* regulated most aspects of nuns' lives: the type of clothing they could wear, what they were supposed to eat, the occasions when they should pray, when they were allowed to talk, and how they were to be reprimanded by the abbess. Despite the obvious piety of many nuns, some did not adhere to the precepts to which they were supposed to be devoted. Numerous accounts tell of nuns wearing gold and silk finery, gossiping, employing servants, and occasionally even indulging in sexual activities with male monks. The bishops overseeing the nuns of Zamora were horrified to discover in 1279 that many of the nuns were having sexual intercourse with the local friars.

Perhaps the evidence showing some nuns' reluctance to follow church ordinances can be better understood in light of the fact that convents drew their populations from the most elite families in Europe. Nuns were by nature aristocrats, and in fact had to bring a significant amount of wealth with them when they entered their religious lives. For many rich families, however, this endowment was far less costly than a dowry, and thus sending daughters into nunneries was a relatively inexpensive alternative to marrying them off. Many aristocrats also sent their daughters knowing that they would receive an education. Outside of home tutors, the learning provided by the convent was virtually the only channel through which medieval women could learn to read and write. The famous scholar and nun Saint Hildegard of Bingen (1098–1179) exemplifies the typical background and potential educational training of female monastics. Born in Germany to a noble family, she gained the ability to read and write as a young woman in a convent. Hildegard far excelled most of her medieval sisters, however, in the extent of her learning and the degree of public power she eventually possessed. Nuns and others today continue to sing musical compositions written by Hildegard, and she achieved great fame in her time for her medical and religious writings. She was leader of her convent at Bingen and also corresponded with some of the most famous political and religious leaders of her era.

As the Middle Ages drew to a close, nunneries grew fewer and more impoverished. Fewer aristocrats donated to convents, because other types of spiritual donations were becoming popular. Whereas the act of establishing a nunnery or paying for nuns to pray for their patrons had been an important source of the convents' revenues, in the Later Middle Ages, emphasis shifted to the power of the church ceremony of the Mass to help the souls or even physical well-being of individuals. Since only priests could preside over a Mass, nunneries were unable to capitalize on this lucrative service.

Another reason for the gradual decline in nunneries was the growth of other female religious professions in the Central and Late Middle Ages, professions that often were more attractive to the growing population of women in cities. These included beguines and anchoresses. The former were eventually censured by the institutional church; the latter received its approval. Beguines, flourishing in towns especially in thirteenth- and fourteenth-century Germany and the Netherlands, did not live by any papally sponsored rule, lived unenclosed public lives, and were unregulated by higher church authorities—which explains why ecclesiastic and even political officials had little tolerance for them. Although the beguine movement at first attracted elite women, it eventually became popular among the poor. Beguines could be widowed, single, or married, and they might take up or leave their religious profession throughout their lives. A defining feature of the beguines was that they led a life of poverty in imitation of Christ. Corresponding with this was a focus on providing charity to others and often an emphasis on physical self-denial in imitation of Christ's final sufferings. Thus, many beguines worked with the sick and the poor while living the most meager of existences. The beguine Mary of Oignies had a reputation of such great holiness that in her last years, the only food she was reported to have taken was the Eucharist wafer from the Mass.

In sharp contrast to the beguines, who inspired fear among church and political officials, were anchoresses, women who lived in prayerful ascetic solitude. Such women never made up a large percentage of the religious profession but nevertheless were important as an example of the diversity of women's religious experiences. The term "anchoress" is derived from the Greek *anachoretes,* or "one who has withdrawn," and indeed refers to women whose piety led them to the most extreme sort of solitude. A woman who wished to become an anchoress was in effect declaring herself dead to the world. Often she would even have a burial ceremony, complete with dirt tossed upon her body before she retreated into a cell, her tomb. In the Central and Late Middle Ages, when anchoresses were most numerous in western Europe, the woman's cell would usually be attached to a church, with one window through which others could pass food and another into the adjacent church so that the anchoress could hear Mass. Her cell door would be locked and sealed. An anchoress's life was thereafter spent in prayer and often fasting. Obviously, such women's lives were strictly controlled, which may explain why the hierarchical church sanctioned their existence.

Despite the terrible sacrifices that anchoresses made, they nevertheless could achieve a powerful position in their local—and sometimes wider—societies. Hardships demonstrated their holiness, so many anchoresses were sought out for spiritual guidance. The English mystic Julian of Norwich was one of the most famous anchoresses. In 1373, when she turned 30 years old, she began to have mystical visions about which she wrote in the *Revelations of Divine Love.* She was not condemned by the church authorities: Many people sought Julian's advice and admired her philosophical writings—as an anchoress confined to a cell, she was less threatening to the status quo than an unenclosed woman would be.

The Holy, the Hell-Bound, and the Outsider: Women's Religious Practices

MYSTICS. Of course, all medieval people participated in a variety of Christian practices—they were not just the prerogative of the professional religious. Whereas most of this activity—attending Mass, receiving the holy rituals known as sacraments, giving wealth to the institutional church or to charity—was considered mundane, medieval society did consider some practices unusual. Among them was the close, irrational connection with God that mystics experienced, the set of beliefs deemed heretical by the church hierarchy, and witchcraft: All were atypical, and yet most people knew about these things and either embraced or shunned them, depending on their point of view. Interestingly, women had a high profile in each of these practices, and perhaps this was because the institutional routes to power in the medieval church were effectively closed to women. Unable to attend universities, barred from performing the most important Christian rituals, some women sought avenues outside of the traditional venue of the church to practice their beliefs.

Mystics were some of the most respected women in medieval society, and although the church was often wary of their power because they professed such a close connection with Jesus, they had credibility without having to fit inside the framework of the institutional church. Although both male and female mystics existed, mysticism was often more associated with women. Perhaps this was because women were thought to be emotional and illogical, and mystics needed these qualities so that they could have direct contact with God—whether through dreams, visions, or spiritual revelations. Most mystics came from the wealthier medieval families and, despite such exceptions as Julian of Norwich, most had little formal education.

A mystic's life was a hard one for several reasons. First, it was a spiritual path that required a great deal of commitment, and women were usually expected to devote their time to the household or in gainful employment. Thus, Dorothea of Montau's husband beat her because she neglected her shopping and cooking in favor of her religious endeavors. Second, mystics willingly gave up their family wealth and worldly comforts—much like anchoresses and nuns were expected to do. Third, part of a mystic's special relationship with Jesus entailed a physical identification with Christ's sufferings before death and on the Cross. Thus, mystics often subjected themselves to great physical distress. Dorothea of Montau mimicked the Crucifixion by praying with her arms extended in the form of a cross and then imitated the burial of Christ by lying down "with the entire weight of her body supported only by toes, nose, and forehead."[10]

Medieval mystics aimed to gain forgiveness of their sins through their self-punishment, but another way that they struggled to gain eternal salvation was through assisting the poor and ill. Sometimes these two holy avenues to paradise coincided. For example, Catherine of Siena strove to help others by her own suffering by drinking pus from the wounds of lepers. Indeed, she apparently spoke of the pus to her biographer, saying "Never in my life have I tasted any food and drink sweeter or more exquisite."[11] Angela of Foligno washed the hands and feet of one leper in a basin, and then drank the water used to clean the sores. A scab from one of the leper's wounds had fallen into the water, and when it stuck in Angela's throat, it miraculously tasted like the Eucharist (the wafer used in the Mass). Considering the fact that lepers were considered to be polluted and were shunned by most of society, these women's ministrations were deemed even holier.

As odd as medieval mystics might seem to a modern audience—or perhaps not so odd, given the proliferation of Buddhist, Sufi, and Christian practices that include a mystical element—they were considered not freakish, but rather unusually holy, by medieval society as long as they earned the approval of church authorities. Indeed, these women often had committed followings of people who sought their counsel. The connection that they had with Christ was thought to have made them an intercessor between God and humanity—an entity who could entreat God on behalf of mortals, similar to the role imputed to the Virgin Mary. Furthermore, many believed that the sufferings endured by mystics did not just atone for their own sins, but could also expiate the sins of others. Thus, the most successful mystics were held in high esteem by their communities.

HERETICS AND WITCHES. Two practices condemned by all political and ecclesiastical officials throughout the Middle Ages were those of heresy and witchcraft. Women who were found guilty of either were harshly punished, often by death. Heresy refers to religious beliefs or practices that the institutional church did not sponsor, and became a problem for the church hierarchy in the Central Middle Ages. Those whom the church labeled heretics of course thought that the church's interpretation of Christianity was incorrect and that their own ideas were right. For instance, several important Christian mystics were eventually branded as heretics by the church: The special access to Christ they proclaimed did not automatically lead to their acceptance. These women continued to consider themselves good Christians. In some heretical communities, women were allowed to play an important public role, even though this was atypical. For instance, one heretical group called the Waldensians allowed women to consecrate the Eucharist, and there were many female leaders among the heretical society of Cathars. This leadership may have been attractive to some heretical women, but the majority of heretical groups taught familiar ideas about the subordinate position that women occupied in society and in their religious movements. Authorities sought the elimination of all heretics: Whereas some members of these groups were able to avoid death by making a full confession and publicly atoning for their beliefs, many others were executed.

Witchcraft was practiced in medieval Europe, just as it was in ancient Greece and Rome—by both genders, although it seems to have been more prominent among women. Perhaps this is because medieval society's distinctions between "magic," "prayer," "science," and "healing" were often vague. Thus, priests who chanted the prayer "Hail Mary" over a field to make the crops grow were considered to be neither doing anything outrageous nor sorcerers. Many women who used herbs and incantations for healing and whose activities passed benignly under the radar of officials have therefore left limited records. The women who were prosecuted as witches were those whose activities threatened or destabilized their local societies. To a modern audience, the accusations against these women might sound like a fabricated excuse to punish them. For instance, in 1459 Catherine Simon of Andermatt allegedly caused illness to people, death to livestock, and avalanches by making a pact with the devil. Despite cases such as Catherine's, complaints of witches in the Middle Ages were relatively few. The era of infamous witch hunts had not yet arrived.

JEWS.   Jewish people were the largest group of non-Christians in medieval Europe and, because of their separate religious identity and Christian-inspired animosity, they often suffered mob violence, prejudice, and abuse at the hands of authorities. By the Central Middle Ages, most European Jews lived in cities, where they played a critical role in the urban economy as moneylenders—a practice called usury, which was forbidden to Christians. Jews had lived throughout Europe during the Roman Empire and the Early Middle Ages, but were most accepted by the general populace in parts of Spain that were under Muslim control. During the Central Middle Ages, attacks against Jews reached brutal proportions as Crusaders traveling over land routes massacred communities wholesale. Jewish chroniclers testify to the slaughter of women, children, and infants by Christian warriors intent on punishing people they branded "Christ-killers." From the thirteenth through fifteenth centuries, Jews were periodically expelled from their homes and countries, as English, French, and Spanish rulers ousted or forcibly converted them. Like the Jewish population generally, Jewish women were part of medieval society and yet treated as outsiders. For instance, their marriage patterns, with partnerships arranged by parents that included dowries, were similar to those of their Christian neighbors. A Jew named Eleazar of Mainz described expectations of female behavior in the will he left for his family, writing that "the rules applying to women . . . [include] modesty, sanctity, reverence."[12] These were of course also traits for women that were lauded by medieval Christian authors. Like their Christian neighbors, Jewish urban women practiced a variety of trades, although there was a disproportionately high number of women engaged in moneylending and medical practices. On the other hand, Jewish women's lives differed, not merely by the oppression all Jews experienced, but because of their separate religious and cultural practices. Unlike their Christian peers, for instance, Jewish women were expected to bathe regularly.

THE UNEASY LEGITIMACY OF FEMALE PUBLIC POWER

Since Europe had a variety of political systems during the Central and Late Middle Ages, women's experiences with public authority differed across the region. Generally, the northern and western parts of Europe allowed more opportunities for women than did other areas. Regardless, very few options were open to women in public offices at the local level or to those who were not wealthy and descended from noble lineage. Rare exceptions existed: Joan of Arc is the most famous. Born into a peasant family in 1412, Joan started receiving visions from God, telling her to lead an army to assist the embattled French King Charles VII against the English—who had been fighting for decades on the Continent during the Hundred Years' War. Donning men's clothing, Joan succeeded against improbable odds in a number of battles. Her taking up of arms was not a criticism of the traditional all-male army, but instead represented the medieval characteristics of mysticism, pilgrimage, and French identity. She did in fact enable King Charles to be crowned in the important city of Rheims, and her actions effectively turned the long conflict against the British. Unfortunately, the British armies eventually captured Joan in 1431, and their allies burned her at the stake for heresy—even though many witnesses considered these charges trumped up for political motives.

More typical roles as public authorities were those of queen and noblewomen, and here medieval Europe differed from civilizations such as Gupta India or the Abbasid Caliphate in that women were sometimes expected to take on the political duties normally done by men, a practice that in part came about because European male leaders so often left their lands to fight in wars or serve their lords. Thus, sometimes queens took on the tasks that kings were expected to do: to oversee a kingdom's finances, to hear the council of his nobles, to pronounce judgment in court, and to conduct foreign relations in peace and in war. As the author Christine de Pisan suggests in her fifteenth-century work *The Book of Three Virtues*:

> If the lady is charged with the government . . . she will go to the council
> on the days when it meets, and there she will show such presence, such
> bearing, and such a countenance as she sits on her high seat that she
> will indeed seem to be their ruler, and everyone will revere her as a wise
> mistress of great authority.[13]

Christine was well acquainted with the goings-on in the courts of French royals and magnates, and both men and women thought her writings carried great merit. Blanche of Castile (d. 1252) is an example of a queen who governed France without her husband for a long duration, put down revolts, made alliances with estranged nobles, and even squelched a rebellion by university students and professors in Paris.

Along the same lines, noblewomen occasionally governed their husbands' estates, deciding what their servants should plant, defending their castles from attacks, overseeing the local bishop or priests' activities, or making purchases of new lands. Again, Christine de Pisan's writings reflect the expectations of such women, for she urges the ladies who oversee great estates to have a solid understanding of their finances to avoid overspending, and to learn about farming so that they can best advise the servants. On a daily basis such women should go over their lands to supervise the workers, and they should rise early to do so, for "in the household where the mistress lies late abed things rarely go well."[14] The English lady Eleanor de Montfort (d. 1275), wife of the famous attempted usurper Simon, was engaged in litigation practically her whole life to secure lands and finances while running her vast household, and, at one point, even defended her husband's castle from enemies. Although these public duties did fall upon queens and noblewomen, they were considered masculine and normally better undertaken by men. Social commentators clearly preferred that such women allow their husbands to assume the most important tasks of running the realm, and, in fact, women had no formal role in a king's council of advisors.

In fact, the political expectation that men of importance should spend a great deal of their lives engaged in battle or serving their monarchs at a royal court miles away from their estates is the central reason that such power was ever granted to women. As we have seen in other regions, societies in which men have had to live long periods away from their bases of power have traditionally turned to their wives for support in overseeing their interests at home. This situation allowed for the strong role that women played in the public arena during the Central and Late Middle Ages, described explicitly in Christine de Pisan's writings:

> As most often knights, squires, and other gentlemen must travel to follow the wars, it befits their wives to be wise and able to manage their affairs capably, because they must spend much of their lives in their households without their husbands, who are often at court or even in distant countries.[15]

Other occasions when queens and noblewomen could overtly take on the public duties normally entrusted to men included times when their husbands had died and their sons were either too young to assume power or were traveling away from their estates, as was the case with Blanche of Castile.

Women who did rule in place of men could expect more frequent challenges to their political authority than their male counterparts, and in some parts of Europe women were less likely to be able to govern even in extreme circumstances. In places such as Hungary—where there was civil war, where the succession was disputed, or where the tradition of women inheriting was not well established—women had difficulty assuming power. Such was the case, for example, of Matilda, daughter of King Henry I of England. Because he lacked a legitimate male heir (he had sired numerous bastard children, but their rights to govern would have been challenged), toward the end of his life Henry called on the most important nobles of England to swear to recognize his daughter, and her children, as heirs to the throne. As one contemporary writes, Henry, "in that thunderous voice which none could resist, compelled rather than invited men to take the oath."[16] Matilda spent years in civil war vying with those who decided against upholding their forced pledges to the king, until her son Henry II finally came of age and began a successful reign.

Queens and noblewomen assumed public roles other than acting as default rulers when the males in their lives were absent. Queens had the most significant public duties, and most important of these was the provision of male heirs. For a queen, bearing children was in fact a public responsibility, and the coronation ceremony that marked her assumption to power reflected the significance of her fertility when she was consecrated with blessed oil. Both queens and noblewomen also had to publicly demonstrate their holiness, whether by donating large amounts of money to charities or ecclesiastical establishments, or by building a reputation for leading a devout and prayerful life. Finally, in the manner of the wives of modern heads of state, queens and noblewomen were expected to be gracious hostesses. This aspect of these elite women's careers enhanced the reputation of the king or lord, and perhaps belonged to the tradition of arranging marriages to promote peace. After all, if her husband needed to chastise or command visiting officials, the tone of such encounters could be softened by the queen or lady's countenance.

As with other civilizations examined in this book, elite women sometimes managed to have non-institutional influence in public affairs through their force of character and closeness with their husbands, sons, or other powerful male authorities. Thus did the French and English Queen Eleanor of Aquitaine (d. 1204) manage a long public career, despite being imprisoned for many years by her husband King Henry II. As a young wife of King Louis VII of France, she and her husband joined a group of Crusaders—an activity of great daring for an aristocratic woman. Later, she left her French husband to marry Henry Plantagenet, the future king of England. She directed the careers of several of her royal sons—at one point raising an enormous ransom for King Richard, who had been captured while off crusading. Finally, she spent a great deal of time in the south of France at her family's base in Aquitaine, where she cultivated French courtly literature called *romances* and troubadour culture—both traditions in which women played a relatively high-profile part.

Queens and noblewomen's married lives differed enormously from their poorer female counterparts in the medieval period, and not merely because of the material comforts they enjoyed. Marital age was considerably lower for elite women: Engagement could in effect occur in their infancy, although the church decreed that the legal age for marriage was 12 for girls and 14 for boys. Medieval elite brides married so young because of the important political alliances their marriages wrought. For instance, during the Hundred Years' War, peace between the feuding countries of France and England was temporarily secured by the marriage of the English King Henry V to Catherine, the daughter of King Charles VI of France. Another motivation for aristocratic marriage was wealth: When a woman's inheritance was significant, she became a desirable bride. Thus, the Emperor Charles IV gained a great deal of land with each of his four marriages. Of course, these financially motivated betrothals could only occur in places where women were able to inherit either lands or offices in lieu of male heirs, or where women received a dowry of lands. This was the case in England, France, the Netherlands, the Kingdom of Sicily, and the Crusader states, but not, for example, in northern Italy. Even in France, women were barred in the fourteenth century from being able to transmit the crown to their sons by the Salic Law. This development had less to do with any desire to curtail the authority of royally born women, however, than with the goal of ensuring that the French crown would not be passed to the English.

As was the case for noble and royal women in many of the societies discussed here, medieval elite women were expected to leave their homes and move into their households of their husbands' families upon marriage. Such arrangements could bring about great loneliness for the young brides, who were often only able to bring along a few servants or an ecclesiastic advisor as companions. Journeys to their homelands were often infrequent, and the husband's family often accepted the new wife grudgingly. Blanche of Castile, who had herself faced homesickness when she first married, became a challenging mother-in-law to Marguerite of Provence, jealously monopolizing her son's time. According to one source, Queen Blanche was the "woman who hated [Marguerite] most."[17] Once, when Marguerite lay in desperate pain after a dangerous childbirth, Blanche told her son to leave his wife's side. Marguerite apparently retorted, "Alas! Whether I live or die, you will not let me see my husband!"[18]

CONCLUSION

The overall situation for Western European women who lived during the Central and Late Middle Ages varied too greatly to be generalized. Although their position in society was expected to be, like all the other sedentary civilizations we have examined in this book, subordinate to men's, nevertheless women did sometimes enjoy relatively good fortune regarding their economic, political, and religious power compared with many of their sisters from other civilizations.

For instance, although they were shut out of the university system, many elite medieval women received some degree of academic education. Indeed, writers such as Hildegard of Bingen, the French *trobairitz*, Julian of Norwich, and Christine de Pisan composed works that still remain with us. Since peasant women in northern Europe and many women living after the Black Death married later, they were able to have more leverage in their choice of marriage partners than women in many other societies. Inheritance regulations and dowry rights—especially in the north—often benefited women, whether they were widows claiming their former husband's estates as their own or trying to exert some degree of political control over their deceased partner's lands. On the other hand, married women usually had little ability to control their financial matters, and their claim to their birth family's fortunes was far less than a Muslim woman from the Abbasid era's share. For common women, work opportunities in textile production, brewing ale, and milling grain were profitable in the Central Middle Ages, but declined in the Late Middle Ages as men monopolized these trades. Certainly the degree of economic control afforded to many medieval women surpassed their sisters in many other early civilizations.

Indeed, because of the frequent absences of noblemen and kings from their lands, aristocratic wives and queens were sometimes expected to take on their husbands' public duties.

In terms of the arena of medieval religion, women had a great impact, as we have seen was the case for all of the other civilizations discussed in this book. Whereas the most popular religious profession for women in the Central Middle Ages was that of a nun, as time went on other spiritual avenues opened up, such as those of the anchoress, the beguine, or the mystic. As we have seen with mystics in other civilizations, the Christian mystics earned an unusual degree of public acceptance, since they were holy women whose close contact with God could bring assistance to their communities. Female spiritual entities also figured prominently in this period in terms of the powerful women saints to whom so many people prayed. Even God—for there were no goddesses in medieval civilization—could be portrayed with the feminine characteristics of a nurturing mother to sinful, needy children.

Despite these relatively positive aspects about medieval women's lives and opportunities, the medieval period was no paradise for the female gender. As in other civilizations, young girls were valued less than male children. And medieval European marriage was not based on romantic love but on familial economic and political interests. Medieval women on the whole earned less money for their work than men, and they—like all sedentary civilizations discussed in these chapters—were normally excluded from public power. The ability of a woman to take up a religious profession actually decreased during these centuries—and those who opted for the life of an ascetic only earned the esteem that came with the job through years of terrific self-sacrifice. For every Mary that the male theologians recorded, they saw a hundred Eves, with the attributes of treachery, seduction, and pride thought intrinsic to the supposedly weaker sex.

◖ CONCLUSION ◗

> *By God, if women set to writing stories*
> *As do these scholars in their oratories*
> *They would have told more wickedness of men*
> *Than all of Adam's race could right again.*[1]
> (*Geoffrey Chaucer,* Canterbury Tales)

Geoffrey Chaucer's satirical account of the life of an ordinary English woman has intrigued scholars for centuries. His portrayal of the Wife of Bath suggests he was empathic toward women, and his words above ring true. If historians had more real women's voices from the premodern era, how different would their story have been from the narrative of world history as we know it today? Furthermore, would women have placed the story of patriarchal oppression as centrally as we have done here?

Given the paucity of women's voices, integrating the disciplines of world history with women's history during the premodern era becomes a complex task, as there is so much that we still do not know about women's experiences across cultures. Historian Gerda Lerner once asserted that, "Only by looking at a long time span and by comparing different histories and cultures can we begin to see major developmental patterns and essential differences in the way historical events affect women and men."[2] Our textbook has attempted to do just that by providing a comparative analysis of seven different periods in human history and evaluating the factors that patterned women's lives, especially identifying those that led to constraints or freedoms.

As revealed in the preceding chapters, there were periods in the premodern era when women's lives became more constricted compared with other times. Why is it that civilizations on the whole have considered women to be innately inferior to men? Why have they been regularly shut out of politics and institutional education? Their sexuality so controlled? Their rights to property limited? The value of their work less esteemed? Although there is probably no complete answer to these questions, we can consider some explanations for them.

In hunting-gathering cultures, gender parity was most possible because of the centrality of women's labor, flexibility in family patterns, and limited social hierarchy. Although this began to change with village life and the domestication of animals, it was not until the development of cities beginning around 3500 BCE, and the governments that ran them,

213

that deep inequalities began to emerge. This was the largely the result of land ownership emerging as the primary means of accumulating wealth in society. Not everyone could own land or other resources, which meant that over time wealth accumulated in the hands of privileged few. This exclusive group wanted to retain their wealth within the family units. One way to ensure that was to make patrifocal family structures more commonplace. Also, it became necessary to closely scrutinize women's sexual behavior in order to guarantee patrilineal descent. As a result, women's reproductive roles started taking precedence over their other roles in society. Ideals of womanhood shifted, in some cases reinforcing inequities, in other cases actually directly causing new ones.

Another consequence of acquiring and retaining familial property was that the institution of marriage underwent changes, often to the detriment of women. For example, in ancient Athens, Gupta India, and the Abbasid caliphate, child and arranged marriages became common, and premarital sexual relations were largely frowned upon. The elite men in many of these societies practiced polygamy, whereas women could no longer have multiple partners. The custom of giving dowry to the groom's family became a common feature in many cultures, indicating women's relative loss of independence in negotiating a marriage contract.

In addition, wealthy classes wished to display the hallmarks of a distinct "elite" culture that would distinguish them from other social groups. Often this came at the expense of women's freedom. For example, some elite practices such as veiling or seclusion (among some upper-class women in ancient Mesopotamia, Classical Athens, and later in the Islamic world) were introduced to signal special status in society. Although the practice was aimed at preserving the chastity of women and constricting their social mobility, in reality, it was associated with a man's honor and status in society. Another custom that was restrictive to women but viewed as an elite tradition was foot binding in Song China.

Women's condition continued to decline with the emergence of complex states that were interested in shaping a monolithic identity among their subjects. Ancient Mesopotamia, Classical Athens, Gupta India, Song China, the Aztec Empire, and the Abbasid caliphate all displayed an increasing concern to define women's behavior, especially during times of insecurity brought about by fears of outside invasions or internal political strife. Since political power rested in the hands of relatively few privileged men, they mandated laws that placed legal restrictions on women. For example, the Code of Hammurabi, *Laws of Manu*, Confucius's Three Obediences, and the Sharia all contained guidelines for women's behavior in their societies.

An important consequence of many state laws was that women in these societies lost their legal autonomy and became legally dependent on men. The texts cited above all echoed the same precepts: that a woman throughout her life cycle was not considered a separate entity. She was dependent on her father before marriage, her husband when married, and finally her son after she became a widow. In addition, such laws also imposed restrictions on women's ability to divorce, their freedom to explore pre- and extramarital relationships, and even their ability to inherit property. Strict punishments were meted out to women who committed adultery, whereas men had multiple sexual relationships with relative impunity.

The main factors that prompted men to limit women's roles in societies cross-culturally were therefore: (1) the urgent need to preserve familial property and keep it within the family units, which was accomplished by controlling women's sexuality; (2) the innate desire of this privileged group in society to create practices reflective of their status, which often occurred by constricting women's roles in society; and (3) the excessive use of state power to mandate women's behavior, which often arose during times of economic and political insecurity.

One goal throughout this book has been to portray women as active agents in the various patriarchal structures. Given their limitations, how have women helped shape the religion, economics, and politics of their respective cultures? Certainly, the relative parity women might have achieved in one area did not indicate women's positions in all levels of their societies.

RELIGION

Women have figured largely in the fertility rituals of most ancient societies, such as Mesopotamia, Classic Maya, Classical Athens, Gupta India, and Tang China, but the inclusion of female deities in these ancient polytheistic cultures did not necessarily translate into better treatment for women in a society. Nevertheless, goddess worship demonstrates the importance of femininity to a culture's conception of the divine.

Although women's public role in religion declined in many states, such as in the Gupta Empire, Song China, the Aztec Empire, and the Abbasid caliphate, often their importance as keepers of religious traditions among their families remained strong. State-endorsed religions did not always have negative effects: They offered a means to place restrictions on women, but they also offered alternate autonomous paths for women in monastic life.

For instance, most of these world religions censured women's sexuality, since great emphasis was put on purity and pollution. In many religions, menstruating women were regarded as impure and not allowed to participate openly in religious ceremonies. On the other hand, women have traditionally played important roles in sects that emphasized mysticism, as was the case with women shamans, Sufi mystics, and Christian saints. By focusing on an irrational connection with the divine, women could circumvent the mandatory religious training normally open only to men. Although all the world religions placed importance on women fulfilling their familial roles, some, such as Buddhism and Christianity, allowed women to join monastic orders to pursue their spiritual and intellectual goals.

One notable difference among states' treatment of women through public religion can be seen in Gupta India, where Hinduism was championed as a shaper of public morality: Women's roles became universally restricted. On the other hand, in both the Roman Empire and Tang China, where the cult of Isis and Buddhism, respectively, were supported by the government as an optional way to participate in public spirituality, women experienced benefits of government-supported religion.

POLITICAL LIFE

Nowhere were women's lives more affected by the development of urban civilizations as in the political arena. During the premodern urban era, political power rested primarily in the hands of privileged few in society—the male landowning class. Despite the lack of opportunities in general for women in public positions of authority, nevertheless in several societies women could occasionally exercise power indirectly. The most common way was to use their personal charm to sway leaders, as did the Abbasid queens Khaizuran and Zubaida. In other examples, women manipulated the political institutions directly by acting as rulers for their absentee husbands or regents until their minor sons attained the maturity enough to take over the reins. We have seen this trend in the peoples of Classical Sparta, the Bedouins of Muhammad's time, or late medieval Europeans. Rarest were women who ruled directly in their own right, such as Zac K'uk of the Maya city-state Palenque and Wu Zhao of Tang China.

ECONOMIC LIFE

The power of the expanding states we have examined rested on the resources created by women's productive labor (both enslaved and free female laborers) and the reproductive activity of women. Textile production had a special place in women's history, since it was usually considered a women's field of activity. The tending to domestic chores, birthing children, and child rearing have also traditionally been women's economic contributions. Nevertheless, women in most urban civilizations participated in a wide variety of economic activities. They have played a central role in certain professions such as midwifery, spinning, weaving, basket making, and pottery. Indeed, women may have even invented agriculture, finding the food value of plants that began the agricultural revolution. Significantly, they have been victims of the slave trade of many regions.

Several factors have traditionally led to the decline of women's economic autonomy. First, as familial property became important, women were often excluded from receiving formal inheritance or controlling their own finances. Second, when a particular trade undertaken by women rose in status, men often began to monopolize it. We have seen this in the case of textile manufacturing and brewing in late medieval Europe. Finally, among elite families of many civilizations, such as the Aztec Empire, it became a sign of social status to keep women out of commercial activities. However, women retained their relative economic independence in some regions. For example, in Southeast Asia, the Abbasid caliphate, and Meso-American civilizations, women could inherit property and negotiate trade transactions that then gave them more social freedoms.

Our aim has been to increase the awareness of the rich diversity and patterns in women's early history among our students. We hope that by reading this textbook, readers will learn to appreciate the common patterns of women's experiences cross-culturally and recognize the differences that shaped world societies.

 NOTES

INTRODUCTION

1. Simone de Beauvoir, The *Second Sex*, trans. H. M. Parshley (New York: Alfred A. Knopf, 1980).
2. Betty Friedan, *The Feminine Mystique* (New York: Norton and Company, 1963).
3. Kevin Reilly, foreword to *Women in World History*, vol. I , *Readings from Prehistory to 1500*, Sarah Shaver Hughes and Brady Hughes (New York: M. E. Sharpe, 1995), xi.
4. Ibid., xvi.

CHAPTER ONE

1. A. Kinney, "Women in Ancient China," in *Women's Role in Ancient Civilizations*, ed. B. Vivante (Westport, CT: Greenwood Press, 1999), 9.
2. Guity Nashat and Judith E. Tucker, *Women in the Middle East and North Africa: Restoring Women to History* (Bloomington: Indiana University Press, 1999), 33.
3. E. W. Barber, *Women's Work: The First 20,000 Years* (New York: W. W. Norton, 1994), 170.
4. R. Westbrook, "Social Justice and Creative Jurisprudence in the Later Bronze Age Syria," *Journal of the Economic & Social History of the Orient* 44, no. 1 (March 2001): 37.
5. V. Leon, *Uppity Women of Ancient Times* (Boston: Conari Press, 1995), 16–17.

CHAPTER TWO

1. Guy Davenport, intro. and trans., *Sappho: Poems and Fragments* (Ann Arbor: University of Michigan Press, 1965), §20.
2. Aristotle, *On the Generation of Animals*, trans. A. L. Peck (Cambridge, MA: Harvard University Press, Loeb Classical Library, 1963), 103.
3. Sarah Pomeroy, *Goddesses, Whores, Wives, and Slaves: Women in Classical Antiquity* (New York: Shocken Books, 1975, 1995), 65.
4. Euripides, *Euripides: Three Plays: Alcestis, Hippolytus, Iphigenia in Tauris*, trans. Philip Vellacott (New York: Penguin, 1974), line 638, 102.
5. Mary Lefkowitz and Maureen Fant, *Women's Life in Greece and Rome: A Source Book in Translation*, 2nd ed. (Baltimore: Johns Hopkins University Press, 1992), document 32, 12.
6. Ibid., 8.
7. Euripides, *Euripides: Medea and Other Plays*, trans. and intro. Philip Vellacott (New York: Penguin, 1963), lines 248–252, 25.
8. Euripides, *Trojan Women*, ed. and trans. David Kovacs (Cambridge, MA: Harvard University Press, Loeb Classical Library, 1999), lines 643–658, 81.
9. Aeschylus, *Seven against Thebes*, trans. Herbert Weir Smyth (Cambridge, MA: Harvard University Press, Loeb Classical Library, 1963), lines 200–203, 337.

10. Lefkowitz and Fant, *Women's Life,* document 64, 30.

11. Ibid., 51.

12. Ibid., document 35, 14–15.

13. Sue Blundell, *Women in Ancient Greece* (Cambridge, MA: Harvard University Press, 1995), 119.

14. Lefkowitz and Fant, *Women's Life,* document 416, 296.

15. Cornelius Nepos, *Cornelius Nepos: Twenty Lives,* ed. J. E. Barss (New York: Macmillan, 1911), 16 (author's translation).

16. Livy, *The Early History of Rome: Books I–V of The History of Rome from Its Foundation,* trans. Aubrey de Sélincourt (New York: Penguin Books, 1971), 99.

17. Pomeroy, *Goddesses,* 153.

18. Jo-Ann Shelton, ed. and trans., *As the Romans Did: A Sourcebook in Roman Social History,* 2nd ed. (New York: Oxford University Press, 1998), document 36, 28.

19. Ibid., document 326, 290.

20. Pomeroy, *Goddesses,* 159.

21. Shelton, *As the Romans Did,* document 61, 45.

22. Pomeroy, *Goddesses,* 219.

23. Elaine Fantham, Helene Peet Foley, Natalie Boymel Kampen, Sarah B. Pomeroy, and H. Alan Shapiro, *Women in the Classical World* (New York: Oxford University Press, 1994), 363.

24. Shelton, *As the Romans Did,* document 334, 297.

25. Naphtali Lewis and Meyer Reinhold, eds., *Roman Civilization, Volume I: Selected Readings,* 3rd ed. (New York: Columbia University Press, 1990), 549.

26. Lefkowitz and Fant, *Women's Life,* document 179, 153.

CHAPTER THREE

1. David Kinsley, "Kali: Blood and Death Out of Place," in *Devi: Goddesses of India,* ed. John Stratton Hawley and Donna Marie Wulff (Chicago: University of Chicago Press, 1996), 77–78.

2. David Kinsley, *Hindu Goddesses: Visions of the Divine Feminine in the Hindu Religious Tradition* (Berkeley: University of California, 1986), 72.

3. The notion of purity pollution emphasized by the Brahmins implied that the three upper castes were considered to be ritually pure and therefore should prevent themselves from becoming polluted through any interaction with the lowest caste and untouchables. Therefore, over time the caste system became very rigid due to fears of pollution through inter-caste dining and miscegenation, which then was strictly prohibited.

4. Wendy Doniger O'Flaherty, *The Rig Veda: An Anthology* (New York: Penguin, 1981).

5. Ibid., verse 7, 111.

6. Ibid., verses 5 and 6, 291.

7. Ibid.

8. *The Laws of Manu,* trans. Wendy Doniger with Brian K. Smith, verses 48–40, 48 (New York: Penguin, 1991).

9. Ibid., ch. 9, verse 94, 208.

10. Daiva, the second form of marriage, was when a father married off his daughter to a Brahmin priest in return for officiating a family sacrificial ritual. In this way, Brahmins could acquire many wives. Often it was symbolical (that is, not consummated).

In a Prajapatya marriage, a legal guardian gave the girl away instead of her father. Asura, Paishacha, and Rakshasa were considered to be the lowest forms of marriage and were usually performed without the consent of the bride's father or legal guardian. For example, it could result from rape, capture, or forcible drugging of the bride.

11. Doniger and Smith, *Laws of Manu*, ch. 5, verse 148, 115.

12. Ibid., ch. 3, verses 8–11, 44.

13. Ibid., ch. 3, verses 61–62, 49.

14. Ibid., ch. 9, verse 14, 198.

15. Ibid., ch. 5, verse 154, 115.

16. Ibid.

17. Ibid., ch. 5, verse 150.

18. Ibid., ch. 5, verse 17, 198.

19. Ibid., ch. 5, verse 155, 115.

20. Dorrane Jacobson, "Golden Handprints and Red-Painted Feet: Hindu Childbirth Rituals in Central India," in *Unspoken Worlds: Women's Religious Lives,* ed. Nancy Auer Falk and Rita M. Gross (Belmont, CA: Wadsworth, 1989), 59–72.

21. Quoted in P. Thomas, *Indian Women Through the Ages* (New Delhi: Asia Publishing House, 1963), 231.

22. Doniger and Smith, *Laws of Manu*, ch. 9, verse 65, 205.

23. Ibid., ch. 5, verse 160, 116.

24. Quoted in A. L. Basham, *The Wonder that Was India,* (New York: Grove Press, 1954), 185.

25. Ibid., 185–186.

26. V. Lina Fruzzetti, *The Gift of a Virgin: Women, Marriage and Ritual in Bengali Society* (New York: Oxford University Press, 1990); Werener Menski, "Marital Expectations as Dramatized in Hindu Marriage Rituals," in *Roles and Rituals for Hindu Women,* ed. Julia Leslie (Rutherford, NJ: Fairleigh Dickinson University Press, 1991).

27. Doniger and Smith, *Laws of Manu*, ch. 8, verse 416, 196.

28. Kinsley, "Kali: Blood and Death," 77.

29. Rita M. Gross, "Hindu Female Deities as a Resource for the Contemporary Rediscovery of the Goddess," in *The Book of the Goddess Past and Present,* ed. Carl Olson (New York: Cross Road, 1983), 217–230.

30. Kinsley, *Hindu Goddesses,* 116.

31. Ibid.

32. Ibid., 120.

33. Ibid., 122.

34. John S. Sharp, *The Experience of Buddhism: Sources and Interpretation* (Belmont, CA: Wadsworth, 1995), 53.

35. Ibid., 55.

36. Ibid.

37. Nancy Falk, "The Cases of Vanishing Nuns: The Fruits of Ambivalence in Ancient Indian Buddhism," in *Unspoken Worlds: Women's Religious Lives,* ed. Nancy Falk and Rita Gross (Belmont, CA: Wadsworth, 1989), 164.

38. Ibid.

39. "The central tenet of *Mahayana* Buddhism is the concept of *bodhisattva* ('he who has the essence of Buddhahood'), a compassionate and loving savior who rather than selfishly abandoning the world, pauses at the threshold of nirvana to reach down to help all

mankind attain liberation from sorrow and rebirth through his grace." Stanley Wolpert, *A New History of India* (New York: Oxford University Press, 2004), 70.

40. Vajrayana, also known as Thunderbolt, is now commonly practiced in Tibet and Nepal. Both Tantric Hinduism and Buddhism believed the divine to be feminine. Both believed that the right way to worship the divine was through *maithuna*, sexual union of men and women. However, the only way one could achieve this ideal state of maithuna was by perfecting eight different forms of yoga. Controlling the body and breath were central for the ideal maithuna to happen, and that could be achieved only through intensive practice of yoga.

41. See Miranda Shaw, *Passionate Enlightenment, Women in Tantric Buddhism* (Princeton, NJ: Princeton University Press, 1994).

42. Anthony Reid, *Southeast Asia in the Age of Commerce, 1450–1680,* vol. I (New Haven: Yale University Press, 1988), 6.

43. Ibid.

44. Ibid., 137.

45. Sarah and Brady Hughes, *Women in World History,* vol. I, *Readings from Pre-History to 1500* (New York: M. E. Sharpe, 1995), ch. 12, 207.

46. Quoted in Reid, *Southeast Asia,* 146.

47. S. Abeyasekere, "Slaves in Batavia: Insights from a Slave Register" (pp. 286–314) and A. vander Kraan, "Bali: Slavery and Slave Trade" (pp. 315–340) in *Slavery, Bondage and Dependency in South East Asia,* ed. Anthony Reid (New York: St. Martin's Press, 1983).

48. Quoted in Reid, *Southeast Asia,* 149.

49. Quoted in Reid, *Southeast Asia,* 150.

50. Ibid., 85.

51. Ibid., 1148.

CHAPTER FOUR

1. Susan Mann, "Grooming a Daughter for Marriage" in *Marriage and Inequality in Chinese Society,* ed. T. R. Watson and P. B. Ebrey (Berkeley: University of California Press, 1991), 209.

2. V. Hansen, *The Open Empire: A History of China to 1600* (New York: Norton, 2000), 183–184.

3. Lady Zheng, "Book of Filial Piety for Women," trans. P. Ebrey, in *Under Confucian Eyes, Writings on Gender in Chinese History,* ed. S. Mann and Y. Cheng (Berkeley: University of California Press, 2001), 47–50, 52, 54–55, 62–63.

4. P. Ebrey, *The Inner Quarters, The Lives of Chinese Women in the Sung Period* (Berkeley: University of California Press, 1993), 33, 37, 40–42.

5. F. Bray, *Technology and Gender, Fabrics of Power in Later Imperial China* (Berkeley: University of California Press, 1997), 116.

6. J. Zang, "Women and the Transmission of Confucian Culture in Song China" in *Women in Confucian Cultures in Premodern China, Korea and Japan,* ed. D. Ko et al. (Berkeley: University of California Press, 2003), 130.

7. Zang, "Transmission of Confucian Culture," 127; Bray, *Technology and Gender,* 128–129.

8. P. Ebrey, *Women and the Family in Chinese History* (London: RoutledgeCurzon, 2002), 29.

9. Ibid., 29.

10. Ibid., 30.

11. Ibid., 69.

12. Zang, "Transmission of Confucian Culture," 130.

13. Ebrey, *Inner Quarters,* 160–161.

14. Zang, "Transmission of Confucian Culture," 128.

15. Hansen, *The Open Empire,* 277–278.

16. Zang, "Transmission of Confucian Culture," 131.

17. F. Du and S. Mann, "Competing Claims on Womanly Virtue in Late Imperial China," in *Women in Confucian Cultures in Premodern China, Korea and Japan,* ed. D. Ko et al. (Berkeley: University of California Press, 2003), 224.

18. Zang, "Transmission of Confucian Culture," 133; S. Sievers, "Women in East Asia" in *Women in Asia, Restoring Women to History,* B. Ramusack and S. Sievers (Bloomington: Indiana University Press, 1999), 182.

19. Hansen, *The Open Empire,* 362–363.

20. S. Cahill, "Discipline and Transformation: Body and Practice in the Lives of Daoist Holy Women of Tang China" in *Women in Confucian Cultures in Premodern China, Korea and Japan,* ed. D. Ko et al. (Berkeley: University of California Press, 2003), 268–269, 215.

21. Sievers, "Women in East Asia," 174, 177.

22. Cahill, "Discipline and Transformation," 270.

23. Hansen, *The Open Empire,* 160.

24. S. Cahill, *Transcendence and Divine Passion: The Queen Mother of the West in Medieval China* (Stanford, CA: Stanford University Press, 1993), 6–7, 34.

25. This phrase has become well known, perhaps after Francis K. Hsu's important work *Under the Ancestors' Shadow: Kinship, Personality and Social Mobility in Village China* (Anchor Books, 1948; reissued Stanford: Stanford University Press, 1967) and *Under the Ancestors' Shadow: Chinese Culture and Personality* (New York: Columbia University Press, 1948).

26. S. Cahill, "Discipline and Transformation," 259.

27. Jiang Zhiqi, "Biography of the Great Compassionate One of Xiangshan" trans. Chun-tang Yu, in *Under Confucian Eyes: Writings on Gender in Chinese History,* ed. S. Mann and Yu-Yin Cheng (Berkeley: University of California Press, 2001), 31–32.

28. V. Hansen, *Changing Gods in Medieval China, 1127–1276* (Princeton: Princeton University Press, 1990), 22, 167.

29. Cahill, *Transcendence and Divine Passion,* 44–45.

30. S. Wawrytko, "Prudery and Prurience" in *The Sage and the Second Sex, Confucianism, Ethics and Gender,* ed. Chenyang Li (Chicago: Open Court, 2000), 182, 179.

31. Ebrey, *Women and the Family,* 16–18.

32. M. Abramson, "Deep Eyes and High Noses, Physiognomy and the Depictions of Barbarians in Tang China," pp. 119–159; and I. Leung, "Felt Yurts Neatly Arrayed, Large Tents Huddle Close, Visualizing the Frontier in Northern Song Dynasty," pp. 192–219, in *Political Frontiers, Ethnic Boundaries and Human Geographies in Chinese History, 960–1127,* ed. N. Di Cosma and D. Wyatt (London and New York: Routledge Curzon, 2003).

CHAPTER FIVE

1. George Stuart, "Yucatan's Mysterious Hill Cities," *National Geographic* 201, no. 4 (April 2002): 54.

2. Linda Stephen Neff, "Labor and Lowland Terrace Agriculture" in *Ancient Maya Women,* ed. Traci Ardren (Walnut Creek, CA: AltaMira Press, 2002), 41.

3. Andrea Stone has revealing details about women's ideals of beauty in her article "Women in Mesoamerica" in *Women's Roles in Ancient Civilizations*, ed. B. Vivante (Westport, CT: Greenwood Publishing, 1999), 292–312. See also Rosemary Joyce, "Beauty, Sexuality, Body Ornamentation and Gender in Ancient Meso-America" in *In Pursuit of Gender: Worldwide Archaeological Approaches*, ed. Sarah Milledge Nelson and Myriam Rosen-Ayalon (Walnut Creek, CA: AltaMira Press, 2002), 82, 88.

4. Stone, "Women in Mesoamerica," 295.

5. Ibid., 298–299.

6. John Gerry and Meredith S. Chesson, "Classic Maya Diet and Gender Relationships" in *Gender and Material Culture in Archaeological Perspective*, ed. Moira Donald and Linda Hurcombe (London: Macmillan Publishers, 2000), 250–264.

7. Karen O. Bruhns and Karen E. Stothert, *Women in Ancient America* (Norman: University of Oklahoma Press, 1999), 163.

8. Cynthia Robin, "Gender and Maya Farming: Chan Noohol, Belize," in Ardren, *Ancient Maya Women* (see note 2), 12–20.

9. Linda Neff, "Gender Divisions of Labor," 31–51.

10. Andrea Stone has a rich portrayal of Maya women and politics in "Women in Mesoamerica," 300–302, 309–311.

11. Bruhns and Stothert, *Women in Ancient America*, 14–20.

12. Traci Ardren, "Death Became Her: Images of Female Power from Yaxuna Burials," in Ardren, *Ancient Maya Women* (see note 2), 68–88.

13. Matthew Looper, "Women-Men (and Men-Women): Classic Maya Rulers and the Third Gender," in Ardren, *Ancient Maya Women* (see note 2), 173.

14. Ibid., 180–182 ff.

15. June Nash, "Gendered Deities and the Survival of Culture," *History of Religions* 36, no 4 (May 1997): 333.

16. Esther Pasztory, *Aztec Art* (Norman: University of Oklahoma Press, 1998), 218.

17. Michael E. Smith, *The Aztecs* (Malden, MA: Blackwell Publishers, 1996), 139.

18. Inga Clendinnen, *Aztecs: An Interpretation* (Cambridge: Cambridge University Press, 1991), 153.

19. Ferdinand Anton, *Women in Pre-Columbian America* (New York: Abner Schram, 1973), 18.

20. Smith, *The Aztecs*, 137.

21. Clendinnen, *Aztecs: An Interpretation*, 158.

22. Ibid., 166.

23. Miguel León-Portilla, *The Aztec Image of Self and Society: An Introduction to Nahua Culture*, ed. J. Jorge Klor de Alva (Salt Lake City: University of Utah Press, 1992), 195.

24. Arthur J. O. Anderson, "Aztec Wives," in *Indian Women of Early Mexico*, ed. Susan Schroeder, Stephanie Wood, and Robert Haskett (Norman and London: University of Oklahoma Press, 1997), 73.

25. Clendinnen, *Aztecs: An Interpretation*, 174.

26. Ibid., 170.

27. Sarah Shaver Hughes and Brady Hughes, *Women in World History*, vol. 1, *Readings from Prehistory to 1500* (Armonk, NY and London: M. E. Sharpe, 1995), 231.

28. Nash, "Gendered Deities," 346.

29. Louise M. Burkhart, "Mexica Women on the Home Front: Housework and Religion in Aztec Mexico," in *Indian Women of Early Mexico* (see note 24), 33.

30. Clendinnen, *Aztecs: An Interpretation*, 160.

31. Joyce Marcus, *Mesoamerican Writing Systems: Propaganda, Myth, and History in Four Ancient Civilizations* (Princeton, NJ: Princeton University Press, 1992), 227.

32. Hughes and Hughes, *Women in World History*, 231.

CHAPTER SIX

1. All suras are taken from *The Koran*, translated with notes by N. J. Dawood (New York: Penguin, 1990).

2. Elizabeth Warnock Fernea and Basima Qattan Bezirgan, eds., *Middle Eastern Muslim Women Speak* (Austin: University of Texas, 1999), 2.

3. Quoted in Fernea and Bezirgan, *Muslim Women Speak*, 33.

4. Quoted in Wiebke Walther, *Women in Islam from Medieval to Modern Times* (Princeton, NJ: Markus Wiener Publishers, 1995), 74.

5. Madelain Farah, *Marriage and Sexuality in Islam* (Salt Lake City: University of Utah Press, 1984), 6, 40.

6. Sarah and Brady Hughes, *Women in World History, Vol. I, Readings from Prehistory to 1500* (New York: M. E. Sharpe, 1995), 204.

7. Ibid.

8. Ibid., 194.

9. Quoted in Walther, *Women in Islam*, 205.

10. Ibid., 183.

11. See Abu Hamid Al-Ghazali, *Advice to Kings* (Cairo: Al-Aszhar University Press, 1968).

12. Ibid.

CHAPTER SEVEN

1. Jennifer Ward, *Women in Medieval Europe: 1200–1500* (New York: Longman, 2003), 24.

2. Joseph and Frances Gies, *Women in the Middle Ages* (New York: Harper Perennial, 1991), 11.

3. Ibid., 52.

4. "A Talk of Ten Wives on Their Husband's Ware," in *The Trials and Joys of Marriage*, ed. Eve Salisbury, The Consortium for the Teaching of the Middle Ages (Kalamazoo: Medieval Institute Publications, Western Michigan University, 2002), 95.

5. Ward, *Women in Medieval Europe*, 53.

6. "Ballad of a Tyrannical Husband," in *The Trials and Joys of Marriage*, ed. Eve Salisbury, The Consortium for the Teaching of the Middle Ages (Kalamazoo: Medieval Institute Publications, Western Michigan University, 2002), 85–88.

7. Judith M. Bennett, *Ale, Beer, and Brewsters in England: Women's Work in a Changing World 1300–1600* (New York: Oxford University Press, 1996), 18.

8. Cited in Wendy R. Larson, "Who Is the Master of This Narrative? Maternal Patronage of the Cult of St. Margaret," in *Gendering the Master Narrative: Women and Power in the Middle Ages*, ed. Mary C. Erler and Maryanne Kowaleski (Ithaca, NY: Cornell University Press, 2003), 94.

9. Karen A. Winstead, ed. and trans., *Chaste Passions: Medieval English Virgin Martyr Legends* (Ithaca, NY: Cornell University Press), 62–69.

10. Cited in Caroline Walker Bynum, *Holy Feast and Holy Fast: The Religious Significance of Food to Medieval Women* (Berkeley: University of California Press, 1987), 210.

11. Ibid., 172.

12. Cited in *Women's Lives in Medieval Europe: A Sourcebook,* ed. Emilie Amt (London: Routledge, 1993), 291.

13. Charaty Cannon Willard, trans., "The Franco-Italian Professional Writer: Christine de Pizan," in *Medieval Women Writers,* ed. Katharina M. Wilson (Athens, GA: University of Georgia Press, 1984), 351.

14. Ibid., 354.

15. Ibid., 353.

16. W. L. Warren, *Henry II* (Berkeley: University of California Press, 1973), 12.

17. M. R. B. Shaw, trans., *Joinville and Villehardouin: Chronicles of the Crusades* (New York: Penguin Books, 1988), 316.

18. Ibid.

CONCLUSION

1. Geoffrey Chaucer, "The Wife of Bath" (ca. 1387) in *The Past Speaks: Sources and Problems in English History,* Vol. I, *1688,* ed. Lacey Baldwin Smith and Jean Reeder Smith (Lexington: D.C. Heath, 1993), 175.

2. Gerda Lerner, *The Creation of Feminist Consciousness, From Middle Ages to Eighteenth Century* (Oxford: Oxford University Press, 1993), 15.

SUGGESTED READINGS

CHAPTER ONE

Adovasio, J. M., O. Soffer, and J. Page. *The Invisible Sex: Uncovering the True Roles of Women in Prehistory.* New York: Harper Collins, 2007.

Barber, E. W. *Women's Work: The First 20,000 Years.* New York: W. W. Norton, 1994.

Ehrenberg, M. *Women in Prehistory Oklahoma Series in Classical Culture.* Vol. 4. Norman: University of Oklahoma Press, 1990.

Gero, J., ed. *Engendering Archaeology: Women and Prehistory.* Malden, MA: Blackwell, 1991.

Hughes, S., and B. Hughes. *Women in Ancient Civilizations: Essays on Global and Comparative History.* Washington DC: American Historical Association, 1998.

Lerner, G. *The Creation of Patriarchy.* New York: Oxford University Press, 1987.

Nashat, G., and J. E. Tucker. *Women in the Middle East and North Africa: Restoring Women to History.* Bloomington: Indiana University Press, 1999.

Vivante, B., ed. *Women's Role in Ancient Civilizations.* Westport, CT: Greenwood Press, 1999.

CHAPTER TWO

Blundell, Sue. *Women in Ancient Greece.* Cambridge, MA: Harvard University Press, 1995.

Cantarella, Eva. *Pandora's Daughters: The Role and Status of Women in Greek and Roman Antiquity.* Translated by Maureen B. Fant. Baltimore, MD: Johns Hopkins University Press, 1987. First published in the Italian language in 1981 as *L'ambiguo malanno.*

Clark, Gillian. *Women in Late Antiquity: Pagan and Christian Lifestyles.* New York: Clarendon Press, 1993.

D'Ambra, Eve. *Roman Women.* New York: Cambridge University Press, 2007.

Fantham, Elaine, Helene Peet Foley, Natalie Boymel Kampen, Sarah B. Pomeroy, and H. Alan Shapiro. *Women in the Classical World.* New York: Oxford University Press, 1994.

Gardner, Jane F. *Women in Roman Law and Society.* Bloomington and Indianapolis: Indiana University Press, 1991.

Lefkowitz, Mary, and Maureen Fant. *Women's Life in Greece and Rome: A Source Book in Translation.* 2nd ed. Baltimore, MD: Johns Hopkins University Press, 1992.

Pomeroy, Sarah. *Goddesses, Whores, Wives, and Slaves: Women in Classical Antiquity.* New York: Shocken Books, 1975, reprinted 1995.

———. *Spartan Women.* New York: Oxford University Press, 2002.

Shelton, Jo-Ann, ed. and trans. *As the Romans Did.* 2nd ed. New York: Oxford University Press, 1998.

CHAPTER THREE

Alterkar, A. S. *The Position of Women in Hindu Civilization.* 2nd ed., 3rd. rep. Delhi: Motilal Banarsidass, 1978.

Basham, A. L. *The Wonder That Was India: A Survey of the Culture of the Indian Subcontinent before the Coming of the Muslims.* New York: Grove Press, 1954.

Chakravarti, Uma, and Kum Kum Roy. "Breaking Out of Invisibility: Rewriting the History of Women in Ancient India." In *Retrieving Women's History: Changing Perceptions of the Role of Women in Politics and Society,* edited by S. Jay Kleinberg. Oxford, England: Berg/UNESCO, 1988.

Chandra, Moti. *The World of Courtesans.* New Delhi: Vikas Publishers, 1973.

Falk, Nancy Auer. "The Case of the Vanishing Nuns: The Fruits of Ambivalence in Ancient Indian Buddhism." In *Unspoken Worlds: Women's Religious Lives in Non-western Cultures,* edited by Nancy Auer Falk and Rita M. Gross. San Francisco: Harper and Row, 1980.

Hawley, John Stratton, ed. *Sati: The Blessing and the Curse: The Burning of Wives in India.* New York: Oxford University Press, 1994.

Hoerner, I. S. *Women in Buddhism under Primitive Buddhism: Laywomen and Almswomen.* Delhi: Motilal Banarsidass, 1975.

Kinsley, David. *Hindu Goddesses: Visions of the Divine Feminine in Hindu Religious Tradition.* Berkeley and Los Angeles: University of California Press, 1986.

Jain, Devaki, ed. *Indian Women.* New Delhi: Ministry of Information and Broadcasting, Government of India, 1975.

Reid, Anthony. *Southeast Asia in the Age of Commerce, 1450–1680.* Vol. 1,*The Lands below the Winds.* New Haven, CT: Yale University Press, 1988.

CHAPTER FOUR

Bray, F. *Technology and Gender: Fabrics of Power in Later Imperial China.* Berkeley: University of California Press, 1997.

Cahill, S. *Transcendence and Divine Passion: The Queen Mother of the West in Medieval China.* Stanford: Stanford University Press, 1993.

Ebrey, P. *The Inner Quarters: The Lives of Chinese Women in the Sung Period.* Berkeley: University of California Press, 1993.

———. *Women and the Family in Chinese History.* London: RoutledgeCurzon, 2002.

Hansen, V. *Changing Gods in Medieval China, 1127–1276.* Princeton: Princeton University Press, 1990.

Ko, D., et al., eds. *Women in Confucian Cultures in Premodern China, Korea and Japan.* Berkeley: University of California Press, 2003.

Li, Chenyang, ed. *The Sage and the Second Sex: Confucianism, Ethics and Gender.* Chicago: Open Court, 2000.

Mann, S., and Y. Cheng. *Under Confucian Eyes: Writings on Gender in Chinese History.* Berkeley: University of California Press, 2001.

Ramusack, B., and S. Sievers.*Women in Asia: Restoring Women to History.* Bloomington: Indiana University Press, 1999.

Watson, T. R., and P. B. Ebrey, eds. *Marriage and Inequality in Chinese Society.* Berkeley: University of California Press, 1991.

CHAPTER FIVE

Anton, Ferdinand. *Women in Pre-Columbian America.* New York: Abner Schram, 1973.

Ardren, T. *Ancient Maya Women.* Walnut Creek, CA: AltaMira Press, 2002.

Bruhns, K. O., and Karen E. Stothert, eds. *Women in Ancient America.* Norman: University of Oklahoma Press, 1999.

Claassen, C., and R. A. Joyce. *Women in Prehistory: North America and Mesoamerica; Regendering the Past.* Philadelphia: University of Pennsylvania Press, 1997.

Clendinnen, Inga. *Aztecs: An Interpretation.* Cambridge: Cambridge University Press, 1991.

Donald, M., and Linda Hurcombe, eds. *Gender and Material Culture in Archaeological Perspective.* London: Macmillan, 2000 and New York: St. Martin's Press, 2001. Page references are to Macmillan edition.

Hughes, Sarah Shaver, and Brady Hughes. *Women in World History.* Vol. 1, *Readings from Prehistory to 1500.* Armonk, NY and London: M. E. Sharpe, 1995.

Joyce, R. *Gender and Power in Prehispanic Mesoamerica.* Austin: University of Texas, 2001.

Nash, June. "Gendered Deities and the Survival of Culture," *History of Religions* 36, no. 4 (May, 1997).

Nelson, S. M., and M. Rosen-Ayalon, eds. *In Pursuit of Gender: Worldwide Archaeological Approaches.* Walnut Creek, CA: AltaMira Press, 2002.

Pasztory, Esther. *Aztec Art.* Norman: University of Oklahoma Press, 1998.

Schroeder, Susan, Stephanie Wood, and Robert Haskett, eds. *Indian Women of Early Mexico.* Norman and London: University of Oklahoma Press, 1997.

Stone, Andrea. "Women in Mesoamerica." In *Women's Role in Ancient Civilizations,* edited by B. Vivante, 292–312. Westport, CT: Greenwood Press, 1999.

CHAPTER SIX

Abbot, Nabia. *Aishah the Beloved of Muhammad.* Chicago: University of Chicago Press, 1942.

———. "Women and the State in Early Islam, I. Muhammad and the First Four Caliphs." *Journal of Near Eastern Studies* I (1942a): 106–126.

———."Women and the State in Early Islam, II. The Umayyads." *Journal of Near Eastern Studies* I (1942b): 341–361.

———. "Women and the State on the Eve of Islam." *The American Journal of Semitic Languages and Literature* 58 (January-October 1941): 259–285.

Ahmed, Leila. *Women and Gender in Islam: Historical Roots of a Modern Debate.* New Haven, CT: Yale University Press, 1992.

Ahsan, Muhammad Manazir. *Social Life under the Abbasids.* London: Longman, 1979.

Farah, Madelain. *Marriage and Sexuality in Islam.* Vol. 1, part 1. Salt Lake City: University of Utah Press, 1984.

Ibn Battuta. *Travels in Asia and Africa.* Translated by H. A. R. Gibb. London: George Routledge. 1929.

Keddie, Nikki, and Beth Baron. *Women in Middle Eastern History: Shifting Boundaries in Sex and Gender.* New Haven, CT: Yale University Press, 1991.

Mernissi, Fatima. *Beyond the Veil: Male and Female Dynamics in Modern Muslim Society.* Bloomington: Indiana University Press, 1987.

CHAPTER SEVEN

Amt, Emilie, ed. *Women's Lives in Medieval Europe: A Sourcebook.* London: Routledge, 1993.

Bennett, Judith M. *Ale, Beer, and Brewsters in England: Women's Work in a Changing World, 1300–1600.* New York: Oxford University Press, 1996.

Bynum, Caroline Walker. *Holy Feast and Holy Fast: The Religious Significance of Food to Medieval Women.* Berkeley: University of California Press, 1987.

Erler, Mary C., and Maryanne Kowaleski, eds. *Gendering the Master Narrative: Women and Power in the Middle Ages.* Ithaca, NY: Cornell University Press, 2003.

Hanawalt, Barbara A. *The Ties That Bound: Peasant Families in Medieval England.* New York: Oxford University Press, 1986.

Herlihy, David. Opera Muliebria: *Women and Work in Medieval Europe.* New York: McGraw-Hill, 1990.

Karras, Ruth M. *Common Women: Prostitution and Sexuality in Medieval England.* Oxford: Oxford University Press, 1996.

Parsons, John Carmi, ed. *Medieval Queenship.* New York: St. Martin's Press, 1993.

Pernoud, Régine. *Joan of Arc: By Herself and Her Witnesses.* Lanham, MD: Scarborough House, 1994. First published in the French language in 1962 as *Jeanne d'Arc par elle-même et par ses témoins.*

Ward, Jennifer. *Women in Medieval Europe: 1200–1500.* New York: Longman, 2003.

Winstead, Karen A., ed. and trans. *Chaste Passions: Medieval English Virgin Martyr Legends.* Ithaca, NY: Cornell University Press, 2000.

◀ INDEX ▶

231